A HISTORY OF GAME THEORY, VOLUME 1

Did Game Theory exist before 1944?

Game Theory – the formal modelling of conflict and cooperation – first emerged as a recognized field with the publication of John von Neumann and Oskar Morgenstern's *Theory of Games and Economic Behavior* in 1944. Since then, game-theoretic thinking about choice of strategies and the interdependence of people's actions has influenced all the social sciences. However, little is known about the history of the theory of strategic games prior to this publication.

In this volume, the history of strategic games (from their origins to 1945) is traced through the work of

- nineteenth-century economists, such as Cournot and Edgeworth;
- voting theorists, including Lewis Carroll;
- conflict theorists, Richardson and Lanchester;
- probabilists, such as Bertrand, Borel and Ville;
- later economists, notably Stackelberg and Zeuthen.

This authoritative account of the history of game theory concludes with a historical perspective on the achievement of von Neumann and Morgenstern, and an appraisal of the reception of their book.

Mary Ann Dimand, a doctoral student at Yale University, teaches economics at Albion College, MI, USA. **Robert W. Dimand** is Professor of Economics at Brock University, Ontario, Canada, and the author of *The Origins of the Keynesian Revolution* (1988). Mary Ann and Robert Dimand edited (together with Evelyn Forget) *Women of Value: Feminist Essays on the History of Women in Economics* (1995).

ROUTLEDGE STUDIES IN THE HISTORY OF ECONOMICS

A HISTORY OF GAME THEORY, VOLUME 1

From the beginnings to 1945

In alphabetical order:

Mary Ann Dimand and Robert W. Dimand

London and New York

First published 1996
by Routledge
2 Park Square, Milton Park, Abingdon, Oxfordshire OX14 4RN

Simultaneously published in the USA and Canada
by Routledge
711 Third Avenue, New York, NY 10017

First issued in paperback 2014

Routledge is an imprint of the Taylor and Francis Group, an informa company

Reprinted 2000

Transferred to Digital Printing 2005

British Library Cataloguing in Publication Data
A catalogue record for this book is available from the British
Library

Library of Congress Cataloguing in Publication Data
Dimand, Mary Ann., 1960–
A history of game theory / by Mary Ann Dimand and
Robert W. Dimand.
p. cm. – (Routledge studies in the history of economics)
Includes bibliographical references and index.
Contents v. 1. From the beginnings to 1945.
1. Game theory – History. I. Dimand, Robert W.
(Robert William)
II. Title. III. Series. HB144.D56 1996 519.3'09–dc20
96-5078 CIP

ISBN 13: 978-0-415-07257-1 (hbk)
ISBN 13: 978-1-138-00660-7 (pbk)

To John P. Mayberry
Game theorist and friend

CONTENTS

PREFACE

Examining the early history of game theory has been an extremely enjoyable project – one which has led to fascinating byways and to many interesting speculations. Among the elements of the work which we have enjoyed are our contacts with game theorists and historians of thought.

Many of the sources mentioned in this volume will appear in a collection, *The Foundations of Game Theory*, edited by M.A. Dimand and R.W. Dimand (forthcoming from Edward Elgar Publishing), making them much more easily accessible to readers of this work.

We would like to thank Roy Weintraub, Duke University, and *History of Political Economy* for including us in an engrossing conference on the development of game theory, and all participants there for the enormous amount we learned from them.

We would also like to thank Rob Leonard not only for conversation with him at that conference, but later and sequentially as he worked and works also on the history of game theory. Similar thanks to Christian Schmidt, whose work on the history of game theory is invariably inspiring. We thank Christian and l'Association Charles Gide pour l'Etude de la Pensée Economique as well for inviting Bob to present the material which has become Chapter 8 of this book at a conference in Paris, and for supporting his travel.

We are grateful to the Dean of Social Sciences at Brock University for financial support of this project on a number of occasions.

We would like to thank all of our game theorist friends for interesting conversations, but especially John P. Mayberry, Martin Shubik, Monique Florenzano and David Pearce.

Special thanks to Judy Klein for her helpful remarks on material, much of which has become Chapter 4. That there are reproduced diagrams in this volume is due to Judy. We also thank Martin Osborne and Paul Walker for correcting an error in our remarks on Todhunter, and Nicolas Chaigneau and Philippe LeGall for correcting a minor error in our discussion of Edgeworth and for introducing us to Marcel LeNoir's work.

We are indebted to the *Economia delle Scelte Pubbliche (Journal of Public Finance and Public Choice*), *History of Economics Review, History of Political Economy,* and the *Revue d'Economie Politique* for permission to use material which has appeared in their pages, in a different form.

Many thanks as well to Alan Jarvis of Routledge, who has been a kind, helpful and most patient editor.

Because this is a joint work, and one in which the apportionment of credit is unusually easy, we would like to state who did what. (Renegotiation has occurred: this is an equilibrium statement.) The original idea of study in this area was Bob's, and it is only because of his invitation that Mary Ann began work on these topics. In the final manuscript, Mary Ann is the primary author of Chapters 1 through 5, although she discussed them with Bob and derived much helpful advice from him. As well as conceiving this project, Bob is the primary author of Chapters 6 to 9, with Mary Ann contributing substantially as a coauthor.

1

INTRODUCTION
Defining game theory and its history

This book is about the history of game theory up to and including von
Neumann and Morgenstern (1944) – i.e. it discusses the history of an economic
concentration for over 200 years before the concentration was named, and ends
with its demarcation as a separate field. The continued study of the economics
of Aristotle and, indeed, Adam Smith shows that there is no novelty in this: we
can learn from our predecessors.

To discuss a literature we call game theory before the term was invented, we
must define what problems and approaches we include under this rubric:
authors did not label their work with a term which did not yet exist. The first
section includes a discussion of the structure of the book within this context.

Moreover, since there are many possible approaches to examining the history
of a discipline or concentration, we would like to define the task we attempt in
this book – and also what tasks we are not attempting. This is the subject of the
second section.

We would also like to make a distinction between game theory and
conceptual tools (of which probability theory and treatment of preferences
under uncertainty are particularly prominent for this period). Some of this
literature, as well as intellectual connections between its proponents and game
theorists in our sense, are discussed in the third section.

In the fourth section, we discuss some literature of interest to historians of
game theory which we have nonetheless chosen not to examine in the body of
the book. This literature, including Pascal's Wager, focuses on works which can
receive, or have received, more game-theoretic interpretation.

A brief conclusion sums up the matter of this introductory chapter.

DEFINING GAME THEORY

When non-cooperative game theory is introduced as a classroom topic, many
instructors introduce a game as an event tree with certain properties (e.g. a
structure representing perfect memory). Cooperative games are typically
defined as sets of players and of imputations for different subsets of players.
In the classroom, game theory is implicitly demarcated as the study of the

1

properties of such games, of ways to analyse such games and of game-construction by optimizing agents.

In discussing the analytical work of writers before von Neumann and Morgenstern, the typical definitions of a 'game' do not function. The concept had not been invented, and the relationship of topics which have since been embraced by game theorists to each other was often not recognized.

For the purposes of this book, we define game theory as the (relatively) rigorous analysis of situations of strategic interdependence.[1] In such situations, the entire payoff structure faced by one player depends on decisions, or 'moves', made by other players. This produces a situation of what Émile Borel called 'psychological uncertainty': a stochastic element is introduced not by some truly random process, but by player A's lack of knowledge about the play of other agents.[2] If the risk of a strategically interdependent situation can be quantified, some sort of theory of behaviour under risk is still necessary for the analysis of agent behaviour.[3]

The problems of information and uncertainty are intimately linked in problems of the sort which denominate game theoretics. Players may suffer uncertainty because they do not know what moves others have made, are making, or will make. For this reason, each player must form some inference about the moves of others to rationally choose among his or her own potential moves. The structure of a game, including its payoffs, may greatly affect the conjectures A makes about B's behaviour. However, since A's conjectures about B's behaviour affect A's actions, B has an incentive to influence those conjectures.

Morgenstern (1928), who presented the much-cited and deliberated example of Holmes and Moriarty, discussed the recursion problem in a situation of strategic interdependence without well-defined payoffs. He also suggested that, if both players could work out who would win the game, they might as well make each other the appropriate payments at the outset rather than playing.

> Sherlock Holmes, pursued by his opponent, Moriarty, leaves London for Dover. The train stops at a station on the way, and he alights there rather than travelling on to Dover. He has seen Moriarty at the railway station, recognizes that he is very clever and expects that Moriarty will take a faster special train in order to catch him in Dover. Holmes' anticipation turns out to be correct. But what if Moriarty had been still more clever, had estimated Holmes' mental abilities better and had foreseen his actions accordingly? Then, obviously, he would have travelled to the intermediate station. Holmes, again, would have had to calculate that, and he himself would have decided to go on to Dover. Whereupon, Moriarity would again have 'reacted' differently. Because of so much thinking they might not have been able to act at all or the intellectually weaker of the two would have surrendered to the other in

the Victoria Station, since the whole flight would have become unnecessary. Examples of this kind can be drawn from everywhere. However, chess, strategy etc. presuppose expert knowledge, which encumbers the example unnecessarily.

(1928; translated in Morgenstern 1935a, 173–4)

The Holmes–Moriarty problem has been set up as a two-player game with payoffs leading to a well-defined solution (by von Neumann and Morgenstern), though not precisely that of Conan Doyle. Without parameterization, the problem of Conan Doyle's short story 'His Last Bow' would seem insoluble, serving, as Morgenstern (1935a) used it, to illustrate the problem of mutual perfect foresight in many situations of strategic interdependence. Such games as chess not only 'presuppose expert knowledge', but inherently possess more structure than Holmes' (and Moriarty's) problem – they are correspondingly easier to reason about, and it is not surprising that early workers on strategic interdependence typically set up and analysed specific games. Another question suggested by Morgenstern's pre-1944 remarks is whether game theory (as well as the theory of decision under uncertainty) constitutes specialized knowledge, whether it is a positive depiction of rational behaviour or yields normative recommendations for strategy choice.[4]

Magnan de Bornier remarks in an aside that 'game theory... developed largely from mechanical models such as Cournot's: game theorists still consider him a precursor' (Magnan de Bornier 1992, 638 fn15). However, the sorts of problems we call game-theoretics (certainly including Cournot's 1838 work) were not assembled as the stuff of a particular study, game theory, until long after Cournot wrote. A singularly interesting aspect of examining early work analysing situations of strategic interdependence is seeing how thinkers who were not indoctrinated in game theory thought about handling the informational problems they faced. We contend that an interesting feature of such early work is that many of the methods used to deal with problems such as those of player conjecture are not notably more mechanical than those used by present-day game theorists. Many of the weaknesses of early examinations of problems of strategic interdependence are weaknesses in present-day game theory. Looking at early work makes it easier to see 'mechanical' elements in more recent game theory – not all of which have been inherited from Cournot.[5]

Chapters 2 and 3 discuss work on market structure, particularly duopoly, much of which is already recognized as game theoretic in nature, as Magnan de Bornier suggests. Authors in this area essayed analysis of the 'reasonable' actions and reactions of producers of substitute goods. Coeval with Cournot's more famous duopoly model was his discussion of bilateral monopoly, in which producers of complementary goods interact strategically. For Cournot, bilateral monopoly was an opening into verbal discussion of a general equilibrium model with emphasis on the production side. Later writers, however, became more interested in the strategic aspects of the problem: Edgeworth's discussion

3

of the indeterminacy of equilibrium in an exchange economy with few agents is notable. This literature is examined in Chapter 4.

Political science, initiated by William Riker, became a fruitful area for game-theoretic analysis. Under the successive parliamentary reforms of the nineteenth century, however, many English economists wrote on the properties of various voting schemes and to advocate particular systems. Chapter 5 examines this literature, setting Charles Lutwidge Dodgson's (Lewis Carroll's) stunning achievement of a two-stage game-theoretic model in *Principles of Parliamentary Representation* in the context of other works. Because many readers may not be familiar with the history and literature of proportional representation, we review the background literature in that chapter, and at greater length than its game-theoretic content merits by our definitions, in order that the meaning of Dodgson's model will be transparent.

Chapter 6 addresses analyses of military strategy and pacifist strategy, which oddly share similar theoretical roots. We touch lightly on Sun Tzu's *The Art of War* before turning to the work of the military modeller Frederick Lanchester and the pacifist theorist Lewis Fry Richardson.

The remaining chapters centre on issues which are more familiar to modern game theorists. Chapter 7, on the definition of equilibrium in situations of strategic interdependence (including the maximin approach[6]) and issues of equilibrium existence, focuses primarily on Borel and on von Neumann (1928a, b). We also discuss James Waldegrave's seventeenth-century solution to the card game '*le Her*' as a very early example of a mixed strategy[7] maximin equilibrium, and Zermelo (1913). In Chapter 8 we discuss further work by Borel, his student Jean Ville, and René de Possel, while Chapter 9 examines von Neumann and Morgenstern (1944) in the historical perspective of the earlier literature and of contemporary reviews.

APPROACH TO THE EARLY LITERATURE

A number of approaches are possible in writing any history of a discipline. An old-fashioned approach is that of Todhunter, whose *History of the Theory of Probability* (1865) recounts every scrap of literature he knew of, which had a bearing on probability theory. To do such work today would be to invite a remark like that of Winston Churchill: 'Pray take away this pudding; it has no theme'. Another approach, which few historians of thought deliberately adopt, but of which they often accuse each other, is the canonization of precursors.[8] (One risks such accusations by comparing the earlier and later literatures.) Another relatively recent approach is to discuss the development of the discipline as such. One may, like Leonard (1992), argue that work which was not influential in the core development of the discipline is not worth mentioning for that reason. This approach is more directly concerned with the sociology of knowledge than with the content of the intellectual work in that discipline.

We have chosen to take a different approach which, though far from unusual, is not easily distinguished by description. As intimated at the end of the last section, we think it worthwhile to read early analyses of questions, which were later seized upon by game theory, for themselves. We find them interesting as early approaches to handling such complex problems and feel that they retain interest in providing approaches which now, paradoxically, often seem new. Moreover, examination of such work provides an appropriate context for looking at the achievement of von Neumann and Morgenstern, even in (the many) cases where von Neumann and Morgenstern were unaware of the literature upon which they made a substantial advance.

Where earlier literature has been cited or seemed to us to merit comparison with later work, we remark on this. We make no claims of completeness in such cross-referencing, however, because of both the size of the later literature and our own obliviousness to appropriate correlations. Moreover, some of the literature discussed here may not be transparently game-theoretic: in these cases we have bolstered our own arguments with quotations from later economists and game-theorists.

Where we know of an association, interaction or influence between writers, whether these are contemporaries or not, we make mention of it. We agree that the sociology of knowledge is of interest itself, although advancing this study is not our primary aim. In addition, certain claims of priority for earlier writers seem to merit examination (notably Maurice Fréchet for Borel's priority over von Neumann's 1928 proof of the existence of maximin equilibrium), and on these occasions we consider such claims.

Our approach, then, is eclectic with respect to the three approaches described at the beginning of this section. It is our belief that our strategy of looking above all at the literature which was available before von Neumann and Morgenstern is a worthwhile one.

INDIRECT FOREBEARS

Probability theory

The study of strategic interdependence not only requires the ability to treat risk, but also the earliest works in both probability and game theory derived from consideration of gambling games. Early analysis of games of pure chance, such as hazard or craps, stimulated the development of probability; later analysis of card games and Morra, with more strategic content, marked the birth of game-theoretic analysis. The existence of some probability theory would seem, then, to have been a precondition for game-theory. Readers with particular interest in this area are strongly advised to refer to the invaluable Todhunter (1865) and to Stigler (1986). Moreover, a number of probabilists contributed to the development of game-theoretic models and tools: Borel and his students (discussed in Chapters 6 and 7) are particularly notable.

The relatively late start of probability theory (e.g. as compared with geometry) would seem to be due to the irregularity of hand-made dice as much as anything else. Iterated throws of ancient dice have shown that they typically do not yield a uniform distribution for display of their sides, and that the differences in distribution are idiosyncratic. Where randomization devices differed so widely, deriving laws of probability would have seemed far from natural.

Todhunter (1865) traces the origins of probability theory from a fifteenth-century commentary on Dante's *Divine Comedy*. Daniel Bernoulli, who presented a solution of the St Petersburg Problem which bears a strong relationship with game theory (see below), was, like other Bernoullis, an important probabilist. James Waldegrave's mixed strategy maximin solution of the game *'le Her'* (discussed in Chapter 7) stands strongly on probabilistic roots. Probabilists concerned themselves with the properties of voting systems, which have become an important area within applied game theory (see Chapter 5 for an account of nineteenth-century analyses of proportional representation which take the perspective of strategic interdependence). Cournot, who pioneered the most widely used equilibrium concept in the course of analysing duopoly, also figured as a probabilist.

One of the most useful tools supplied to later game theory by probability theory was Bayes's Theorem. John Harsanyi (1967, 1968) originated the theory of games of incomplete information, using initial move by nature (which chooses the 'type' or initial situation of each player, unbeknown to others) and Bayesian updating by players. Bayesian updating provides a method for players to process information on the nature of an opponent from his or her play during early stages of a game, and has been useful for the analysis of situations in which the exact preferences, or 'type', of another player are inferred in a multi-stage game, such as Cho and Kreps (1987). (Where preferences are assumed risk-neutral and the physical payoff is money, such inference problems do not exist.) Developed by the Englishman, the Reverend Thomas Bayes (1763), this method uses the formula for determining the probability that a given event will occur, given information that the event falls within a smaller set than the entire event space.

Let S be the entire event-space, $S_1 \subset S$ be the event space in which it is known that the event has fallen, which is an event in itself, and S_2 be the event of interest. (For an example, see note[9]). This formula is $\text{Prob}(S_2|S_1) = \text{Prob}(S_1 \cap S_2)/\text{Prob}(_1)$, where Prob(s) indicates the probability that event s occurs, | can be read 'given that', and $\cap$ indicates intersection.

If, however, we are interested in the probability that the event S_1 has occurred, given that event S_2 has occurred, we can use the above formula to substitute for $\text{Prob}(S_1 \cap S_2)$, yielding $\text{Prob}(S_1|S_2) = \text{Prob}(S_1 \cap S_2)/\text{Prob}(S_2) = \text{Prob}(S_2|S_1)\text{Prob}(S_1)/\text{Prob}(S_2)$ (for an analogous example, see note[10]). In the realm of game theory, we might construct a game in which a player knows that another is of one of two types (e.g. 'diligent' or 'lazy') which are characterized by different preferences. The rational player can then be modelled as inferring the other's type from his or her play: this also provides a rationale for bluffing for the other player.

Valuable as the contributions of probability theory have been for the study of strategic interdependence, they do not themselves constitute game theory. It seems likely, however, that gaming manuals which advise appropriate play of card games, chess and the like, which often have a substantial probabilistic component, contain some game theoretic material. We have not made any extensive search of such material. However, a précis of some interesting material from one such work, John Arbuthnot's, is presented below.

Arbuthnot

The 1692 *Of the Laws of Chance, or, a Method of Calculation of the Hazards of Game* is a gaming manual attributed to John Arbuthnot by Todhunter and reproduced as under that authorship by the Early English Text Society. According to Todhunter, it reproduces work by the early probabilist Christian Huygens, with some added material. It furnishes an example of some interesting features in such works, particularly in view of the author's stance:

> I call that Chance, which is nothing but want of Art; that only which is left to me, is to wager where there are the greatest number of Chances, and consequently the greatest probability to gain; and the whole Art of Gaming, where there is anything of Hazard, will be reduc'd to this at last, *viz.* in dubious Cases, to calculate on which side there are most Chances; and tho this can't be done in the midst of Game precisely to an Unite, yet a Man who knows the Principles, may make such a conjecture, as will be a sufficient direction to him; and tho it is possible, if there are any Chances against him at all, that he may lose, yet when he chuseth the safest side, he may part with his Money with more content (if there can be any at all) in such a Case.
>
> ... The Reader may here observe the Force of Numbers, which can be successfully applied, even to those things, which one would imagine are subject to no Rules. There are very few things which we know, which are not capable of being reduc'd to a Mathematical Reasoning, and when they cannot, it's a sign our Knowledge of them is very small and confus'd; and where a mathematical reasoning can be had, it's as great folly to make use of any other, as to grope for a thing in the dark when you have a Candle standing by you.
>
> (Arbuthnot 1692, Preface)

While Arbuthnot's work is probabilistic, his approach is that of advising readers on the strategic matters of how much, and on which side, to bet. Moreover, he suggests that mathematical methods furnish a tool kit which the player can employ to choose the 'safest side', and at least 'part with his Money with more Content (if there can be any at all) in such a Case'. That is, probability outfits a normative tool which advises players on what to do. Alternatively, it could be interpreted as describing the behaviour of a 'good player' or 'rational agent'.

Arbuthnot's approach to valuing the lotteries specifically embodied an hypothesis on player preferences over lotteries:

> ... I shall make use of this Principle, *Ones Hazard or Expectation to gain any thing, is worth so much, as, if he had it, he could purchase the like Hazard or Expectation again in a just and equal Game.*
>
> For *Example*, If one, without my knowledge, should hide in one Hand 7 Shillings, and in his other 3 Shillings, and put it to my choice which Hand I would take, I say this is as much worth to me, as if he should give me 5 Shillings; because, if I have 5 Shillings, I can purchase as good a Chance again, and that in a fair and just Game.
>
> (1692, 3–4)

On this principle, players value a lottery with a probability of 0.5 of gaining each of 3 shillings and 7 shillings equally with a lottery with a probability of 0.5 of losing 10 shillings and a probability of 0.5 of gaining 20 shillings, at 5 shillings. That is, Arbuthnot assumes that agents have a constant marginal utility of income and hence are risk neutral, and satisfy the expected utility hypothesis. Preferences under risk are thus affine in both payoffs and probability.

That the hypothesis of risk neutrality gives rise to a paradox, in the sense that it yields predictions which seem 'unreasonable' in the light of actual behaviour, was the focus of the St Petersburg Paradox which Bernoulli (1738) addressed: this is discussed below. That the assumption of expected utility maximization also gives rise to such a paradox is the crux of the Allais Paradox. While the problem of non-linear utility of income is relatively easy to deal with by assuming that players know each other's utility functions, non-expected utility is more difficult to deal with. Von Neumann and Morgenstern finessed this issue by axiomatizing agent valuation of lotteries. Subsequently, game theorists with concerns in this area typically construct and deal only with games with pure strategy solutions. However, if we take Arbuthnot's (and Huygens's and de Moivre's) assumption as a datum, it is still of interest to look at his further arguments.

Arbuthnot used his framework to address what Todhunter termed the Problem of Points, which confronts the issue of gauging the value of a player's position in an unfinished game:

> ... if I should play with another on this condition, that the Victory should be to the Three first Games, and I had gain'd one already; it is still uncertain who shall first gain the third; yet by a demonstrative

reasoning I can estimate both the Value of his expectation and mine, and consequently (if we agree to leave the Game unperfect) determin [sic] how great a share of the Stakes belong to me, and how much to my Play-fellow; or if any were desirous to take my place, at what rate I ought to sell it.

(1692, 2–3)

Using his stated utility hypotheses, Arbuthnot considered the proportion of a pre-existing pot which players should be allotted if the game is stopped before it's finished, based on players' (*ex ante*) probability of winning each stage of the game. While Arbuthnot's treatment is based on agents whose asymmetry is supplied by their status in an unfinished game, an extension (which was made by other authors) permits asymmetry to come from differential skill levels. This can be generalized to asymmetry due to rules of the game. Similarly, this method can be used to evaluate the proportion of the pot each player might claim before the game is started. In approaching this sort of issue, work on the Problem of Points looks like a forebearer of game value and of the Shapley value.

The St Petersburg Paradox

The St Petersburg Paradox epitomizes a weakness of the assumption of risk neutrality. (Its name is derived from the fact that Bernoulli, who provided a solution to the problem (1738), then resided in St Petersburg and published it in a St Petersburg journal.)

The problem asks how much a player should be willing to pay for a lottery in which a randomizing device such as a coin gives a probability of 0.5 of ending the game on a given coup. If the game is ended at the first coup, the player receives 2 francs, if at the second, 4 francs, if at the nth, 2^n francs. The game is of indefinite length: the probability that the game ends at the nth coup is $(0.5)^n$. The expected monetary value of this lottery is:

$$\sum_{n=2}^{\infty}(0.5)^n(2)^n = \sum_{n=1}^{\infty} 1 = \infty.$$

The infinite expected monetary value of the lottery suggests, if we accept Arbuthnot's assumptions, that a player should be willing to pay an infinite amount to play it. It seems clear, however, that no player would do so. Bernoulli suggested that players might not value successive monetary gains in the same way, and proposed a utility of income function which exhibits risk-aversion: $v = ln(y)$, where y is the increment to income from playing the lottery. With a utility of income function displaying decreasing returns, a player will only pay a finite sum to play this lottery.

The assumption of risk-aversion thus yields answers to problems of choice under uncertainty, such as most of those addressed by early game theorists,

9

which seem to describe agent behaviour better than the answers yielded by risk-neutrality. Although game theorists have typically simply assumed that the value of payoffs to players is known to all players, it seems credible that solution of this problem aided the rise of game theory, if it was not strictly necessary for future work.

Another branch of mathematics, the development of fixed point theorems, has been extremely useful to game theorists in proving the existence of equilibrium, however it is defined. In fact, mathematical economists interested in games, such as Shapley, have worked to extend fixed point theory. Interestingly enough, a number of those working in fixed point theory in the 1930s were associated not only with each other, but also with important figures in the game-theoretic sphere, in the group which created *The Scottish Book*.

Fixed point theorems and *The Scottish Book*

For most economists, the primary use of fixed point theorems is as tools for proving that an equilibrium exists for a problem, even if that equilibrium might be prohibitively difficult to find. They have served this purpose for models of general competitive equilibrium, as well as for game theory. The basic idea of fixed point theory is this: consider two spaces, A and B, which are supposed to have properties such as convexity and compactness,[11] with A bearing a particular relation to B (often $A=B$), and mapping h from A to (or onto) B, which satisfies certain continuity properties. Then there is some point $x \in A$ such that $x \in h(x)$. (Readers interested in fixed point theory and its history are strongly advised to consult Border (1985).)

By choosing the mapping h sufficiently carefully, a fixed point theorem proves the existence (but not uniqueness) of an equilibrium. Where the strategy set for a game has convexity and compactness, which the possibility of mixed strategies gives to most such sets, a sufficiently continuous and cleverly chosen mapping has a fixed point. Due to the choice of mapping that fixed point must be an equilibrium for the game. (One such mapping might be one from the set of all possible strategy profiles to itself, in which for each player i, $h(s) \equiv h(s_1, \ldots s_i, \ldots)$) has as its ith element the strategy which yields i the highest possible payoff given the strategies of other players. A fixed point of this mapping is a Cournot–Nash equilibrium.)

The earliest and simplest fixed point theorem is that of Brouwer (1912): in this version a compact convex subset of $\Re^m$ is mapped onto itself by means of a continuous function. The lemmas of Sperner and of Knaster, Kuratowski and Mazurkiewicz in the 1920s applied the same ideas to the simplex[12] and to the convex hulls of sets of points. In 1941, Kakutani published the fixed point theorem perhaps most widely used by economists, in which the properties required for $h(\cdot)$ are less strict: it need only be an upper hemi-continuous correspondence.

While these and later fixed point theorems have been remarkably useful for game theorists and other mathematical economists, the work is not in itself game theory by our definitions. However, in 1935 (Ulam 1981, 3), not long after von Neumann (1928) presented the first proof of the existence of maximin equilibrium, a group of mathematicians including fixed point theorists and strategic interdependence theorists met regularly at the Scottish Café (Café Szkocka) in Lwów, Poland, after Polish Mathematical Society meetings. Among their activities was the setting of mathematical problems for solution, often with prizes offered. These problems were recorded in *The Scottish Book*.

Regular members of this group included the important mathematicians Banach, Mazur, Ulam and the ubiquitous Erdös, early strategic interdependence theorist Steinhaus, and fixed point theorist Kuratowski. Since sessions at the Scottish Café succeeded Mathematical Society meetings, there were frequent visitors: problems were also contributed to *The Scottish Book* by game theorists Fréchet (nos. 117 and 118), von Neumann (no. 163) and Knaster (no. 182).

As Granas (1981, 45) notes, the theory of KKM-maps (Knaster–Kuratowski–Mazurkiewicz-maps) related closely to a number of *The Scottish Book* problems, especially problem 54.[13] Other problems which refer to games focus more on the properties of sets and mappings than on the matter we have defined as game-theoretics.

Problem 54, contributed by Schauder, runs as follows:

(a) A convex, closed, compact set H is transformed by a continuous mapping $U(x)$ on a part of itself. H is contained in a set of type (F). Does there exist a fixed point on the transformation?

(b) Solve the same problem for arbitrary linear topological spaces or such spaces in which there exist arbitrarily small convex neighbourhoods. [A solution exists for spaces of type (F_0); in the more general theorem, H need not be compact; only $U(H)$ is assumed compact.]

Mauldin adds the remark:

This problem has led to an incredible number of fixed point theorems.... The second and third parts of the problem have a positive solution; the first part of Problem 54 is still unsolved.

(1981, 124)

In his Scottish Book Conference lecture, Kac discusses the 'Ulam game' as one 'we of course all remember', in which

Player One picks a zero or one and Player Two picks a zero or one, and then one constructs what Tony Martin called a decimal binary (which is an excellent name for what ordinary mortals call simply a binary). If it falls

11

into a set E Player One wins, and if it is not in E Player Two wins. The question is: Is there a winning strategy for either one of the players?

(Mauldin 1981, 19–20)

This game, however, serves to focus attention on the nature of sets rather than of strategically interdependent choice, with the game's rules functioning to delineate a particular set of mappings from which players seek optima. One of the difficulties of this problem is that the series of zeros and ones which constitute the binary may be of infinite length. Depending on the nature of E, it may or may not be possible to learn whether a given point belongs in it. Kac emphasizes Steinhaus's deliberations on classifying types of sets as 'constructible' or the reverse, and the puzzle bears a clear relationship to Gödel's Theorem.

Problems 43 and 67 are similar in their focus on the properties of sets.[14]

Despite the period and participants of *The Scottish Book*, it is not clear that progress in the study of strategic interaction *per se* occurred in this group. It seems credible enough that conversations between participants were fruitful in the area which was to become game theory, as they were in other areas. However, *The Scottish Book* provides no evidence on this point.

WORKS WHICH CAN BE GIVEN GAME-THEORETIC INTERPRETATION

A number of publications which can be given (and, often enough, have been given) game-theoretic interpretations nonetheless fail to satisfy us as early works in game theory. Although appraisal of situations of strategic interdependence has often been the subject of these works, they usually fail to pass our criterion of analytical rigour.[15] Steven Brams, for instance, has written game-theoretic castings of many stories from the Bible in *Biblical Games* (1980), but we do not feel that these stories offer a rigorous analysis in themselves.

In ancient and early literatures themselves, it is not unusual to see perfectly good *solutions* to games given, with little or no reasoning accompanying them. Walker (1995) opens his outline of the history of game theory with this entry:

The Babylonian Talmud is the compilation of ancient law and tradition set down during the first five centuries AD which serves as the basis of Jewish religious, criminal and civil law. One problem discussed in the Talmud is the so called marriage contract problem: a man has three wives whose marriage contracts specify that in the case of his death they receive 100, 200 and 300 respectively. The Talmud gives apparently contradictory recommendations. Where the man dies leaving an estate of only 100, the Talmud recommends equal division. However, if the estate is worth 300 it recommends proportional division (50, 100, 150), while for an estate of 200, its recommendation of (50, 75, 75) is a complete mystery. This particular Mishna has baffled Talmudic scholars for two millennia. In 1985[16], it was recognized that the Talmud anticipates the modern theory of cooperative games. Each solution corresponds to the nucleolus of an appropriately defined game.

(1995, 1)

Fascinating though this sort of intellectual archaeology is, it does not fall under our heading.

Also in the realm of faith, but in philosophy as well,[17] Pascal's famous Wager may be interpreted in a game-theoretic fashion.

Pascal

Pascal argued the advantages of religious faith with an imaginary 'rationalist', and posited that

A game is on, at the other end of this infinite distance, and heads or tails will turn up. What will you wager? According to reason you cannot do either; according to reason you cannot leave either undone.
... Yes, but wager you must; there is no option, you have embarked on it.... You have two things to lose: truth and good, and two things to stake: your reason and your will, your knowledge and your happiness. And your nature has two things to shun: error and misery. Your reason does not suffer by your choosing one more than the other, for you must choose. But your happiness? Let us weigh gain and loss in calling heads that God is. Reckon these two chances: if you win, you win all; if you lose, you lose naught. Then do not hesitate, wager that He is.

(1950, 117–19)

Pascal's Wager has been represented in a decision-theoretic context by Chimenti (1990).[18] This formulation differs from game theory only in that it isn't specifically formulated as a 'game against nature'. As in a game against nature, the probability of the state 'a caring God [in Pascal's sense] exists' is unknown. However, Chimenti seems to be interested only in pure strategy solutions, and he does not explicitly discuss, as a game-theoretic modeller typically would, the rationalist's decision criterion.

The Wager can be considered a game of imperfect information between the rationalist and 'nature'. 'Nature' has previously determined whether there is a god who cares about the behaviour of human beings: the rationalist, however, does not know which state exists. The rationalist can choose to believe or choose not to believe; belief has a finite mundane cost: call it B. If the rationalist believes and there is a god observant of human behaviour, he or she gains 'all', which might be considered eternal bliss, or a payoff of ∞. Otherwise, she has lost the costs of belief, B, during her lifetime, decreasing the payoff of a life

13

without the pains of faith, which we denote G. If the rationalist does not believe and Pascal's God exists, she loses from God's disapprobation. If we assume that eternal damnation is the reward of non-belief in this case, the payoff can be given as $-\infty$. Otherwise, temporal belief-costs are saved and the payoff is G. Let the rationalist's prior probability that Pascal's God exists be denoted q. The rationalist's pure strategies are to believe or not to believe: she can also randomize over these strategies. Let the probability of believing, to be determined by the rationalist, be p. The rational sceptic then solves the problem

$$\max_p \; q[p(\infty) + (1-p)(-\infty)] + (1-q)[p(G-B) + (1-p)G]$$

or, equivalently,

$$\max_p \; q(2p-1)\infty + (1-q)(G-pB).$$

So long as q, the prior probability that Pascal's God exists, is greater than zero, the rationalist's optimal strategy is to believe with probability one. According to Pascal, one cannot be sure that such a God does not exist. In this case, what is to be gained by a believer if God exists is indeed 'all': prospective losses are by comparison 'naught', since they are finite? Prudence then dictates that even a purely self-interested rationalist believes in Pascal's God.

This approach, like Chimenti's, is more decision-theoretic than game-theoretic. Approaches to games against nature vary: Luce and Raiffa (1957) discuss several. A rationalist might choose instead to use a max-min criterion (fundamental to von Neumann and Morgenstern), choosing a strategy (pure or mixed) which maximizes the minimum which is received across all states of nature. The minimum payoff from belief is $G - B$, from unbelief $-\infty$: this criterion also dictates belief.

The minimax risk criterion is one in which the player minimizes the maximum payoff loss from use of a strategy. Belief yields no payoff loss or regret if God exists, but unbelief yields infinite loss or regret. If Pascal's God does not exist, belief generates a loss (regret) of B, and unbelief none. The maximum payoff loss from belief, then, is finite B, but that for unbelief is ∞ – hence a rationalist following this criterion also chooses to believe.

Suppose, however, the rationalist believes the universe to be malevolent, desiring her downfall. In this case, the universe might be conjectured to prefer the state in which the rationalist is worse off, and might be believed to minimize the maximum payoff to the rationalist. In this case, Pascal's God will not exist, and the rationalist should not incur the cost of belief.

Jean-Jacques Rousseau and Adam Smith

Ordeshook (1986) and Fudenberg and Tirole (1991) quote Rousseau (1755) as remarking that

If a group of hunters set out to take a stag, they are fully aware that they would all have to remain faithfully at their posts in order to succeed; but if a hare happens to pass near one of them, there can be no doubt that he pursued it without qualm, and that once he had caught his prey, he cared very little whether or not he had made his companions miss theirs.

Ordeshook uses this passage as a demonstration of the instability of coalition under some circumstances, while Fudenberg and Tirole employ it as a game of 'stag hunt' to discuss multiple equilibria and the riskiness of equilibria. With two players, for example, the product of joint stag-hunting might be two utiles for each player, while the payoff to lone stag-hunting is zero and that for lone hare-hunting is one utile. In this case, both joint stag-hunting and double lone hare-hunting are Nash equilibria: a player's deviation from joint stag-hunting causes her (as well as the other player) a reduction in payoff. A player who deviates from hare-hunting and attempts to hunt stag when the other adheres to hare-hunting experiences a loss in utility which, however, is not shared by the other.

Each situation is a pure strategy equilibrium. However, a hunter's payoff from hare-hunting is not affected by the other's behaviour, while that from stag-hunting is. Thus, there is no risk associated with hare-hunting, while a stag-hunter risks desertion by his or her partner. This risk increases as the number of hunters required to bring in a stag increases.

It is interesting to compare the game of 'stag-hunt' derived from Rousseau with a passage from Smith (1776). Comparison points out a fundamental feature of the matter of game theory. Discussing price in an 'early and rude state of society', Smith stated that

If among a nation of hunters, . . . it usually costs twice the labour to kill a beaver which it does to kill a deer, one beaver should naturally exchange for or be worth two deer. It is natural that what is usually the produce of two days or two hours labour, would be worth double of what is usually the produce of one day's or one hour's labour.

(1776, I.vi.1, 65)

Not only did Smith assume that double labour need not be supplied by two individuals, but he wrote in the context of exchange and price and, implicitly, a market. Where such exchange is possible, partners in beaver-hunting can contract in advance to pay a fine in deer for deserting a beaver-hunting partnership. It is less clear that such an option exists in the 'stag-hunting' game. The context of game theory is one in which there is no market, or no perfect market. This applies to problems in the realm of gambling, firms operating in the same imperfect market, situations of adverse selection or moral hazard, and many others. Where perfect markets exist, there is no opportunity for strategic behaviour. Often, the introduction of new markets into a problem eliminates its game-theoretic properties, just as a market for rights obviates the problem of externalities in Coase (1960), by changing the rules or incentives faced by players. Such concerns have been the concern, primarily, of game theory of a later period than that covered in this volume, in the realms of coordination devices and mechanism design.

Ortmann and Meardon (1995) represent Smith's *Theory of Moral Sentiments* (1759) and *Wealth of Nations* (1776) in game-theoretic forms. They formalize the socialization of behaviour Smith addressed as games of reputation in which social sanctions cause the rational person to adhere to social norms. Nonetheless, neither Rousseau nor Smith wrote in analytical ways about strategic interdependence.

In this section, we have discussed some works which consider situations that can be, or later have been, interpreted in game-theoretic terms. We have addressed those which have struck us, and other authors, as most interesting. Many works left undiscussed here can be cast in such forms, often with profit. However, the works themselves do not satisfy our definition of early game theory because of their style or imprecision. Here, we have recounted a few works of particular significance in terms of game theory, as well as giving examples of literature which will not be extensively discussed in later chapters.

CONCLUSION

This chapter is intended to stake out the territory we survey in the body of this book, and to mark our approach, which is to look at how mathematicians, economists and other writers approached problems of strategic interdependence. This permits us, additionally, to look at von Neumann and Morgenstern's book, in which game theory as a proper concentration was delimited, in the context of earlier work.

In succeeding chapters, we will look at treatises on the behaviour of firms when they have market power; trade among small numbers when prices are not necessarily the negotiating instrument (and when they are), the outcomes of voting rules, and war, among other strategic games. In some of these essays, writers applied old tools to new questions; in others, they devised new methods. Chapters 7 and 8 discuss the more conscious development of a mode of analysing situations of strategic interdependence, and Chapter 9 the great leap forward made by von Neumann and Morgenstern, and how it was received.

Von Neumann and Morgenstern established game theory as a distinct, recognized field. Most earlier writers were working on specific problems rather than on constructing a mode of thought, and many of them had remarkably little influence until after *The Theory of Games and Economic Behavior* had been published. The works of Stackelberg and Zeuthen were not recognized primarily for the new methodology embodied in them, but primarily as straightforward, though significant, contributions to industrial organization theory. Émile Borel, Jean Ville and René de Possel seem to have acted as an independent nucleus which might have developed a theory of games and strategic behaviour – perhaps a very different one! – but the rigours of working for occupied France during World War II, if nothing else, prevented this.

Our story is not one of precursors or forefathers. It is the story of (mostly isolated) attempts to answer questions, and of the beginning of a study which classed these questions together in an attempt to answer them better.

2

STRATEGIC INTERDEPENDENCE
Cournot and Duopoly

Cournot's (1838) treatments of monopoly, duopoly, and bilateral monopoly were almost incredibly early and prescient

1 in their mathematization of economic problems;
2 in their use of graphical illustrations; and
3 in their treatment of fundamentally game-theoretic problems of strategic interdependence of optimizing agents.

Recognition of Cournot's eminence has become almost axiomatic to economists. One of the most familiar treatments of duopoly and the most-frequently employed equilibrium concept in game theory have been named after him: Cournot duopoly and Cournot–Nash equilibrium. Before Cournot (1838), writers on strategic interdependence such as Sun Tzu, Pascal and Waldegrave had formulated problems in the fields of war, ethics or card games. It was Cournot who first gave a rigorous analysis of market structure, and he gave it from a game-theoretic perspective.

That Cournot's massive contribution went unrecognized for a remarkably long period is commonplace to economists.[1] It was long widely thought that Bertrand (1883) was the first thinker to recognize Cournot's work. Although Dimand (1988) has shown that Cherriman (1857, reprinted in Dimand 1995) reviewed Cournot intelligently, work stemming from Cournot's did not blossom until after Bertrand, and that was based, curiously enough, on a misunderstanding of Bertrand (see Magnan de Bornier (1992) for a discussion of what Bertrand actually said).

Considering the economics of monopoly and equilibrium analysis, Schumpeter said that

> The chief performance was Cournot's and the period's work may be described as a series of successful attempts to develop his statics of straight monopoly and as another series of much less successful attempts to develop and to correct his theories of oligopoly and bilateral monopoly. Second honors are divided between Marshall and Edgeworth.
>
> (Schumpeter 1954, 976)

Cournot's early use, not only of explicitly mathematical models, but of diagrammatic illustration of his propositions, was remarkable in itself. It was not until Shubik informed Nash and the profession (Shubik 1955: cf. Shubik 1992) of Cournot's priority in the use of Cournot–Nash equilibrium that Cournot's writing was recognized as an important contribution to game theory before game theory was invented as a separate approach.[2] Cournot's work on economic equilibrium followed earlier papers by him on the necessary conditions for static physical equilibrium (see Prékopa 1980, 535–6).

According to Morgenstern (in a paper clearly intended to promote game theory as a modelling stratagem for economists):

> In the background . . . is the undeniable and disturbing fact, already well known to Cournot, that when there are but few participants in a market, they reflect about each other's behavior and try to set their course accordingly. Here, indeed, is the crux of the matter. . . .
>
> (1948, 10)

Morgenstern identified the two issues with which game theory has perhaps dealt most frequently:

1 strategic interdependence; and
2 the role that conjectures players make about each other's behaviour has in determining the equilibrium outcome(s).

Strategic interdependence is the essential stuff of game theory. In a situation of strategic interdependence, each player's choice of action affects the payoff structure faced by other players in response to their feasible actions. Thus, in order for a modeller to cling to optimizing agents, players must be modelled as making some sort of inference about the actions of other players, and as processing these inferences. Morgenstern (1928) illustrated the dilemma facing either an optimizer or the modeller of optimizers in his example of Holmes and Moriarty: where each leaves a train depends on his beliefs about the other's beliefs about his beliefs about . . . etc. He later said that 'One may be easily convinced that here lies an insoluble *paradox*' (1935b, 1976a). Cournot leapt over the problem of modelling players' conjectures on their opponents' play and the processing of such conjectures simultaneously by employing what later became known as the Nash equilibrium concept.

Friedman states that

> Probably the first great game theorist was Cournot (1838) who invented the *non-cooperative equilibrium* in the context of theoretical industrial economics.
>
> (1992, 353)

Cournot's characterization of what was to become non-cooperative equilibrium is, implicitly, what has become the commonest description (due to Harsanyi 1966): the inability of agents to make binding contracts with each other.

In this chapter and Chapter 4, we re-examine the significance of Cournot as a game theorist before von Neumann and Morgenstern, and look at the controversies founded on his work from a game theoretic perspective. The themes that arise are those of strategic interdependence and definition of an outcome (which Cournot successfully handled by a method savouring of unconscious finesse); definition and lack of definition of the rules of the game players act within; and the formation of conjectures by players – the latter two of which early writers in particular combined with dynamic concerns. In the first section we discuss Cournot's work. The second examines the works of his critics from Bertrand to Smithies and Savage. Chapter 3 addresses the work of his heirs, Zeuthen and Stackelberg, and deals with the allied areas of the dominant firm and monopolistic competition models.

COURNOT AND DUOPOLY

Cournot was the first to formulate and give the solution of the monopolist's problem mathematically: his familiar model may be considered a particular sort of game. Positing a producer of effectively infinite quantities of mineral water at zero cost, he supposed that this monopolist maximizes revenue (hence profit) subject to market demand for mineral water. The demand curve faced by the monopolist is a reaction function to the monopolist's choice of price (or quantity) of output. Subject to the constraint imposed by this reaction curve, the monopolist maximizes profit. While consumers and the single producer are all players of the game, each consumer is too small (in an economic sense) to affect the outcome, and the use of a demand relation[3] as a reaction curve is perfectly sound.

Opening his chapter on competition, Cournot stated that

> Every one has a vague idea of the effects of competition. Theory should have attempted to render this idea more precise; and yet, for lack of regarding the question from the proper point of view, and for want of recourse to symbols (of which the use in this connection becomes indispensable), economic writers have not in the least improved on popular notions in this respect.

> (1838, 79)

That is, mathematics is necessary to clarify the effects of competition in different regimes, and to yield precise answers to questions of firm behaviour. Cournot took the competition of finite numbers of producers as paradigmatic of competition more generally, and began by assuming two identical producers of identical mineral water at zero cost. (The role of numbers in distinguishing perfect competition from other market forms in general, rather than partial, equilibrium models began to be recognized as a more complex matter with Edgeworth (1881). See Chapter 4.) This separated the role of competition in the quantity realm from any other factor: firms were symmetric with respect to cost and demand, and ineluctably symmetric with respect to the nature of their output. As Schumpeter noted,

> Cournot's example, two springs that produce mineral water of identical quality, suggests an assumption that has been almost universally adopted in the later discussion of duopoly, namely, the assumption that the cost structures of the duopolists are exactly alike. This seems to bring out the pure logic of the duopolistic situation. Actually it defines a very special case and represents an element of duopolistic situations that is particularly important for the more general case of oligopoly and enables us frequently to narrow down ranges of indeterminateness. Cournot's procedure may be excused by invoking the privileges of the pioneer. But those who dealt with the problem after him should realize that they did not gain but lost something by making the same assumption. As it was, only Marshall seems to have been fully aware of this.
>
> (1954, 979, n22)

Given the period during which Schumpeter was assembling his material, the remark about the symmetry assumed by later writers aside from Marshall seems rather odd. Other writers, notably Stackelberg, Hotelling and Zeuthen, relaxed symmetry assumptions with interesting results. Perhaps the celebration of imperfect competition (monopolistic competition), in which cost variation is possible but was not really stressed, affected Schumpeter's perspective. Models building on Cournot's while dropping various forms of symmetry will be discussed in the next chapter.

Cournot's assumption of identical products, with producers able to meet any demand, led to symmetry from the demand point of view, so that where p is the (one) price of spring water and subscripts 1 and 2 denote the two firms, $D = f(p) = D_1 + D_2$, in notation similar to that used to analyse monopolist behaviour. Cournot assumed furthermore that

> each {of the two producers} independently will seek to make this income as large as possible.
>
> We say each independently, and this restriction is very essential, as will soon appear; for if they should come to an agreement so as to obtain for each the greatest possible income, the results would be entirely different, and would not differ, so far as consumers are concerned, from those in treating of a monopoly.
>
> (1838, 79–80)

That is, in modern terms, where the two producers can come to a binding agreement to maximize joint profit, the game becomes a cooperative one, and consumers face the monopoly price and joint output. The remaining game-theoretic problem, not addressed by Cournot, is the producer's division of profits.

Cournot then changed the problem (because 'it will be convenient') to that

21

of the dual, where $p = f(D)$. Thus the income (and profits) of firm i are $D_i f(D) = D_i f(D_1 + D_2)$ (1838, 80). While it makes no difference to the equilibrium price and quantity whether a profit-maximizing monopolist who knows the demand function he or she faces uses price or quantity as her instrument, use of price or quantity as instruments makes a crucial difference where there is more than one producer. Cournot expressed no explicit recognition of this fact and, in fact, phrased his prose explanation in terms of *price* adjustment. It is interesting to note that, in his treatment of bilateral monopoly, he equally casually assumed that price was the instrument used (see Chapter 4).[4]

The general answer to the question of what outputs will be chosen by two identical zero-cost producers who wish to maximize their profits is that we do not know what outputs they will produce. $D_1 f(D_1 + D_2)$ depends not only on 1's output but on 2's (and vice versa); 1's *ex ante* profit-maximizing output depends on 1's conjecture as to 2's output. Cournot seems to have confused his independence assumption, which yields a non-cooperative game, with player conjectures of opponent passivity:

> Proprietor (1) can have no direct influence on the determination of D_2: all that he can do, when D_2 has been determined by proprietor (2), is to choose for D_1 the value which is best for him. This he will be able to do by properly adjusting his price, except as proprietor (2), who, seeing himself forced to accept this price and this value of D_1, may adopt a new value for D_2, more favourable to his interests than the preceding one.
>
> Analytically this is equivalent to saying that D_1 will be determined in terms of D_2 by the condition
>
> $$\frac{d[D_1 f(D_1 + D_2)]}{dD_1} = 0$$
>
> (1838, 80)

and vice versa for D_2.

This leads immediately to the familiar system of equations (Cournot 1838, 81) for a pair of duopolists:

$$f(D_1 + D_2) + D_1 f'(D_1 + D_2) = 0, \tag{1}$$

$$f(D_1 + D_2) + D_2 f'(D_1 + D_2) = 0. \tag{2}$$

This pair of equations yields conventional reaction curves (unnamed by Cournot) for the two duopolists, depicted in Cournot's Figure 2. Simultaneous solution of the two equations (yet another form of symmetry) yields the well-known Cournot–Nash equilibrium for duopolists.

Cournot's discussion of equilibrium stability makes clear the strength of his assumption that each player i takes her opponent j to be passive to i's alteration of quantity marketed:

> The state of equilibrium corresponding to [the intersection of the

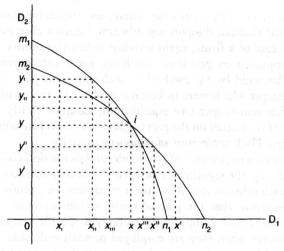

Figure 2.1

reaction curves] is . . . *stable*: i.e. if either of the producers, misled as to his true interest, leaves it temporarily, he will be brought back to it by a series of reactions, constantly declining in amplitude, and of which the dotted lines of the figure give a representation by their arrangement in steps.

(1838, 81)

The dotted lines depicted show a cobweb-style adjustment as producers move along their reaction curves (which assume opponent passivity) in response to the opponent's last-period output. In each period, then, i takes j's last-period output to be the one j will advance this period, *although this conjecture is actualized only at Cournot–Nash equilibrium*. In discussing the stability of equilibrium, Cournot used the reaction curves to illustrate the successive quantity 'moves' of the two duopolists. That is, he not only used the reaction curves to *locate* his equilibrium, but implicitly assumed that they showed the reactions of a duopolist to an opponent's last-period output. (See figure 2.1)

In so doing, he used a fundamentally static, one-period model in a pseudo-dynamic way. His duopolists are assumed to maximize profits period by period, rather than maximizing the present discounted value of output over a specific time horizon. Even if he had distinctly assumed a zero rate of discount for each duopolist, Cournot employed an assumption of successive conjectures by agents which is, as early reviewers noted, inherently fishy. Until the duopolists arrive at their equilibrium outputs, their conjectures about opponent behaviour are wrong in each period. This, a form of what is now called time-inconsistency, has helped lead to the literature of equilibrium refinements. Early debate on this subject will be discussed in the next section.

Cournot distinguished his duopoly result from that of monopoly. When a producer offers one-half the lower monopoly output (attempting to achieve the monopoly price and joint profit maximization), the other will follow

23

self-interest, as dictated by its reaction curve, and successive reactions drive the system to the Cournot duopoly equilibrium. Cournot then expanded his analysis to the case of n firms, again arriving at familiar results.

Cournot's approach to problems involving agent interdependence was substantially flavoured by his method in analysing monopoly although he introduced concepts which were to become vital to the theory of games. In order to develop non-cooperative equilibrium, Cournot tacitly assumed a particular type of conjecture on the part of players, a conjecture which we will call the 'Cournot–Nash conjecture' of opponent passivity.

Cournot stated the importance of agent independence in decision-making in his model, realizing the significance of agents' inability to make a binding contract with each other so that they might maximize joint profit. He failed, however, to recognize that his pair of optimization problems, and hence reaction functions 1 and 2, implicitly embody a specific conjecture as to opponent(s)'s moves when they are employed to analyse dynamics. In these optimization problems, each agent takes as given the strategy/strategies of opponent(s). This immediately eliminates the sort of recursion problem Morgenstern considered. Each agent thinks of her strategy as 'small', as each consumer facing a monopolist thinks her reaction 'small', within an inter-dependent system with small numbers!

In a world of strategic interdependence, this assumption takes the analysis of play as far as it can go in the direction of neo-classical *ceteris paribus*. One supposes that each player formulates her best response to each strategy profile which her opponent(s) might supply; this best-response relation is a reaction correspondence or, more usually, a reaction function. Cournot–Nash equilibrium occurs where no player would change her strategy in response to those played by her opponent(s): this can be represented by the intersection of reaction correspondences or functions. Nonetheless, although Cournot did not (and, at the time, scarcely could, giant though he was) phrase the situation in this way, *in equilibrium all agents' expectations are fulfilled*, and all agents are optimizing subject to these correct expectations.

As Pearce (1984) and Bernheim (1984) note, in Cournot–Nash equilibrium agents are getting things 'right'. This enables each agent to take the quantity/quantities set by the other player(s) as given, even as the agent optimizes: *in equilibrium*. Cournot–Nash equilibrium says nothing about the dynamics of the situation, unless agents make Cournot–Nash conjectures of opponent passivity. Moreover, the general solution to the problem of Cournot's two strategically interdependent producers of mineral water is that *we cannot know what the outcome will be* – not, that is, without making some supposition on the reasoning processes of the agents. Cournot implicitly made such a supposition – perhaps the simplest one – but seemingly tied it up with the 'independence' of agents' output decisions.

Work on equilibrium concepts has been part of a still-continuing effort to generalize the predictions of economic models on the outcome of agents' actions in situations of strategic interdependence: such concerns, however, arose rather late. Once the economics discipline began to read Cournot, their immediate attention was fixed on other problems. Do firms really act in this way, using quantity as an instrument, and with the symmetry implied by simultaneous play? This set of questions may be considered as an implicit discussion of what rules-of-the-game duopolists (or oligopolists) play under, and led to new and sometimes richer models. Arguments frequently appealed to an artificial sort of dynamics in which Cournot's basically static model was used (as he used it in discussing equilibrium stability) as the framework. A more genuinely dynamic version of the model was not employed until Frisch (1933) considered conjectures of interdependence and Smithies and Savage (1940) considered the effect of duopolist conjectures and learning in a multi-period model. Attention to asymmetries on the demand side (due to location or other forms of differentiation) and on the production side (due to producers with different costs or the ability to move first) led to richer models, which, however, did not directly engender a more general theory of games.

CRITICS OF COURNOT

Nichol, also author of 'Tragedies in the life of Cournot', wrote of Cournot's work that

> If Cournot had had the advantage of competent criticism during his own lifetime, no doubt he would have set forth unmistakably all the assumptions of his own analysis. *Thus much useless controversy might have been avoided.*
>
> (1934, 91)

Nichol referred primarily to the question of whether agents use price or quantity as their instrument, noting that, in competition, it does not matter which agent(s) name price and which quantity (nor does it under monopoly), while it does in the study of duopoly. We do not, however, regard the controversies incited by Cournot's model as useless *even in this limited case.* Controversies following Cournot embodied consideration, though admittedly rather inchoate consideration, of questions of multiple equilibria, of dynamics in player conjectures and of what the rules of the games they play *are* or *should be*. The literature of equilibrium and equilibrium refinement continues to address the 'reasonableness' of equilibrium concepts and methods of reducing the set of equilibria to more 'reasonable' and more stable ones. Game theorists after von Neumann and Morgenstern have become much more careful than Cournot was in defining the rules within which the players of a game work: however, the question of rule-setting and payoff-setting has been directly addressed only fairly recently, in the literature on mechanism design[5] which arose from reflection on principal-agent problems.

25

Cherriman and Fauveau

Cherriman (1857), a Canadian mathematician who wrote what may have been the first review of Cournot (1838), largely confined himself to praising and celebrating the precision of Cournot's mathematical modelling. He restricted his criticism to complaints about the later chapters of Cournot, which he found overly 'literary' and commonplace as contemporary political economy.

Fauveau has been discussed by Ménard (1978) and Ekelund and Hébert (1990) as forerunner of Bertrand. However, Fauveau (1867) thought that if one duopolist fixes the quantity it supplies, the other could not fix the selling price, so that being first to fix quantity makes a duopolist the market leader, in the sense of Zeuthen rather than of Stackelberg (Theocharis 1993, 66–7).

Fauveau, however, noted the peculiar nature of the out-of-equilibrium conjectures made by Cournot's duopolists:

> Unfortunately, one hypothesis, which is necessary for the correctness of these results, appears to us to be wrong. The author assumes that each producer can fix his sales without this changing the sales of other producers, a thing which is not true. He cannot, in effect, modify his own sales without changing his selling price, which will cause a change in the sales of his competitors.
>
> (1864; as translated in Theocharis 1993, 66)

In noting the incorrectness of agent conjectures (out of Cournot–Nash equilibrium), Fauveau was indeed a precursor of Bertrand. As Magnan de Bornier (1992) ably shows, the work of Bertrand, the best-known critic of Cournot, is also most miscited. As he says, 'While Bertrand is often referred to, he is never quoted, and probably never read, which perhaps explains why his criticism is "well-known" ' (Magnan de Bornier 1992, 624).

Bertrand

Bertrand is commonly referred to as the originator of the 'Bertrand duopoly model', in which agents use price, rather than quantity, as their strategic instrument. While the outcome of the one-period monopoly problem does not depend on whether the monopolist sets price or quantity to maximize profit, the instrument makes a crucial difference where two duopolists produce identical products, which must have the same price for both to sell. Where they choose quantities of output and permit the market to give the price,[6] output (price) in Cournot–Nash equilibrium is greater (less) than that of a monopolist and less (greater) than that of a competitive market. In the so-called Bertrand model, however, where competition is by means of price and producers satisfy the demand which they experience, competition results in a price which is (at least arbitrarily close to) that of competitive equilibrium, and therefore to a joint output (at least arbitrarily close to) competitive output.

Magnan de Bornier establishes that Bertrand's concern about Cournot's duopoly model was: why do the duopolists not collude to offer the monopoly output and reap monopoly profits between them? This concern, however, sets aside Cournot's deliberate statement that he separated his model from the outcome which would occur if the duopolists could come to such an agreement. Indeed, Cournot's concern with the effect of degree of competition on a good's output and price would evaporate if it were to be assumed that producers could make such agreements: why should not *any* finite number of zero-cost producers agree to joint profit-maximize? The number of producers would play no role at all in the total output. The intelligent reader of Bertrand might well extend Bertrand's criticisms to a concern about Cournot conjecture of the sort expressed by Fauveau. A wider extension to a duopoly model in which price, rather than quantity, is used as the instrument of competition by producers, however, is further from Bertrand's text.

Magnan de Bornier quotes a particularly pregnant passage:

> Cournot assumes that one of his proprietors will reduce his prices to attract buyers to him and that the other will, in turn, reduce his prices even more to attract business back to him. They will only stop undercutting each other in this way when either proprietor, even if the other abandoned the struggle, has nothing more to gain from reducing his prices. One major objection to this is that *there is no solution under this assumption*, in that there is no limit in the downward movement. Indeed, whatever the common price adopted, if one of the proprietors, alone, reduces his price he will, ignoring any minor exceptions, attract all the buyers and thus double his revenue if his rival lets him do so. If Cournot's formulation conceals this obvious result, it is because he most inadvertently introduces as D and D_1' the two proprietors' respective outputs and by considering them as independent variables he assumes that should either proprietor change his output then the other proprietor's output could remain constant. It quite obviously could not.
>
> (1883, 503; as translated by Margaret Chevaillier and cited in
> Magnan de Bornier 1992, 631–2, emphasis added)

On the basis of Bertrand's review *per se*, Magnan de Bornier argues that Bertrand's 'two obvious misunderstandings of Cournot appear: the belief that given Cournot assumptions, price differentiation could happen, and a mis-reading of the meaning of conjectures'(1992, 633).

Magnan de Bornier states that it is reasonable to suppose that when Bertrand said 'no solution . . . , in that there is no limit in the downward movement' that's what he meant, not that a zero-profit zero-price solution was unacceptable. He connects this with Bertrand's misunderstanding about the possibility of price differentiation. However, Bertrand is correct about the lack of a solution for duopolists who use price as their instrument (though not about the lack of a limit) even with a common price, so long as what consumers trade for

27

the identical spring water (whether that is money or beans) is perfectly divisible. There is then 'no solution' in the sense that $\inf(P) = 0$ (or $\inf(Q) = \inf[D(p)] = \inf[D(0)])$, which is the competitive solution, but infinitely divisible price suggests that this infimum will not be reached but merely approached.[7]

Magnan de Bornier argues that, like Fauveau, Bertrand attributed Cournot conjecture to Cournot – rather than to the duopolists Cournot modelled – and that this is Bertrand's (and Fauveau's) mistake rather than Cournot's. Magnan de Bornier cites Cournot's account of a duopolist producing out of equilibrium as being 'punished for his mistake' (Cournot 1838, 90) to show 'that Cournot was perfectly aware that he attributed incorrect conjectures to his proprietors' (630–1). To state that Cournot did not err in the conjectures he assumed his duopolists made, *even though these were consistently wrong out of equilibrium*, because he recognized his assumption that they made mistakes, seems rather sophistical. Even if Cournot fully appreciated that his assumption about duopolists' conjectures meant that their conjectures were refuted time and again, is this not (at least potentially) a fault of his model?

Edgeworth and Multiple Equilibria

Magnan de Bornier traces the 'legend' of the price-competing duopoly model through Pareto, Edgeworth, Marshall and Fisher, all of whom he holds responsible, in some part, for the misattribution of this model to Bertrand. 'Summing up these early comments on the Cournot–Bertrand debate,' he says,

> it is quite clear that today's contrast between quantity-models and price-models was not an issue. The contrast then was between models with a determinate solution and models without a determinate solution, a result of the influence of Edgeworth and Fisher. In the twenties, there may have seemed to be a general agreement on this point [i.e. that Cournot's model yielding determinate equilibrium had failed].
>
> (1992, 640)

As Edgeworth, whose interest in indeterminate equilibrium will be discussed further in Chapter 4, summed up his perspective on the problem in 1889,

> The significance of this proposition [about indeterminate equilibrium] has been missed by many of those who have treated the subject without aid of the appropriate apparatus. Some fail to see that there is any peculiarity in the bargain between isolated units. Another discerns the indeterminateness of the bargain only in the special case in which the article exchanged is a large indivisible object, like a house. Another limits the difficulty to the case of a single negotiation as distinguished

28

from a contract which, as in the actual labour market, may be modified from time to time. Another tells us that in such a bargain the most anxious party gains least.

All these phrases seem to obscure the cardinal distinction that perfect competition tends to a determinate settlement, whereas in a *régime* of combination a principle of adjustment is still to seek. What is that principle?

(1889, 499)

The 'principle of adjustment' which Edgeworth sought has been elusive, if it is to be viewed as unique.

For Edgeworth, small numbers tend to lead to indeterminacy. Indeed, there can be such a problem with a 'Bertrand' model. Vives (1993) describes Edgeworth as showing that there is no price indeterminacy problem under duopoly (substitute products) in the price-instrument model so long as the marginal cost of production is increasing: prices cycle within bounds. Moreover, indeterminacy declines as product differentiation increases and as the number of firms increases. With complementary products, however, there exists a price equilibrium which may not obtain as conjectures if others' play is a problem.

In a review of Amoroso's work, however, Edgeworth (1922) argued in favour of indeterminacy on a quite different ground: that players may have an incentive to change the rules. In an example from Amoroso, first mover (in the Stackelberg sense described below) of quantity Primus in a duopoly receives lower profits from the optimal output than the second mover of quantity, Secundus.[8] Surely, if this is the case, Primus will retaliate by lowering the price of the good. Yet then Secundus can retaliate likewise, and 'the price will again descend, again to mount' (Edgeworth 1922, 404). That is, when the rules of the game (quantity adjustment alone) result in undesirable outcomes, why would the players adhere to them? Edgeworth discussed a change to price adjustment: he might equally have discussed competition for the role of Secundus in the duopoly.

The theme of making rules acceptable to potential players has been taken up first by the literature of threat points, then by that on mechanism design, with its emphasis on the participation constraint. Edgeworth's emphasis, however, did not lie on such issues. Rather, while he did not doubt the mathematical correctness of equilibria such as that derived by Amoroso, he doubted the efficacy of such definitions of equilibrium in describing firm behaviour.

By 1929, however, Chamberlin remarked that

> Duopoly is not one problem, but several. The solution varies, depending upon the conditions assumed, being, with minor exceptions, determinate for each assumption made. It is indeterminate only in so far as the best choice between these assumptions is in doubt.... [However,]

Uncertainty [about opponents' strategies and knowledge] may render the outcome indeterminate....

(1929, 91, 92–93)

The search for such a principle of adjustment in cases of small numbers continued to be pursued for some time, before being set aside for other concerns. In so far as such a principle has been achieved, it has probably in the realm of game theory, and especially of mechanism design, and here largely via explicit modelling of firm conjectures and incentives. Kaldor (1934) and Sweezy (1939) recognized the importance of conjectures in analysing firm behaviour, and in fact Sweezy was thought to have found a unifying principle in the kinked demand curve. Stackelberg worked extensively on firm incentives in an imperfectly competitive market. These treatises will be discussed in the next section.[9]

Issues of dynamic adjustments within a Cournot-type game, and the existence of convergence to a unique equilibrium, were less studied. In two interesting pieces, however, Frisch (1933), one of the founders of dynamic analysis in economics, and Smithies and Savage (1940) took two very different approaches to this question.

Dynamics and Frisch

Frisch's 1933 paper on types of market, which looks to have been intended as an advertisement for the use of dynamic methods, was framed quite explicitly in terms of the 'rules of the game' binding participants. Following Bowley, agents are divided into two strategic types. Agents with 'elementary adaptation' can bid (to buy or sell) quantity alone, bid price alone, or offer an 'option' of a price–quantity combination (or accept or refuse such an offer). Other agents are classed as being in models in which each agent has the ability to set only some of the parameters which define the economic environment. In this case, conjectures about the behaviour of other players are important, including the conjectures of players as to what the rules of the game are.

Let z_i^h indicate parameter i^h, over which agent h has control, so that $(z_1^1,\ldots,z_\alpha^1;\ z_1^2,\ldots,z_\beta^2;\ldots;\ z_1^m,\ldots,z_\gamma^m)$ is the entire set of variables (which would now be called the strategy profile). Frisch characterized models by the matrix of reactions (in elasticity form) which each agent h *conjectures* would result in variable z_j^k (controlled by k) from a change in z_i^h (controlled by h): $z_{ji}^{kh} = (\partial z_j^k/\partial z_i^h)(z_i^h/z_j^k)$ for all i, h, j, k. Let this matrix be denoted by z. An assumption of sanity dictates that $z_{ii}^{hh} = 1$ for all h, i. If the model is characterized by Frisch as one with autonomous action, z has zeros everywhere but such entries. Otherwise, the model is one with conjectural behaviour. If there exists h such that $z_{ji}^{kh} = 0$ unless $k = h$, then h believes itself passive or powerless before k such that $z_{ij}^{hk} \neq 0$. Frisch called this situation 'action supérieure'. It should be noted that agents' conjectures

30

determine this matrix, rather than mechanical rules-of-game, although these can be represented.

Where $r^b = r^b(z_1^1, \ldots, z_\alpha^1; z_1^2, \ldots, z_\beta^2; \ldots; z_1^m, \ldots, z_\gamma^m)$ represents b's payoff from the entire set of variables (which would now be called the strategy profile), yet another matrix Ω can be made up, using z. A typical element of this matrix is $\omega_i^b = (\partial r^b / \partial z_i^b)(r^{bj}/z_i^b)$, where the first term sums up not only the direct effect of a change in z_i^b on b's payoff, but also the conjectured indirect effects from the reactions of other players. Ω then indicates the direction of changes each player would like to make in variables under its control from an initial position.

Frisch illustrated the dynamics given by Ω in a simple phase diagram, in which he blithely assumed the existence of only one equilibrium, and dynamics such that there was convergence from any point to the equilibrium (which was thus a sink). While movement from a region of strategic complementarity to one of strategic substitution (or vice versa) causes fluctuation in the choice variables, there is convergence to the unique equilibrium and 'centre of attraction'.

While this phase diagram suggests unique equilibrium, it is dependent on the conjectures of players which are embodied in the matrices z and Ω. Frisch showed that four equilibria which can result in a simple case from beliefs of two players that they act autonomously or otherwise. Despite the simplicity of the dynamics in these illustrations, Frisch believed that his approach was a promising one for explaining what forces made economic life one of perpetual oscillation, with static equilibrium never attained (1933, 259).

While Frisch's approach has been much used in macroeconomics, it has not made successful inroads into game theory. Its simplicity becomes merely mechanical unless z (and hence Ω) depends on past observations through the updating of priors about opponent behaviour. Nonetheless, it is of considerable interest to see much of the dynamic problem of Cournot duopoly and allied problems treated so neatly. While Smithies and Savage's approach looks less sophisticated *a priori*, it actually allows more freedom (with little added complexity) in the use of information by the agents modelled.

Smithies and Savage

Smithies and Savage (1940) addressed some of the concerns advanced on the stability of a Cournot outcome without such strong restrictions on duopolist conjectures.[10] Their model tests the effect of conjectures on the convergence of the model, and on the steady state. Their approach, however, was an adaptive one quite dissimilar to Frisch's although they cite him repeatedly for other work. Since they worked in a model with (at least potentially) many periods, they emphasized that the period over which the competitors they modelled maximized (subject to their conjectures) was one in which the (joint) demand curve was stable. They checked the effect of two types of conjecture:

(1) Each competitor assumes that his rival's output, one unit of time from the present, will be a weighted arithmetic mean of their present levels of output. This is a generalization of which the Cournot assumption that one competitor assumes that his rival will maintain a constant output is an extreme special case. At the other extreme one producer will assume that his rival will always produce an output equal to his own . . . . (2) Each competitor assumes that his rival's output will increase for the next unit of time at its present rate.

(1940, 131–2)

While these modes of expectation-formation are quite unlike those assumed in current game-theoretic models, they are not trivial. In the first Case, the information set available to each player is last period's outputs, and any linear use of this data is permitted. In the second, the data is past outputs, and this data is processed in a particular way.

In Case (1), Smithies and Savage found that there was always convergence, and that

If the Cournot assumption [by agents] is made, Cournot's solution will be the solution to the present problem. On the other hand, if it is assumed [by agents] that outputs will be equalized, the solution will be the same as if the competitors acted as a single monopolist.

(1940, 132)

Interestingly, agent assumptions of identical outputs (or, rather, their assuming choices independent of each other's) acts as a coordination device in this model, producing a result which cannot be achieved by autonomous action of the agents, yet which they desire. Aumann (1974) originated the notion of a coordinating device. Zeuthen (1930) noted this phenomenon as well: if individual duopolists assume from the outset that they will sell half the total quantity sold, the total quantity is that of the monopolistic outcome. Such conjectures assume that the two duopolists are

bound together tacitly or expressly, so that either of them can resist the temptation of a small extension of his production which takes nothing from the other party, . . . but if continued would nevertheless make it impossible for him to maintain both present price and production.

(1930, 28)

The dynamics of the model also generate cycles, and incentives to increase and decrease output alternate.

Case (2), however, where the conjectures are dynamic (in that they are rate-related) rather than static,

. . . yields cyclical solutions of similar character to those described above, but, as is fairly evident, we cannot say that stable equilibrium is achieved for all initial conditions . . . .

(Smithies and Savage 1940, 132)

While certainly the proponents of unique equilibrium would find it fairly unnerving to have a change to dynamic conjectures destroy the stability properties (hence number of equilibria) of the model, Smithies and Savage felt that they had salvaged it:

We can say, however, that if the initial outputs are approximately linear over time, the cycles will be damped over a finite period of time and output for each competitor will tend towards the value given by the Cournot solution. If the initial outputs are in fact linear functions of time, the cycles will be damped over any period. We shall argue, further, that the 'explosive' cases are in general cases where it is unreasonable to suppose that linear extrapolation would be used as the method of estimation.

(1940, 132–3)

The 'unreasonableness' of linear extrapolation in this case of output non-linear in time is presumably due to vaguely rational-expectations concerns: where output behaviour is in fact *not* linear in time, accumulated evidence would surely reject such a model of output dynamics.

Frisch *assumed* convergence to an equilibrium which would depend on the conjectures of each player about the responsiveness of others. Smithies and Savage, on the other hand, showed that for a broader class of conjectures as to others' output than Cournot assumed, the system converges to an equilibrium, though not always Cournot's, while for some conjectures no convergence occurs.

CONCLUSION

In modelling duopoly at a remarkably early date, Cournot surmounted the difficulty of defining equilibrium in the presence of strategic interdependence by the Cournot–Nash conjecture of opponent passivity. His model was precise and well specified, and permitted the prediction of output and price in a particular sort of duopoly.

Criticisms of Cournot's model came in several flavours. A number of writers were concerned that the conjectures Cournot attributed to duopolistic agents were systematically wrong out of equilibrium. This led to dynamic concerns which, however, were not very systematically addressed for some time. This strand of the literature parallels the literature of equilibrium concepts.

Other writers expressed concern that Cournot's model did not properly represent the observed behaviour of firms. Some writers focused on the use of quantity (in the formal model) rather than price as the instrument, often attributing their concern to Bertrand. Some argued that the firms would surely collude and offer the monopoly output and price.

Others focused on questions of symmetry, again often on the grounds that the identical cost and perfect substitutability of products of the two firms was 'unrealistic'. Stackelberg and Zeuthen, notably, modelled firms without identical cost functions who differed in market power. Asymmetry can also exist from the demand side. Is the appropriate model of firms in an industry one in which their products are perfectly substitutable? Surely firms differentiate their products, or are themselves differentiated, if only in the beliefs of consumers? Hotelling (1929) originated a mathematical model for studying the strategic behaviour of firms differentiating in one dimension. The literature of monopolistic competition addressed questions of firm behaviour in this case, where the many dimensions of a good lead to a rich strategy space. These literatures are discussed in the next chapter.

3

STRATEGIC INTERDEPENDENCE
Cournot's heirs and asymmetry

Cournot's model of duopoly, discussed in the preceding chapter, opened up a new channel of enquiry in economics: the modelling of firm behaviour in situations of strategic interdependence in which there is more than one firm, but not so many that each is powerless. More immediate criticisms of Cournot's model and dynamic variants are discussed above. This chapter focuses on richer models in which the symmetry of the Cournot model is abandoned, from either the producer's or the consumer's side.

For one firm to move before others, or for a firm to have a different cost function or influence on the market, alters the game considerably. In the first section below, the model of price leadership and Stackelberg's examination of leadership in a market are discussed, as well as the 'kinked demand curve' model of Paul Sweezy, and Hall and Hitch.

Where different firms' products are perceived as differing from the consumer's standpoint, even a small number of firms in a market are no longer symmetric because their products are no longer perfect substitutes. Hotelling's, Chamberlin's and Robinson's models in which firms interact strategically by setting not only price or quantity, but product characteristics, are analysed from a game-theoretic perspective in the second section.

PRODUCER ASYMMETRY

The work discussed in this section expanded on Cournot's duopoly model by examining the results of various forms of asymmetry in producers' power, whether due to size or to priority.

Zeuthen and Stackelberg, whose work on asymmetric market power was pivotal, both agreed and disagreed on the existence and uniqueness of equilibrium. Zeuthen, writing at a time when a belief in the indeterminacy of equilibrium under duopoly was general, felt that equilibrium is determinate under most rules of the game and that the economist's task is to work out which rules obtain, or are 'probable':

The case of *'monopolistic competition'*, i.e. the instance in which several

35

entrepreneurs have at the same time so great a share in the production that they may be, and are, interested in influencing the price even at the cost of some reduction of their own sales, is more complex.... Many economists, therefore, think that no stable equilibrium can be obtained in this instance, but others are of the opposite opinion. The different points of view depend, however, on the choice of hypotheses. If this is realised, it will be understood that it is not true that one solution is correct and the others are wrong, but that the different theoretical instances become more or less probable instances from real life.

(Zeuthen 1930, 24)

The existence of a unique equilibrium under a certain market form does not preclude movement in the economy, as agents may alter the rules of the game. However, the proper role of economics is the analysis of equilibrium under each set of rules, rather than analysis of regime changes.

That theoretically, there is a definite equilibrium in the case of competing monopolies (competition between a few, relatively large enterprises), does not in any way mean that conditions are at all quiet and stable.... Economic theory alone...teaches us that under normal circumstances there will at each given moment be a tendency towards one definite position of equilibrium. The equilibrium which we have here described as 'monopolistic competition' is, however, unsteady not only because the assumptions are constantly changing, but also because the necessary conditions for competing monopolies may entirely disappear owing to the greater advantage either of a struggle for existence or of a combination.

(Zeuthen 1930, 56–7)

Even the economic warfare discussed by Zeuthen (for appraisal of which see Chapter 4) did not address changes in rules, but negotiating power within a given set of rules.

For Schumpeter, Zeuthen's emphasis on defining equilibrium was his greatest contribution to economics. In a preface to the English translation of four essays, Schumpeter stated:

[The] relevant question: properly choosing well defined sets of reasonable assumptions, do we get determined results in the same sense as in the case of simple monopoly, or are we driven to the Edgeworthian conclusion that, as far as purely economic forces go, there is nothing but 'chaos'?

Dr Zeuthen's argument does much to clear up this question. A large group of cases emerges, for various reasons not without claim to the epithetons ornans 'normal', which undoubtedly yield 'determinateness' of equilibrium. Roughly speaking, this group consists of those cases in which each party reacts on what the other does, simply by adjusting the quantity it is willing to supply. There seems to me to be great merit in proving this, and to draw a strong dividing line between such cases and those other ones in which parties to a bilateral monopoly try to fight each other, or dictate their terms to one another, by entirely withdrawing, or threatening to withdraw, what they control ....

(1930, xii)

For Stackelberg, on the other hand, much of the interest of a duopoly model was in how agents worked to change the parameters of the market – this generated his interest in what came to be called Stackelberg conflict, or Stackelberg warfare. His methods for attacking such issues were inadequate, and his success consequently moderate.

Both Zeuthen and Stackelberg were, however, major figures in the modelling of firm behaviour in the slippery realm of imperfect competition, and major thinkers on issues of strategic interdependence.

The dominant firm model

In this familiar model, only one producer in an industry has market power. This producer faces consumers, whose competitive price-taking makes their demand curve a reaction curve, and a 'competitive fringe' of producers. The competitive fringe, with no market power, produces to maximize profit at the dominant firm's price.[1] For this situation to occur, the dominant firm must be the industry's low-cost producer. Production at each price by fringe firms, given by their marginal cost curves, fills demand which is then not available to the dominant firm. This situation can be easily handled analytically by altering the upper portion of the demand curve faced by the dominant firm, from the demand curve for the entire market. Schenzler, Siegfried and Thweatt (1992) have examined the history of the model.

As Reid (1979) has shown, Forchheimer (1908) was, at least in part, an innovator of the dominant firm model before Zeuthen. While Reid acknowledges that Forchheimer's argument was based on a table of figures shown as an example, he shows that a model can be fitted to the figures and contends that this model represents Forchheimer's contribution. Although Forchheimer claimed that the figures were arbitrary, they in fact derive from a linear market demand curve. Forchheimer obtained the equilibrium price and output (within his example) in two cases: when fringe firms produce a fixed amount and when they produce along their marginal cost curves.

Schenzler, Siegfried and Thweatt (1992), with whom we agree, maintain that Forchheimer's presentation does not contain the reasoning to make it much more than an interesting early special case, largely because it is so firmly based on figures, rather than equations. Moreover, Forchheimer's emphasis is not on the strategic interdependence within the situation, but on the solution of the example.

Zeuthen's (1930) perspective had more in common with general

37

equilibrium theory than with game theory: he began his presentation of the dominant firm model by explaining

> A monopoly will always be exposed to competition from substitutes. The same want may generally be satisfied in several different ways, and when a certain minimum of satisfaction has been obtained, different wants will compete with each other for the buying power of consumers. Thus the price conditions of one commodity influence the demand for another....
>
> (1930, 15)

Zeuthen differentiated the dominant firm situation from

> the very important group of cases, in which the partial character of the monopoly is not due to the fact that there are other enterprises outside, but to a limitation in the co-operation of enterprises.
>
> (1930, 17–18)

This is a somewhat curious distinction, as the fringe firms could typically exercise market power if they formed a cartel.

Zeuthen typically favoured diagrammatic analysis. Assuming fringe firm output constant with respect to price, he illustrated the effect on dominant firm output response to varying fringe sector outputs, of the dominant firm's cost structure (1930, Figures VIIIA–D), and also some effects of the shape of the demand curve (1930, Figures VIIIE and IX). He also depicted the more usual case of fringe firms producing along marginal cost curves increasing in price (1930, Figure X).

The situation in which a dominant firm's profits are constrained by both the demand curve and fringe firms producing perfect substitutes is, indeed, game theoretic in that outcomes for both the dominant firm and the fringe depend on each other's actions (and those of consumers, as well). However, the fringe is defined in such a way that its choices in response to a dominant firm move are fairly trivial. This permits the analyst to adjust the equally passive consumer's demand curve by the fringe reaction curve, and derive the dominant firm's optimal output and price just as if it were a monopoly. The susceptibility of the problem to this sort of simplification drastically limited the interest of work in the area, from a game theoretic point of view.

The Stackelberg leader

Heinrich von Stackelberg, most widely known as an originator of the eponymous 'Stackelberg leader' model of duopoly, thoroughly recognized a wide variety of forms of duopoly and oligopoly. Like Cournot, he stated in chapters on imperfect competition (Stackelberg 1952)[2] that

> Monopoly need not always arise in cases where only one seller of a product emerges. It may well be that several small firms may agree to influence

the market by collective action in order to make monopoly gains. Realistic examples are found in the case of cartels. We call such cases, following Eucken, *collective monopoly*.

(1952, 176)

He distinguished carefully between different types, or rules of the game, of imperfect competition, and mentioned Zeuthen-type 'partial monopoly', with a price leader and fringe competition (182).

At a time when the hostilities of World War II (even more than nescience of the German language)[3] would have kept Australians from learning of his work, Heyward (1941) summarized Stackelberg (1934) in the *Economic Record*. He used Stackelberg's diagrammatic style of presentation, which included iso-profit curves as well as Cournot-style reaction curves for firms A and B. Heyward stressed Stackelberg's emphasis on the beliefs of A and B about each other.

For Stackelberg, there were four possible equilibria in a duopoly situation: Cournot equilibrium, what he termed the Bowley Case, and two equilibria in which A (B) acts as a market leader. In the case of 'simple duopoly', represented by Figure 3.1, x represents A's output and y, B's. The point of tangency between B's reaction curve (b) and A's isoprofit map is the output combination which will be realized if A is able to lead in the market, and the tangency between a and B's iso-profit map if B can lead. A (B) can lead only if B (A) believes her immovable. If each party thinks the other will yield, 'Stackelberg warfare' or the Bowley Case ensues: where A plays a_1 thinking B will react with a_2, and B plays b_1, expecting b_2, (a_1,b_2) (labelled π in Figure 3.1) will be realized until one player gives way. Because of the shapes of their indifference maps in this diagram, neither party has the incentive to follow, staying on its reaction curve and behaving like a Cournot duopolist.[4]

In presenting the classic Cournot model of duopoly, Stackelberg (1952) implicitly assumed *ordered* choice of outputs, calling the duopolists 'first' and 'second'. With this presumption in place, the difference between Cournot monopoly and a model with a quantity leader depends primarily on the conjectures of the duopolists:

If the first duopolist takes the supply of the second as a datum, then he adjusts his supply correspondingly, at which the second reacts by an adjustment of his supply. . . . This is the *Cournot solution* of the problem of Duopoly.

(1952, 190)

Stackelberg's geometric presentation of the Cournot model differs from the standard one by the quiet depiction of different cost functions (though, oddly, symmetric reaction curves) in diagrams.

After this exposition, Stackelberg asked:

Must the duopolists really behave in this manner? The first duopolist will

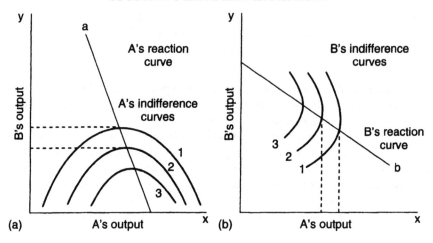

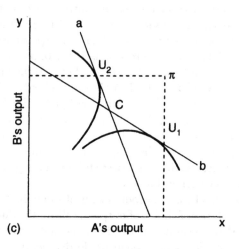

Figure 3.1

notice that his rival always follows suit and adjusts his total supply to that of his own. This reaction by the second one can be taken into account by the first one who can accordingly put on the market that amount of mineral water which will maximise his profits not *before* but *after* the resultant adjustment of his rival's supply. This amount can be called the independent supply of the first duopolist.

(1952, 194)

The 'Stackelberg leader' case (which Stackelberg called '*asymmetrical duopoly*') occurs when the first produces an 'independent' supply and the second a 'dependent' supply. The first duopolist, however, while independent in the sense that the second has not yet produced output to be adjusted to, will consider the second's optimal output while forming his own optimum decision.

Stackelberg was, however, interested in dynamic issues, and questioned the producer's meek acceptance of such rules of the game:

> But this equilibrium is unstable, for the passive seller can always take up the struggle again at any time. Only if one duopolist is, economically speaking, manifestly stronger than the other will he know that he can take up the most favourable market position and that the second will have to content himself with the less favourable one.

(1952, 194)

This point was emphasized by Leontief (1936) in his presentation of Stackelberg's models:

> Should . . . seller A assume that B acts independently, the profit motive will necessarily induce him to direct his own output according to the variation of B's production, i.e. to accept the rôle of a *follower*. Should A believe, on the other hand, that B behaves like a follower himself, A would necessarily take the rôle of a *leader* and determine his own best optimum position, disregarding the momentary output of B, but taking into account that every move which he himself might make will produce a definite reaction on the part of B.

(1936, 555)

However, both Cournot and Bowley positions were inconsistent with the expectations discussed in this passage.

In Stackelberg's view, conflict between duopolists was extremely likely, where the profits between being leader and follower differed.

> . . . the second duopolist could decide to offer his independent supply and to sell at any given price that will make the first duopolist give up the struggle and adjust his supply to that of the second. The first duopolist will then occupy the 'dependent supply' position.
>
> If both duopolists are determined to capture the market, then they will compare the dependent and independent supply positions and seek to attain the more favourable one. As a rule, the position of independence will be more favourable for both.[5] If this is the case, then each duopolist will put that amount of the commodity on the market that will correspond to his independent position and will seek to maintain it until the other decides to give up. A regular trial of strength emerges and no equilibrium position is reached. This can be called *'Bowley's Case'* because Bowley was the first to examine its formal conditions. In special cases, however, it may be more advantageous for each one to adopt the dependent position. In this case, each simultaneously tries to induce the

other to offer his supply first, so that the latter, the competitive supply, is always taken as a datum. Thus Cournot's duopoly position manifests itself and we can call this situation *'Cournot's Case'*. But this result offers just as little chance of an equilibrium solution as the first case. Each duopolist will behave in a different manner from that which his competitors want to force upon him, which would not be that which would secure him maximum profits when his rival's independent supply is given and he is in a dependent position or when he is independent and his rival must adjust his supply.

(Stackelberg 1952, 194)

Either type of struggle is called 'Stackelberg warfare', which automatically yields lower profits to each producer, every period, than submission to the other would deliver. The gains from engaging in such conflict lie in establishing the producer in the desired position in the longer run.[6]

Stackelberg's verbal and graphic explication of this struggle, which focuses on choosing to go off one's reaction function, includes no explicit dynamics, not even a stated number of periods for a horizon or rates of time preference. The producers' differential 'strength', which presumably depends on their relative wealth and cost functions, is not spelled out. (While the ability of a low-cost firm to drive out a high-cost firm is discussed, it is not formally modelled (1952, 203).) The market is implicitly one which cannot be entered by outsiders, and there seems to be no exit or other outside option.[7] For Stackelberg, it is quite possible that the struggle can continue indefinitely if a cartel is not formed and there is no intervention from outside:

It is possible, of course, that the duopolists may attempt to supplant one another in the market so that 'cut-throat' competition breaks out. Only the formation of a collective monopoly or State regulation of the market can bring the battle to an end and restore equilibrium . . . .

(Stackelberg 1952, 194–5)

In a rigorous game-theoretic analysis, if there were perfect information on the wealth, cost functions and rate of time discount, and a finite horizon for the two players, the recursive analysis of subgame perfection[8] would typically indicate a unique equilibrium from the first period. A player who would not win the 'Stackelberg warfare' would submit from the outset. Only in the case where a producer knew her own reserves, cost function and time preference but held only a prior distribution on those of her opponent would conflict actually occur. In an infinite horizon context, as indicated by the Folk Theorem,[9] matters would indeed be as indeterminate as Stackelberg thought.

Stackelberg's primary emphasis, however, was on the indeterminacy of equilibrium under duopoly, though on somewhat different grounds than those cited by Edgeworth in his review of Amoroso. While Edgeworth stressed that duopolists might abandon quantity adjustment in favour of price adjustment with sufficient incentives, Stackelberg focused on the producers' incentives and ability to seize the position of 'leader'.

> We have observed that, apart from the Bowley and Cournot cases, there is an abundance of other possible solutions to duopolistic price formation. All these possibilities represent strategic positions and all are unstable with the exception of the two asymmetrical duopoly positions (and a number of very improbable situations). Accordingly, we are justified in considering duopoly as an *unstable market form* (*gleichgewichtslose Marktform*).
>
> (Stackelberg 1952, 202)

In Stackelberg's view, not only is equilibrium indeterminate under duopoly, but it is likely that effective monopoly will occur, whether because one firm firmly defeats the other, or because the two form a cartel:

> Duopoly is an unstable market form not only in the sense that price is apt to be indeterminate, but much more because it is unlikely to remain as a market form for any length of time. The inherent contradictions in the duopolistic situation press for a solution through the adoption of another market form – monopoly.
>
> (1952, 203)

Stackelberg recognized that any such indeterminacy is not limited to duopoly, unless the number of producers enforces competition. He suggested as well that with a larger number of producers with market power, the number of equilibria increases.

> Duopolistic price formation is found in similar forms in the case of oligopoly. Certainly there are many more possible situations than merely the position of dependence and independence. The number of market positions which can be chosen by oligopolists increases as their number increases. At the same time their individual influence upon the price level diminishes. If the number of oligopolists is sufficiently large and their economic importance is sufficiently small, then the unstable market form of oligopoly is transformed into the relatively stable form of pure competition.
>
> (1952, 203–4)

Stackelberg may have had in mind as a factor which induces many conceivable positions the number of coalitions combinatorially possible with a larger number of players. Coalition is the essential stuff of cooperative game theory, which had not yet been developed. In cooperative game theory, the payoffs to members of each possible coalition are generally well defined. Since the coalition of the whole, that formed by all players, could reproduce any partition of the set of players, the equilibrium imputation[10] must be one for the coalition of the whole – the mathematics of much of cooperative game theory is based on this. For Stackelberg, however, the division of joint profits of a cartel was probably not predetermined.

Stackelberg may also have had in mind the conceivable divisions of producers into those whose output was 'independent', those with 'dependent' output, and those who acted as the fringe competition in a 'partial monopoly' model. In this case, as well, a greater number of producers leads a greater possible number of market positions. However, the incentives underlying any such portion of producers would limit the number of equilibria in an extended Stackelbergian analysis.

For Friedman, Stackelberg's analysis was promising, but ultimately elusive:

> To my mind the Stackelberg leader-follower analysis has always seemed flawed because it appears to beg the very question that it is intended to address; namely the explanation of which markets are characterized by price leadership and which firm emerges as the price leader in such markets.
>
> (Friedman 1992)

In the absence of explicit analysis based on the attributes of firms, Friedman is justified in suggesting that Stackelberg's analysis was not the final answer to such questions. However, as an early accomplishment enriching the duopoly model, and suggesting that the incentives agents experience to change the rules of the game matter, Stackelberg's work still contains matter of considerable interest, which is no longer especially well known.

In contrast with Stackelberg's stress on grasping leadership, Zeuthen (1930, 41–2) initially assumed explicitly that there was no dynamic advantage in being first to change price to capture demand in his rendition of the Hotelling geographic differentiation model, discussed below. His survey of market conditions under 'leadership' (being first to change price) matter is largely diagrammatic and somewhat opaque (1930, 44–5), and he devoted more space to an evaluation of the 'realism' of various models of price leadership (1930, 46–51).

Like Zeuthen's (or Forchheimer's) dominant firm model, Stackelberg's work expanded Cournot's model in the direction of production-side asymmetry. As well as his model of 'Stackelberg leadership', Stackelberg examined cases in which duopolists differed with respect to cost, and in which one played 'Cournot' while the other played 'Bertrand'. While he was much more interested in time or sequence in market structure than Zeuthen, it is somewhat ironic that his model of market leadership is usually conceived of as one exemplifying 'first mover advantage'. Not only did he recognize that the leadership role might be *less* profitable than that of follower, but sequence of moves did not define the roles for him. What mattered, rather, was each firm's prior on the role the other coveted and could seize. Not surprisingly, in an undefined framework of potentially infinite periods, almost anything could happen.

44

The kinked demand curve

In 1939, two papers introducing the concept of a kinked demand curve for an oligopolist in a market with differentiated goods were published: Sweezy's, and Hall and Hitch's.[11] The idea behind the kinked demand curve (one with discontinuous slope) is that the reactions of an oligopolist's opponent(s) differ depending on whether the oligopolist raises or lowers the good's price. The asymmetry in this model consists of the differentiated nature assumed for the goods in the industry.

With differentiated goods, an oligopolist A can raise the price of her output and still sell goods. However, this can be expected to decrease sales if others in the industry do not change their prices. If, on the other hand, A lowers the good's price and the competitor(s) follow, the demand for A's output will not increase as much as it otherwise would. Following Kaldor's (1934) review of Robinson's *Economics of Imperfect Competition*, Sweezy used the concept of an 'imagined demand curve' to make use of what seemed to him reasonable conjectures on the part of any oligopolist A in this situation of strategic interdependence. He suggested that A would reason that, if their cost conditions have not changed, it is not in A's competitor(s) interest to fully match A's price increase, but that, on the other hand, they would fully match any decrease of A's price to maintain their sales. This yields an 'imagined' or conjectured demand curve for A which is more elastic at higher prices than the current one, and less elastic at lower prices, than it would be in the absence of the moves A conjectures the opponent(s) will follow if A's pricing strategy were to change.[12]

Sweezy stresses that a kinked demand curve would not explain how the current price had been arrived at, but merely explain its maintenance. A kinked demand curve of this sort yields a marginal revenue curve which is discontinuous, so that quite a substantial change in A's marginal cost curve is generally necessary for A to be willing to alter the good's price. By focusing on a specific, not unreasonable, form of conjecture on the part of each oligopolist, Sweezy explained the stability of a price array in an industry characterized by differentiated oligopoly. As presented in textbooks such as Scherer (1980), the kinked demand curve model is still used as an explanation of precisely this price stability.

Sweezy hoped that he had arrived at a theory which could be widely generalized for industries characterized by imperfect competition. He stated that

> So far as I know no attempt has yet been made to investigate the characteristics of imagined demand curves, though it should be obvious that such an investigation is desirable. Oligopoly is probably the typical case throughout a large part of the modern economy, and yet the theory of oligopoly can scarcely be said to be in a very advanced state, consisting as it does of a number of special cases which allow of little generalization.

45

My purpose in this note is to show that a very considerable degree of clarification might be introduced into the study of this subject by a systematic inquiry into the nature of imagined demand curves.

(1939, 404)

In focusing on oligopolist conjectures to explain price stability, Sweezy was thinking in the context of strategic interdependence, and thinking in quite a different way to other writers who were interested in price formation. His approach, however, was not very game theoretic in nature. His expressed recognition of strategic interdependence is essentially limited to this passage:

The most obvious consideration in this connection seems to me to be the obvious fact that rivals react differently according to whether a price change is upward or downward. If a producer A raises his price, his rival producer B will acquire new customers. If, on the other hand, A lowers his price, B will lose customers. Ordinarily the reaction to a gain in business is a pleasurable feeling calling for no particular action; the reaction to a loss in business, however, is likely to be some viewing with alarm accompanied by measure designed to recoup the loss. If the cause of the loss is obviously a rival's price cut, the natural reaction is a similar cut.

(1939, 404–5)

Hall and Hitch's (1939) exposition of the same idea of a conjectured kinked demand curve is, if anything, even less game theoretic in nature, as the authors focused on data from surveying producers in an attempt to show the 'reason-ableness' of their model.

Although the conjectured kinked demand curve model is of interest to game theorists as focusing on player conjectures, a good deal is lacking in the early literature on this subject from a game-theoretic perspective. Friedman (1992) discusses Sweezy (1939) as embodying a belief-based theory. Nevertheless, he shows in a model-cum-example that Sweezy-style equilibrium stability is not subgame perfect in all relevant cases.[13]

DEMAND-SIDE ASYMMETRY

Chamberlin, along with Robinson (one of the originators of the model of monopolistic competition),[14] wrote that

Duopoly is not one problem, but several. The solution varies, depending upon the conditions assumed, being, with minor exceptions, determinate for each assumption made. It is indeterminate only in so far as the best choice between these assumptions is in doubt;

(1929, 91)

and that 'Uncertainty [about opponents' strategies and knowledge] may render the outcome indeterminate . . . ' (Chamberlin 1929, 92–3). The earlier section on producer asymmetry (see above) examined some of the situations which early theorists speculated might hold when asymmetry was due to firm characteristics endowed in different models. These characteristics included the size of firms (in the dominant firm model), cost functions (in Zeuthen's and Stackelberg's generalizations of the Cournot model), firmness of purpose (in the quasi-dynamic Stackelberg models), and product differentiation (in the kinked 'imagined demand curve' model of Sweezy, and of Hall and Hitch).

In this section, we discuss the analysis of models of strategic interdependence which, by their focus on differentiation of firms or firm products from the consumer's point of view, allow for firm strategy to include choices of differentiation. That Hotelling's (1929) model of spatial differentiation falls into this class is exceptionally clear. Taking the costliness for consumers of getting to the supplier of a good as a primitive, Hotelling analysed firms' optimal price subject to their location along a line segment, and to a fixed transport cost per unit distance. He extended his analysis to entrant location in the presence of sitting firms. Hotelling's central idea can be applied directly to product characteristics which may be assumed to appear in consumer demand functions (especially when charcteristics differentiation is one-dimensional, like a line segment), with geographic transactions costs directly analogous to tastes for differentiation or specific varieties.[15] Moreover, the model has been extended to analyse other forms of differentiation. Hotelling-style models (usually with differentiation along a circle rather than along a line segment for mathematical convenience) have been used for this purpose for decades, and Hotelling himself recognized that such a parallel existed (Hotelling 1929, 467).

Hotelling's and other geographic models

Hotelling's title, 'Stability in Competition', indicated his position in the dissension between those who believed that duopoly was inherently unstable (as did Edgeworth (see Chapter 2) and Stackelberg (above)) and those who thought that, subject to appropriate assumptions, duopoly and imperfect competition generally were characterized by stable, sometimes unique solutions (like Zeuthen and Sweezy). It may be recalled that Edgeworth thought that duopoly might be unstable because producers might not stand by 'rules of the game' assumed by economists, where they could use more than one instrument, and thus firms' price and quantity sold might see-saw indefinitely. One of Hotelling's aims was to indicate that differentiation, and indeed optimal differentiation, could provide stability by limiting the substitutability of the goods. For Hotelling, differentiation, by permitting firms to set different prices, eliminates the drastic price see-sawing of a 'Bertrand' model. Not only was his model a *tour de force* as a work of mathematical price theory, but

47

Note: Market of length l = 35. In this example a = 4, b = 1, x = 14, y = 16.

Figure 3.2

it is one of the relatively few thoroughly game-theoretic early works on strategic interdependence.

Hotelling began his analysis with two zero-cost firms located at pre-ordained positions A (to the left of B) and B on a unit interval. Hotelling's assumption that firms produce at zero cost not only simplifies the analysis, but connects his model with Cournot's model of mineral water producers, with which he explicitly associated his example. Consumers (who are implicitly assumed identical) are assumed uniformly distributed along the unit interval, in a fashion similar to Aumann's later work using continua of non-atomic[16] agents. The two firms sell to proportions of agents determined by their relative prices and per-unit transport cost c, and demand (out of a potential maximum of 1) is proportional to market share.

Given that each firm produces at zero cost, it is optimal for each to set price to maximize profit and seize a market share which consists of the a (b) consumers to the first (second) firm's left (right) and x (y) of the consumers to A's (B's) right (left). x (and, by duality, y) are determined by the firms's prices p_1 and p_2 and transport cost c. In equilibrium, the following price and market share conditions hold:

$p_1 + cx = p_2 + cy$ (that is, delivered prices are equated)

because

$a + x + y + b = 1$ (all consumers are served).[17]

This permits solution for x and y:

$x = \frac{1}{2}(1 - a - b + (p_2 - p_1)/c)$ and

$y = \frac{1}{2}(1 - a - b + (p_1 - p_2)/c)$,

and of profit equations

$\pi_1 = p_1 q_1 = p_1(a + x) = \frac{1}{2}(1 + a - b)p_1 - p_1^2/(2c) + p_1 p_2/(2c)$ and

$\pi_2 = p_2 q_2 = p_2(b + y) = \frac{1}{2}(1 - a + b)p_2 - p_2^2/(2c) + p_1 p_2/(2c)$.

The form of the profit functions makes it immediately obvious how this model exhibits strategic interdependence, as each firm's profit depends on its rival's price.

In a familiar Cournot-style approach, the firms are modelled as simultaneously differentiating their profit functions with respect to their own prices, and Cournot–Nash equilibrium is derived to determine price and quantity (Hotelling 1929, 472–3). Here, there is potential asymmetry due to the differentiation of firms by location: firms are symmetric if $a = b$. Hotelling analysed price dynamics from an initial disequilibrium as Cournot did, by means of Cournot-conjecture reaction curves. Hotelling did not discuss the role of firm conjectures, but merely followed Cournot's approach.

Although he wrote before Stackelberg, Hotelling's analysis included consideration of iso-profit curves for the two firms: he showed that one firm might gain higher profits by adopting a position which was later termed price-leadership, and permitting the other to react optimally to it, without 'formal agreement' being necessary (1929, 474–5).[18] Hotelling, however, pronounced 'understandings between competitors . . . notoriously fragile', and felt it likely that deviations from Cournot–Nash equilibrium, while they might last for some time, were impermanent: 'As a child's pile of blocks falls to its equilibrium position when the table on which it stands is moved, so a movement of economic conditions tends to upset quasi-monopolistic schemes for staying' at other price combinations (1929, 475–6).

Using the profit function for the second firm in Cournot–Nash equilibrium which he had derived from his opening model, Hotelling also derived the second firm's optimal location (as represented by the measure b) as an entrant, and showed that the second firm would ideally locate arbitrarily close to the first on the line segment, just to the right (left) of a if a is less (greater) than ½.[19]

Hotelling directly applied his examination of location to politics, assuming that political stance could be represented on a left–right line segment. This form of analysis was later taken up by Downs (1957) and remains central to public choice theory. The number of dimensions of differentiation have been proved to be a difficulty with this form of analysis, notably by Gibbard (1973) and Satterthwaite (1975). Hotelling foresaw no such difficulty and, interestingly, simultaneously echoed Greg (1852a):[20]

> In the more general problem in which the commodities purveyed differ in many dimensions the situation is the same. The elasticity of demand of particular groups does mitigate the tendency to excessive similarity of competing commodities, but not enough. It leads some factories to make cheap shoes for the rich, but all the shoes are too much alike. Our cities become uneconomically large and the business districts within them are too concentrated. Methodist and Presbyterian churches are too much alike: cider is too homogenous.
> (Hotelling 1929, 484)

Friedrich Zeuthen had a continuing fascination with Hotelling's model of product differentiation, exhibited by his 1930 and 1933 publications. While Hotelling's primary analytical method was algebraic, Zeuthen, as usual with him, favoured graphical analysis combined with verbal exposition. Zeuthen

(1930, 34–40) summarized Hotelling graphically to show equilibrium price and market share, and gave a literary exposition of firm location. Like Hotelling, he argued that a market which cannot be represented by a line segment and differential transport costs do not alter the primary story of Hotelling's model (1930, 40), and made explicit Hotelling's assumption of no dynamic advantage in making the first price change to capture demand (1930, 41–2).

Zeuthen (1933) made his development of the Hotelling model more explicit. He specifically demonstrated two new solution methods, one graphical and the other arithmetic but not involving the use of calculus.[21] He also explicitly generalized the problem to cases in which firms are less symmetric than in Hotelling's model, and in which firm location cannot be represented as on a line.

Smithies (1941), whose version (with Savage) of Cournot's duopoly dynamic with respect to conjectures is discussed in Chapter 2, also scrutinized Hotelling's model. Here, unlike in that work, his analysis is almost exclusively verbal and expository rather than mathematical. An appendix intended to indicate 'general mathematical methods' is so general as to be not particularly illuminating.

Explaining his motivation by means of the public choice analogy, he explained that

> The very fact that Professor Harold Hotelling's pioneer article explained so successfully the close similarity of the Republican and Democratic platforms in 1928 indicates that something more was needed in 1936. It was probably true to say in 1928 that by moving to the center of electoral opinion neither party risked losing its peripheral support.... Leaving the political analogy, Hotelling's assumption of completely inelastic demand means that neither competitor makes sacrifices at the ends of the market when he invades his rival's territory; thus there is no check on the rivals moving together. Actually, elastic demands do impose such a check and do account for the fact that equilibrium is frequently established, with the competitors free to move but spatially separated.... I suggest ... that it is important to analyze not only the forces that bring them together but also those that keep them apart.
>
> (Smithies 1941, 485)

Smithies allowed for the possibility of an 'outside option' of not buying the good by assuming that aggregate consumption is governed by a downward-sloping (and incidentally linear) demand curve. He assumed that, in equilibrium, all points on the continuum are served, but the opportunity of exit represented by this demand curve nonetheless affects the conjectured outcome, just as the outside option in a mechanism design problem's participation constraint affect the equilibrium contract. (Mueller (1989) notes this aspect of Smithies's system.) In accordance with the public choice analogy with which he opened the paper, Smithies assumed zero relocation costs for producers, even with constant transactions costs for consumers. (This assumption of course reduces the applicability of his speculations to industrial organization.)

Unlike Hotelling, Smithies gave producer conjectures on opponent reaction a prominent role. He considered three cases:

1 'full quasi-cooperation', in which each competitor assumes that the other will match price and establish a symmetric location – as usual, this (very non-Cournot) conjecture leads to the same output and price as a monopoly;[22]
2 one 'quasi-cooperative as to prices and competitive as to locations'; and
3 'full competition', in which producers, as implicitly in Hotelling's model, assume 'that both the price and location of his rival will be fixed independently of his own' (1941, 490).

He was aware of both the limited and extreme nature of the conjectures he considered, and of the verbal imprecision of his essay.

Smithies said that

> The analysis of these problems can be carried out rigorously only by mathematical methods. Although the methods are elementary, their application is complicated.[23] For this reason, and also for the reason that the mathematics do not bring out clearly the economic principles involved, I have attempted to present the whole argument in purely verbal form and to indicate in an appendix the general mathematical methods.[24]
>
> (1941, 486–7)

Unlike writers on the dominant firm model, Hotelling, Zeuthen and Smithies were conscious of the context of strategic interdependence in which they operated. Hotelling (1929) is interesting in modelling an issue (which had only been casually addressed earlier) in a truly game-theoretic manner, although he omits any attention to player conjectures. Zeuthen expanded this model and dealt with it by new methods. Smithies, while avoiding mathematical methods, introduced the player conjectures as important in this context, and, tacitly, the idea of outside options as important for players.

The literature of monopolistic competition, briefly examined below, expanded on Hotelling's view of differentiated oligopoly by considering many possible dimensions of product and firm distinction. In accordance with Hotelling's basic position, the increased differentiation provides, if anything, *extra* stability to conditions faced by consumers. This is, however, due to an assumption of free entry which enabled both Robinson and Chamberlin to employ neoclassical *ceteris paribus* to an even greater extent than Cournot had achieved, almost a century earlier.

Monopolistic competition

In 1933, Chamberlin and Robinson published separate and innovative books on what is now called (in the USA) 'monopolistic competition'.[25] This is widely considered a case of a multiple discovery in the sense of Merton, although Chamberlin spent many years and pages arguing otherwise.[26] In this brief section, little distinction will be made between their work.

Reviewing Robinson's volume, Kaldor remarked presciently that

> Recent work in the theory of duopoly has made it clear that that baffling question [of producers' knowledge and equilibrium] can only be satisfactorily treated by explicitly allowing for the entrepreneur's estimates of his rivals' reactions, as distinct from the actual reaction itself. This, of course, is not easy to do by 'curves'.
>
> (1934, 341)

Less prophetically, to the extent that one fails to see game theory as a major unifying force in the analysis of market structure and firm behaviour, Kaldor continued,

> But does it not seem probable... that a more thorough-going recognition of this factor would both unify and simplify the whole theory of imperfect competition?
>
> (1934, 341)

It is interesting that Kaldor noted the significance of firm estimates of their rival(s)'s reactions, as this was not a point much emphasized by either author.

Chamberlin began his book with explications of duopolistic models, emphasizing the mutual dependence of the situation, and cited Pigou on the importance of firm conjectures and the uncertainty (which Borel called psychological) due to interdependence. For Chamberlin, however, the sources of uncertainty for oligopolists are:

1 Even where they make Cournot conjectures, they do not know whether rivals will use a price or quantity instrument.
2 Uncertainty as to the rationality and horizon of competitors.
3 Uncertainty of their own impact on the market.
4 'Long and variable lags'.

To these factors Chamberlin attributed any indeterminacy of outcome. They are not very closely related to the core ideas of game theory, or to the more interesting causes of multiple equilibria. Robinson, who based her analysis quite firmly on value theory, dealt even less with strategic interdependence.

Both authors employed graphical analysis, perhaps '[returning] to Marshallian orthodoxy' as Smithies did. And, as was the case with Smithies, this technique did not lead to material of great game-theoretic interest. Assuming many firms which might be differentiated in diverse ways, and wishing to say something definitive and general, both Robinson and Chamberlin hit upon free entry as a condition strong enough to force simple answers, in which the operation of firm interdependence is largely limited to entry.

Given differentiation of each firm or its product (which allows monopolistic pricing at marginal cost equal to marginal revenue) and free entry (which, ignoring an integer constraint, drives profits to zero), optimal strategy by each firm is highly determinate. While Robinson elected to examine further issues in factor demand and factor exploitation, and Chamberlin examined higher dimensional diversification decisions, their results are based on this construct. Free entry serves, like perfect competition, to make the interdependence of the firms virtually trivial from the point of view of strategy.

CONCLUSION

Intellectual descendants of Cournot discussed in the previous chapter typically examined Cournot's assumptions about duopolist conjectures or dynamic processes critically, and sometimes extended them. Zeuthen, Stackelberg, Sweezy, Hall and Hitch, Hotelling, Robinson and Chamberlin chose rather to relax the extreme symmetry of the game-form Cournot had chosen for his model. The least of these created new models of interest for the analysis of particular, concrete situations of strategic interdependence. The greatest (definitely Hotelling) pointed out a method of handling an untouched realm, for analysis of interaction in a rigorous and novel fashion.

Bilateral monopoly, another area broached by Cournot (1838), led to further research of even more interest from a game-theoretic point of view than the duopoly literature. This literature is examined in the next chapter.

4

STRATEGIC INTERDEPENDENCE
Bilateral monopoly

In a city that stands in the very centre of Africa, and is rarely visited by the casual tourist, the people had always bought eggs – a daily necessary in a climate where egg-flip was the usual diet – from a Merchant who came to their gates once a week. And the people always bid wildly against each other: so there was quite a lively auction every time the Merchant came, and the last egg in his basket used to fetch the value of two or three camels, or thereabouts. And eggs got dearer every week. And still they drank their egg-flip, and wondered where all their money went to.

And there came a day when they put their heads together. And they understood what donkeys they had been.

And next day, when the Merchant came only *one* Man went forth. And he said, 'Oh, thou of the hook-nose and the goggle-eyes, thou of the measureless beard, how much for that lot of eggs?'

And the Merchant answered him 'I *could* let thee have that lot at ten thousand piastres the dozen.'

And the man chuckled inwardly, and said '*Ten* piastres the dozen I offer thee, and no more, oh descendant of a distinguished grandfather!'

And the Merchant stroked his beard, and said 'Hum! I will await the coming of thy friends.' So he waited. And the Man waited with him. And they both waited together.

'The manuscript breaks off here,' said Mein Herr, as he rolled it up again . . . .
(Lewis Carroll, *Sylvie and Bruno Concluded*)

Carroll's novel, published in 1893 but by his account largely written by 1885, contains this passage describing an initial situation in which the egg merchant acts as a price-discriminating monopolist. When his customers recognize that they can combine to their advantage, however, both buyers and sellers have market power. That 'the manuscript breaks off here' could indicate two things: that Carroll did not know how to solve the problem, or the indeterminacy of price in such a situation.[1]

This is a peculiarly appropriate passage with which to begin a discussion of treatments of what was termed 'bilateral monopoly'. The indeterminacy of outcome in many situations in which strategic interdependence, rather than a market, operates became a theme of economists and remains a focus for game theorists. As in the analysis of duopoly, some of the controversy was based on dynamic concerns, the conjectures of participants and the rules of the game. Edgeworth, however, emphasized the role of numbers of participants in the game. Both themes have remained important. It is interesting to note that von Neumann and Morgenstern recognized bilateral monopoly as part of their domain. Morgenstern wrote in his diary that he had 'started a treatise with Johnny about games, minimax, bilateral monopoly and duopoly. What fun' (quoted by Leonard (1995, 748)).

Cournot (1838), who first mathematized the problem of a monopolist facing buyers without market power and initiated systematic study of duopoly and oligopoly, introduced analytical treatment of a situation in which parties on different sides of an exchange have market power. According to Schumpeter (1954, 976),

> ... the [early neoclassical] period's work [on market power] may be described as a series of successful attempts to develop [Cournot's] statics of straight monopoly and as another series of much less successful attempts to develop and to correct his theories of oligopoly and bilateral monopoly. Second honors are divided between Marshall and Edgeworth.

Edgeworth first analysed bilateral monopoly for the general case of an endowment economy, and emphasized the role of numbers of traders in limiting the indeterminacy of the outcome. Marshall engaged in controversy with Edgeworth over the cause of indeterminacy in such an economy, and has been widely credited with the innovation of offer curves in international trade theory.

Under bilateral monopoly, as under duopoly, more than one party has scope for strategic behaviour. Outcomes depend on their strategies, their expectations of their opponents' strategies, and any 'rules of the game' that might exist. Each party can potentially affect the outcome. Quintessentially game-theoretic situations of this type have been important in the intersection between game theory and mathematical economics from the outset. The study of the effect of the number of traders in bilateral exchange culminated in the work of Shubik (1959a, b), Debreu and Scarf (1963) and Bewley (1973). An outgrowth of the bilateral monopoly literature was to be bargaining theory, via considerations of labour negotiation.

General equilibrium approaches (including those of international trade) frequently assume that agents conjecture that they cannot affect price and thus manipulate post-trade allocation. Combined with convexity and other assumptions, this framework leads to the existence of equilibrium. In simple situations with strong convexity assumptions, the assumptions often lead to a unique equilibrium. They also led to the development of offer curves as an analytical tool which was often combined with a Nash equilibrium concept before Nash (1950a). Shubik told Nash that Cournot had originated this concept before Nash: see Shubik (1992).

Cournot–Nash conjectures are definitely appropriate to situations of general equilibrium with perfectly competitive markets. The crux of game theory, however, is that not only an agent's actions, but the agent's *ideas* about other agents' actions affect the payoffs to other agents. Early approaches to bilateral monopoly could have treated this effect as an externality, and there was, in fact, some emphasis on the result from substituting a monopolist in two materials for Cournot's two monopolists. However, in general economists modelled equilibria as outcomes of *strategies* by the parties involved, and attempted to justify various forms of strategy formation or to explain why strategies, as well as payoffs, might be indeterminate. Such questions are fundamentally game-theoretic.

Early treatments of bilateral monopoly have three features in common. As in the case of approaches to duopoly, economists were concerned at the 'inde-terminateness' of the problem, and generally failed to consider the effect of exchange rules such as bid sequence. The feeling that further analysis would yield a unique 'correct' equilibrium was, however, largely absent from this literature. Second, also as in the duopoly literature but to a lesser extent, writers tended to use basically static models while making dynamic arguments. Third, several related problems were fused under the name 'bilateral monopoly'. Hicks (1935, 16) stated that ' "Bilateral Monopoly" is a phrase which has been applied to two different problems, and it is well to keep them distinct'. While Hicks discussed varying treatments of isolated exchange and of a raw materials monopolist selling to the producer of a monopolized consumer good, Cournot's example of mutual relations between producers led to further study of two or more raw materials producers with market power selling to a monopolist producer of consumption goods, or to a competitive output sector.

The way in which Cournot raised the issue of what was later called bilateral monopoly was rather curious, and curious in a way which had an effect on the subsequent literature. Cournot analysed the case of a producer of brass, who was assumed to use copper and zinc in constant proportions, and supposed copper and zinc productions both to be monopolized industries. This led to a strand of the bilateral monopoly literature in which industries with monopolists and/or monopsonists interacted. This literature, which was not especially successful, is discussed in the first section.

A more promising line of investigation was that of an endowment economy in which a small number of agents trade. This literature, which has modern counterparts in the analysis of the size of the core,[2] examined the problem of 'indeterminate equilibrium' and its relation to the number of agents in a negotiation situation or market – the problem illustrated in the Carroll quote above. This problem led to the famous controversy over Marshall's appendix on an endowment economy in which the only two goods were apples and nuts, and the early literature on the topic will be examined in the second section.

A related area is the application of offer curves to classical and neoclassical international trade, in which the offer curves of two agents (countries) are primary analytical tools. Early work in this area by Marshall (building on Mill) and Edgeworth will be considered in the third section.

Both Marshall and Edgeworth thought that the apparatus of core analysis would be especially useful in the study of negotiation between labour and management. While this area of study was not very fruitful, the models of Pigou and Zeuthen are of interest and are discussed in the fourth section.

INTERACTING INDUSTRIES WITH MARKET POWER

Schmidt (1992) notes that the problems of duopoly and bilateral monopoly are akin in that they cover strategic situations in which two agents make decisions on goods production (and/or trade), but dissimilar in that, under duopoly, the goods are perfect substitutes but are complements under bilateral monopoly. In the former situation, non-cooperative game theory is most natural while non-cooperative concepts arose in the consideration of bilateral monopoly. In the earliest formal model, however, Cournot neglected possible cooperation.

Cournot ([1838] 1927) initiated the examination of industries with market power which interacted in his ninth chapter: 'Of the mutual relations of producers'. He noted that

> it is necessary to inquire according to what laws the profits, which are made by all the producers as a whole, are distributed among the individuals in consequence of the law of consumption for final products. This short summary will suffice to make known what we mean by influence of the *mutual relations* of producers of different articles, an influence which must not be confounded with that of *competition* of producers of the same article, which has been analyzed in the preceding chapters.
>
> ([1838] 1927, 99)

Cournot assumed that copper and zinc are produced by two separate monopolists at zero cost, and are used only to produce brass, which has no other production costs than the purchase of these raw materials. He supposed that m_1 kilograms of copper and m_2 kilograms of zinc were invariably used to produce a kilogram of brass. Where p is the price of a kilogram of brass and p_1 and p_2 those of a kilogram of copper and a kilogram of zinc, respectively, he stated ([1838] 1927, 100) that 'we should have, according to the hypothesis',

(a) $m_1 p_1 + m_2 p_2 = p.$

That is, he supposed that while copper and zinc industries are monopolized, the brass industry operates competitively. This assumption simplified the model considerably. The copper and zinc industries act strategically against each other, and the brass industry acts passively with respect both to them and to buyers of brass. This permitted Cournot to write the demand for brass as $D = F(p) = F(m_1 p_1 + m_2 p_2)$, so that demands for copper and zinc are

(b) $D_i = m_i F(m_1 p_1 + m_2 p_2), \quad i = 1, 2,$

which are known to the producers of raw materials.

By straightforward differentiation, given the conjecture of opponent passivity used in the case of duopoly, Cournot derived reaction curves for the copper and zinc industries with the equations

$$F(m_1 p_1 + m_2 p_2) + m_i p_i F'(m_1 p_1 + m_2 p_2) = 0, \quad i = 1, 2.$$

That Cournot was employing both equations and diagrams in 1838 remains a point to wonder on.

In this situation, unlike the duopoly situation he modelled, Cournot assumed that producers take price, rather than quantity, as their instrument. No reason is given for this difference, and Cournot may have been unconscious that it could have any effect on the outcome of the problem. (In fact, with a linear demand for brass, the reaction curves of copper and zinc producers who use quantity as an instrument are quite different from those Cournot derived.)

By an argument amounting to a statement of symmetry, he arrived at $m_1 p_1 = m_2 p_2 = \frac{1}{2} p$, which, with the offer curve equations, yielded

(c) $F(p) + \frac{1}{2} p F'(p) = 0,$

while one monopolist producing copper and zinc would, by maximizing $p F(p)$, arrive at

(c') $F(p) + p F'(p) = 0.$

Cournot went on to observe that if 'we had supposed n commodities thus related, instead of only two, equation (c) would evidently have been replaced by $F(p) + (1/n) p F'(p) = 0$; from which we should conclude, that the more there are of articles thus related, the higher the price determined by the division of monopolies will be, than that which would result from the fusion or association of monopolists' ([1838] 1927, 103–4).

In addition, Cournot gave an example of a demand curve for brass such that no equilibrium exists in the markets for copper and zinc ([1838] 1927, 104). He also examined the case in which one or another of the raw materials monopolists is endowed with a quantity of mineral which proves binding with respect to the price (and therefore quantity) given by the intersection of the reaction functions ([1838] 1927, 104–5). (While Cournot worked in price space, a discussion at least in part in quantity space is somewhat more intuitive.) In this case, as Cournot noted, the raw materials monopolists would prefer to sell more copper and zinc than is feasible, given the limited endowment of one monopolist. This limits the quantity of brass which can be produced and therefore its price, given by the demand curve for the competitive brass industry. The raw materials monopolists would prefer to charge a lower price for a higher quantity than they can, given the limitation of endowed raw material. His illustration (see Figure 4.1) shows the situation in

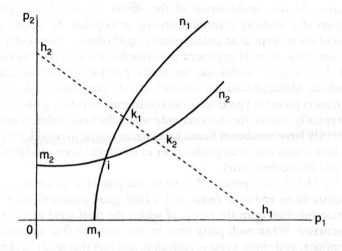

Figure 4.1

price space. The intersection of copper and zinc reaction curves lies strictly inside the line giving the (lower) limit prices of copper and zinc, subject to supplies of raw materials. The copper and zinc reaction curves do not intersect on the limit price line, and Cournot stated correctly that 'from this the conclusion can be drawn . . . that the values of p_1 and p_2 are indeterminate, being subject only to this condition, that the points which would have the values of these variables for coordinates fall on the part . . . of the [price limit] line, which is intercepted between the [reaction] curves . . .' ([1838] 1927, 105).

In the remainder of the chapter, Cournot went on to consider the case in which copper and zinc are produced only at a positive cost, and remarked on the effect of industry cost functions on the shares of profit garnered by copper and zinc monopolists. He also considered the case in which brass production has costs other than the cost of raw materials and, with rightly less sharp results, the case in which copper and zinc have uses other than brass production.

Cournot's ninth chapter successfully analysed a case in which two monopolists are forced to interact by the market for their output, although in a simple case. Thus, he considered interdependent agents other than the famous mineral-water duopolists. As in his analysis of oligopoly, he considered the effect in this simple case of an increase in the number of firms with market power. He indicated the advantage in profit accumulation which accrues to a firm by means of its cost function's relation to that of its opponent, and initiated exploration of the interrelations of firms which use each other's outputs as inputs in a quasi-general-equilibrium framework.

The effects of Cournot's writing on the profession, however, lay largely in other areas. In his consideration of the effects on equilibrium price and production of a quantity constraint on one monopolist, he almost casually introduced the concept of an indeterminate equilibrium – even under the rule of Cournot conjectures of opponent passivity by raw materials monopolists. Second, his simplest model has *one* sector purchasing outputs from two monopolists. Although Cournot assumed that the purchasing industry (brass) had no market power as a producer or as a consumer, facilitating his results, one would typically assume this to occur only where the brass industry consists of an arbitrarily large number of firms. Later writers came to consider the case in which there is only one brass producer, or in which the brass producers form a perfect and frictionless cartel.

Bowley (1924, 62) presented a brief analysis of a situation in which monopolists in an endowed factor and a final good produced via a general production function from the factor, of which the final good producer is the only purchaser. When each party tries to maximize profits, the outcome is indeterminate, aside from a case of collusion, and that this result 'is obtainable with less simple hypotheses; but the method used can be extended to show that universal monopoly of all factors and all production leads to indeterminate results'. While he did not specifically state the cause of indeterminacy, he presumably thought of it as stemming from the same source of indeterminacy he mentioned with respect to duopoly: that the result 'depends on what each producer thinks the other is likely to do' (1924, 38).

Marshall's consideration of Cournot's example led him to contemplate varying rules (sequences of bid) within the market implicitly, and the possibility of combination between the two raw materials monopolists explicitly. The following passage, inserted in the fifth edition of the *Principles*, is worth quoting at length.

> So far it has been assumed that the monopolist can buy and sell freely. But in fact monopolistic combinations in one branch of industry foster the growth of monopolistic combinations in those which have occasion to buy from or sell to it: and the conflicts and alliances between such associations play a rôle of ever increasing importance in modern economics. Abstract reasoning of a general character has little to say on the subject. If two absolute monopolies are complementary, so that neither can turn its products to any good account, without the other's aid, there is no means of determining where the price of the ultimate product will be fixed. Thus if we suppose, following Cournot's lead, that copper and zinc were each of them useless except when combined to make brass: and if we supposed that one man, A, owned all the available sources of supply of copper; while another, B, owned all those of zinc; there would then be no means of determining beforehand what amount of brass would be produced, nor therefore the price at which it could be sold. Each would try to get the better of the other in bargaining; and though the issue of the

contest would greatly affect the purchasers, they would not be able to influence it.

Under the circumstances supposed, A could not count on reaping the whole, nor even any share at all of the benefit, from increased sales, that would be got by lowering the price of copper in a market in which the price of zinc was fixed by natural causes rather than strategic haggling and bargaining. For, if he reduced his price, B might take the action as a sign of commercial weakness, and raise the price of zinc; thus causing A to lose both on price and on amount sold. Each would therefore be tempted to bluff the other; and consumers might find that less brass was put on the market, and that therefore a higher price could be exacted for it, than if a single monopolist owned the whole supplies both of copper and of zinc.... But neither A nor B could reckon on the effects of his own action, unless the two came together and agreed on a common policy: that is unless they made a partial, and perhaps temporary fusion of their monopolies.

(Marshall 1961, v. 1, 494–5)

Later writers were to go from Marshall's rather nebulous discussion to explicit consideration of the effect of specific rules of the market game, and specific, though sometimes implicit, conjectures on the part of raw materials monopolists.

Zeuthen (1930) was perhaps the first to relate Cournot's example to the case of a monopolist facing a monopsonist. He stated that

If, in the third type of case with which we are to deal in this chapter, there are two absolutely monopolistic enterprises or combinations which deliver different materials or services to be used in a fixed proportion by a number of competing producers, they will both be interested in pursuing an active price policy. The dispositions of one party must, however, fit in with those of the other, and *vice versa*, so that the case, just like that of the preceding chapter of two competing enterprises, should in advance seem to be indeterminate. If we consider actual examples, we have in all essentials the same case when two monopolistic concerns face one another as buyer and seller....

(1930, 63)

While he made a distinction between the case postulated by Cournot and that of opposed monopolist and monopsonist, 'In the main, however, the determination of price is the same in both cases...' (Zeuthen 1930, 89).

Zeuthen felt that there was a 'right solution' to the problem of opposed monopolist and monopsonist.[3] His discussion stressed the difference between his and Cournot's analytical frameworks:

The problem is the same as that of a few competing enterprises: What does the individual enterprise determine, price or sales or what? We shall

61

obtain a wrong solution in both cases if either we suppose that one entrepreneur first fixes the price which, with definite sales, will give him the greatest possible profit, or that he fixes the sales which, at a definite price, will achieve the same purpose, leaving the other entrepreneur to fix his sales or prices as the case may be, so that under the actual conditions he gets the greatest possible profit (. . . One solution is obtained where the manufacturer first sets his price and the purveyor of a raw-material or labour sets the price, and the manufacturer on this basis determines how much he wishes to buy). If a distinction were to be made between the position of the parties with regard to price and sales, it would be proper to say that in this case of bilateral monopoly, either party decides his own excess price, whilst the sales of both are necessarily equal. In the case of monopolistic competition, on the other hand, the price must be the same for both; if one party have fixed their sales, the other party are able to fix theirs, and thereby the price.

(Zeuthen 1930, 65–6)

This leads to a general solution for the case in which there may be costs of production for the two monopolists. However, Zeuthen's approach vitiates any discussion like Cournot's of how differing cost functions between the two monopolists affect the profits they can gain.

Zeuthen (1930, 66–8) presented and described diagrams showing the effects of different opponent excess prices on the behaviour of Cournot's model to develop equilibrium. He notes, however, that at the excess prices which yield the monopolists the highest possible profit, 'the individual enterprise will here find an immediate advantage in raising the price, a tendency only to be checked by a belief that the other party is keeping down the price in the common interest of both' (1930, 69). Thus, while he felt that the Cournot–Nash equilibrium was 'correct', Zeuthen recognized that another price point could be chosen given a different conjecture on the part of entrepreneurs.

Following Cournot's analysis of the numbers of raw materials monopolists, Zeuthen underscored the importance of whether monopolists compete or produce complementary products: 'Whilst several competing monopolists set a lower price than a single one, several opposing monopolists, i.e. those whose services supplement each other, set a higher price than would the single monopolist' (Zeuthen 1930, 70–1). (Schmidt (1992) emphasizes that a key difference between duopoly and bilateral monopoly models is that of substitution between goods, and hence strategies, and complementarity between goods and strategies.)

Concerned with the impact of varying conjectures and bid orders, he suggested that

there is undoubtedly a definite solution when there are in a market several competing sellers faced by several mutually competing buyers, and when at the same time each enterprise has a different power of extension (partly owing to an unequal ability to attract customers and partly to greater or smaller proximity to the latter) or when enterprises at the same time have unequal and differently varying costs. This contemporary solution of all questions must be composed of features harmonising with each of the special solutions, [but that f]or the present the treatment of the fundamental questions of detail is bound to be experimental and uncertain, and the attempt at a comprehensive solution must, of course, to a still greater extent be in the nature of a sketch.

(Zeuthen 1930, 76–7)[4]

Zeuthen compiled a table showing price and quantity outcomes with linear demand for final output and identical constant costs of monopolists, depending on the number of raw materials sellers, in some cases with asymmetric market power (1930, 85). He assumes two cases: one in which raw materials monopolists can sell to the entire competitive final output sector, and one in which each input enterprise has a 'power of extension' in selling equal to one plus half the number of raw materials monopolists in its market power class. He shows, like Cournot but for a more complex case, how increases in the number of monopolists drive down the (excess) price.

Zeuthen also discussed how the number of competing raw goods monopolists affect the demand curve faced by each, developing a kinked individual demand curve reminiscent of that of the later Sweezy (1939) (Zeuthen 1930, 91–6).

Stackelberg's *The Theory of the Market Economy* ([1948] 1952, 182–9) contains matter from his (1934) *Marktform und Gleichgewicht*. As in the case of his examination of duopoly, he made explicit assumptions about market dynamics which permitted him to develop several classes of equilibrium outcome. He considered the relations of a monopolist dealing with a monopsonist of her output under simplifying assumptions which lead to four possible equilibria. If the market rules give all market power to the buyer of the intermediate output (the monopsonist) by giving her the first move, the buyer constructs the monopolist's supply curve and can call a demand price to him. The monopsonist can also call an all-or-nothing quantity and price pair to the monopolist, which would create greater profit for her and limits the monopolist's profit to zero (given no fixed cost). Where the rules of the game allow the seller of the raw material (the monopolist) first move, and therefore market power, the monopolist can construct the buyer's demand curve for his product just as a conventional monopolist would. The equilibrium outcome depends on whether he chooses to use the buyer's demand curve like a conventional monopolist, or to force the buyer to operate along her all-or-nothing demand curve by offering only to sell a given quantity at a given cost. Even in the simplified case of strict sequence, the outcome depends on the sequence and on whether the buyer (seller) is allowed to bid price and quantity, or only price. Rather like Marshall, Stackelberg emphasized that this situation is prone to 'trials of power', so that, as in his examination of duopoly, he felt that a market characterized by bilateral monopoly was inherently rather unstable.

THE 'EDGEWORTH BOX', AND APPLES AND NUTS

Cournot's bilateral monopoly model examined the game-theoretic problem of producers with interdependent outcomes and optimal strategies where goods produced are complementary. An exchange economy in which agents' objective functions are utilities derived from consumption of goods which they wish to trade with each other is another form of the same type of problem.

Edgeworth's approach to the problem of small numbers with potential gains from trade in endowed goods was specifically informed by Cournot's work on bilateral monopoly. Hildenbrand (1993, 477) states that

> The important and novel point of Edgeworth's analysis is that he explicitly models the 'degree of competition' by the number of agents who participate in the economy.... Edgeworth introduced a new concept of equilibrium; the *'final settlements'* or, in today's language, the *'core'*.[5]

Edgeworth stated that the importance of the (small) numbers on one side or another of a market (buyers or sellers)

> may have any degree of importance up to the point where a whole interest (labourers or entrepreneurs) is solidified into a single competitive unit.... We shall find the *price* continually diminish as the number of monopolists increases, until the point of complete fluidity is reached. This gradual 'extinction' of the influence of monopoly is well traced by Cournot in a discussion masterly, but limited by a particular condition, which may be called *uniformity of price, not . . . abstractedly* [sic] *necessary in cases of imperfect competition.* Going beyond Cournot, not without trembling, the present inquiry finds that, where the field of competition is sensibly imperfect, an indefinite number of *final settlements* are possible; that in such a case *different* final settlements would be reached if the system should run down from different *initial positions* or contracts. The sort of difference which exists between Dutch and English auction, theoretically unimportant in *perfect competition*, does correspond to different results, *different final settlements* in imperfect competition.
> (Edgeworth 1881, 47–8)[6]

Edgeworth (1881) was the first thinker to make contract curves and offer curves either analytically or casually explicit, and we owe the seeds of what became the 'Edgeworth–Bowley box' to his *Mathematical Psychics.*[7] Nonetheless, Edgeworth's principal concern was not so much with a two-person, two-good endowment economy as with what becomes of final allocations in endowment economies as the number of agents increases. Perhaps because of

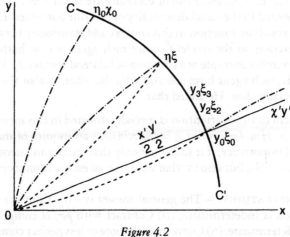

Figure 4.2

this, Edgeworth concentrated on the contract curve to the relative neglect of offer curves.

Offer curves, typically used in the analysis of two-good, two-agent situations, answer the question, 'If the rate of exchange of one good for the other is p, what is an agent's desired final allocation, given her initial endowment?' This immediately implies the post-trade allocation for both parties. Equilibrium occurs where both agents agree on the desired final allocation at the given price p. The formation of offer curves may be looked at in at least two ways. Firstly, they may trace agent reactions to prices proposed by a 'Walrasian auctioneer', or by any other system which the agent cannot affect (including a competitive market). To view offer curves as reactions to an auctioneer's prices is perhaps most traditional. Second, they may trace the reactions of an agent who makes the Cournot or Nash-type conjecture of taking as given her opponents' actions, when players, 'Bertrand'-like, use price as an instrument. Edgeworth placed his emphasis on numbers of agents, and therefore on the degree of competitiveness which lies outside the sanctions of convention or game-rules such as constant use of price as an instrument. He stressed that in the implicit absence of such institutions, the degree of determinateness of final allocation depends on the number of agents: for this purpose, the contract curve is more useful than offer curves could be.

While Edgeworth derived the contract curve in the text at some length (1881, 20–4) and *depicted* offer curves in his illustration (1881, 28), he left derivation and discussion of offer curves (which he called 'demand curves') to his Appendix V, and failed to stress them. Creedy (1986) provides an excellent source on the minutiae of Edgeworth's derivation. Hildenbrand (1993) notes an error in Edgeworth's illustration (see Figure 4.2).

Edgeworth's main interest was the indeterminacy of outcome where numbers of agents in an endowment economy are small. (As a utilitarian, he was also interested in the social desirability of possible outcomes. His use of an additive social welfare function in this context adds symmetry between agents to his deliberation on the model.)[8] Since each agent acts as both buyer and seller, this is another example of a situation of bilateral monopoly. Where there are two goods, each agent buys one and sells the other, so that the correspondence is especially clear. He stated that

> The problem to which attention is specially directed in this introductory summary is: *How far contract is indeterminate* – an inquiry of more than theoretical importance, if it shows not only that indeterminateness tends to prevent widely, but also in what direction an escape from its evils is to be sought.
>
> DEMONSTRATIONS.[i] – The general answer is – (α) Contract without competition is indeterminate, (β) Contract with *perfect* competition is perfectly determinate, (γ) Contract with more or less perfect competition is less or more determinate.
>
> (Edgeworth 1881, 20)

Rather endearingly, the footnote to his demonstrations remarks that he presented

> [i]*Conclusions* rather, the mathematical demonstration of which is not fully exhibited.

Edgeworth's category (α), 'Contract without competition', constitutes a case of two agents. Unless some specific contractual procedure is supposed (a case Edgeworth did not address), any allocation on the contract curve such that each party is at least as well off (in utility) as at the endowment point is a possible final allocation. Edgeworth illustrated this as a Crusoe–Friday economy. He did not discuss the perfectly competitive case at any length, as this result was already well established. It is fascinating, however, to consider Edgeworth's approach to his conjecture for case γ.

He said that

> It is not necessary for this purpose to attack the *general problem of Contract qualified by Competition*, which is much more difficult than the general problem of unqualified contract already treated. It is not necessary to resolve analytically the composite mechanism of a *competitive field*. It will suffice to proceed synthetically, observing in a simple typical case the effect of continually introducing into the field additional competitors.
>
> (Edgeworth 1881, 34)

It was probably the vagueness of this observation that caused Bewley (1973) to assert that it is not clear what Edgeworth meant to say. Edgeworth proceeded, however, to construct what is now known as a replica economy, and to develop the equal-treatment property in much the same way that this was done by

Debreu and Scarf (1963). (Shubik (1959a) treated the game as cooperative, with a utilitarian objective function, and examined the limiting behaviour of solutions as the number of players grows in this cooperative context.)[9] Whether or not Edgeworth thought (incorrectly) that a replica economy is practically the same as an economy which increases in size by means of an increase in agents arbitrarily endowed with goods and tastes, his achievement was an amazing one unequalled for eighty years.

Edgeworth's construction of an economy which increases in size by means of multiplication of agents of each type (a replica economy) in the two-good, two-agent case follows:

> . . . let us now introduce a second [agent of type] X and a second [agent of type] Y; so that the field of competition consists of two Xs and two Ys . . . .

Starting from this point, Edgeworth proved in prose the equal-treatment property, which states that, in equilibrium, two agents of the same type cannot receive different allocations:

> Then it is evident that there cannot be equilibrium unless (1) all the field is collected at one point; (2) that the point is on the *contract-curve*. For (1) if possible let one couple be at one point, and another couple at another point. It will generally be the interest of the X of one couple and the Y of the other to rush together, leaving their partners in the lurch. And (2) if the common point is not on the contract-curve, it will be the interest of *all parties* to descend to the contract-curve.
>
> The points of the contract-curve in the immediate neighbourhood of the limits $y_0\xi_0$ and $\eta_0 x_0$ [utility-equivalents to the initial endowments] cannot be *final settlements*. For if the system be placed at such a point, say slightly north-west of $y_0\xi_0$, it will in general be possible for *one* of the Ys (without consent of the other) to *recontract* with the two Xs, so that for all those three parties the recontract is more advantageous than the previously existing contract. For the right line joining the origin to (the neighbourhood of) $y_0\xi_0$ will in general lie altogether within the *indifference-curve* drawn from the origin to $y_0\xi_0$. For the indifference-curve is in general convex to the abscissa.
>
> (Edgeworth 1881, 35–6)

In this passage, Edgeworth established a quasi-proof of the equal-treatment property very similar to that later used by Debreu and Scarf. As in the later work, he supposes that the players of each 'type' who are worst off among the players of their type defect, and indicates how they can achieve superior allocations by means of trade among themselves. The only substantive difference between this proof and the later one is the assumption of two 'types'.

Edgeworth also demonstrated by a simple example how the core (set of equilibria) of an exchange economy shrinks towards the competitive equilibrium as types of agents are replicated, where subsets of the players could jointly defect and institute exchange among themselves. Again, this quasi-proof in prose is very similar to the one later employed by Debreu and Scarf. Sutton (1993) has attributed this sort of argument focusing on blocking to Edgeworth: he maintains its value in bargaining theory, and remarks that it has been found less valuable in oligopoly theory. Edgeworth and, even more, later writers such as Zeuthen and Pigou, attempted to extend such blocking arguments to the area of industrial organization, though without notable success.

Vilfredo Pareto (1896, §144[1]) later clarified the presentation of 'Edgeworth box' material graphically by first depicting the familiar 'Edgeworth–Bowley' box (see Figure 4.3). However he did not emphasize multiple equilibria within this context, as Edgeworth had done.

> On peut, d'une manière assez élégante, représenter géométriquement les théories de l'échange en suivant la voie ouverte {offer curves, indifference curves} par Mr Edgeworth, et déjà indiquée dans la note du §83 .... Le cas que nous venons de traiter, correspond à celui où le monopoleur prend en considération aussi bien l'ophélimité de ce qu'il vend que de ce qu'il reçoit.

In this passage, Pareto not only offered an appreciation of Edgeworth's work, but connected the problem of an endowment economy with the more general topic of an integrated economy with self-interested agents who have market power. In this sense, he associated his analysis with that of Cournot.

Marshall's review of *Mathematical Psychics* (*The Academy*, 18 June 1881, 457; reprinted 1975, vol. 2, 265–8) gave a presentation of contract curve which was quite correct, but neglected to mention offer curves. Given that Marshall had derived trade offer curves (although incorrectly: see next section), this is somewhat surprising. Marshall did, however, discuss the connection between an Edgeworth exchange economy and international trade in the course of a rather patronizing review:

> He takes barter as his typical bargain, and lets x and y represent, as we have seen, quantities of the two things bartered. No doubt this is the right way of treating some problems of international trade, and what is nearly the same thing, of the trade between the members of different compact industrial groups, whether the groups are formally organised or not. But there are many reasons for thinking that the greater part of economic theory can be dealt with most easily by letting x represent the amount of the commodity dealt in, and y the price of the unit of that commodity expressed in the terms of money, which is supposed provisionally to have a uniform purchasing power.
>
> (Marshall 1975, 267–8)

This passage indicates a peculiarity of Marshall's analysis, which pervades much of his *Principles*, and which was one factor in the controversy over his

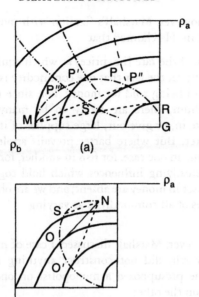

Figure 4.3

appendix on an 'apples and nuts' economy with Edgeworth. As in his consideration of consumer surplus as a measure of welfare, Marshall believed that money was a constant-valued measure of utility, and felt that issues of market power were somehow resolved when an economy was monetary. Even when Marshall dealt with entities which must be large, he *wanted at least the bulk of them* to be small, and felt that this was effectively the case in a monetary economy.

Marshall's Appendix F: Barter (1961, v. 1, 791–3) which dates substantially from the first edition in 1890 considered a two-person endowment economy in which apples and nuts are exchanged. He registered that where successive prices at which there are non-negative gains from trade for both parties move the economy from temporary equilibrium to temporary equilibrium, indeterminacy of final equilibrium outcome within the core is due to changing marginal utility as exchange proceeds. In discussing the sequence of prices such an economy might move through, he cited 'bargaining skill' as a relevant factor. He commented, however, that

> There is, however, one equilibrium rate of exchange which has some sort of right to be called the true equilibrium rate, because if once hit upon it would be adhered to throughout.
>
> (Marshall 1961, v. 1, 791)

This rate of exchange is a competitive equilibrium price.

At this point, however, Marshall's fixation with money as an article with constant utility set in. He claimed that

> This uncertainty of the rate [i.e. price] at which equilibrium is reached depends indirectly on the fact that one commodity is being bartered for another instead of being sold for money. For, since money is a general purchasing medium, there are likely to be many dealers who can conveniently take in, or give out, large supplies of it; and this tends to steady the market. But where barter prevails apples are likely to be exchanged for nuts in one case, for fish in another, for arrows in another, and so on; the steadying influences which hold together a market in which values are set in money are absent; and we are obliged to regard the marginal utilities of all commodities as varying.
>
> (1961, v. 1, 793)

Beyond this, however, Marshall discussed a case of more than two agents, but, unlike Edgeworth, did not construct anything resembling a replica economy. Rather, he presupposed a monopolist on one side of the market and large numbers on the other:

> It is however true that, if nutgrowing had been a chief industry of our barter-district, and all the traders on both sides had large stores of nuts, while only the A's had apples; then the exchange of a few handfuls of nuts would not have visibly affected their stores, or changed appreciably the marginal utility of nuts. In that case the bargaining would have resembled in all fundamentals the buying and selling in an ordinary cornmarket .... The real distinction then between the theory of buying and selling and that of barter is that in the former it generally is, and in the latter it generally is not, right to assume that the stock of one of the things which is in the market and ready to be exchanged for the other is very large and in many hands; and that therefore its marginal utility is practically constant.
>
> (1961, v. 1, 793)

While he rightly supposed that a situation in which an apple monopolist faces competitive nut-sellers creates a situation in which a unique equilibrium occurs, Marshall wrongly connected this to a marginal utility which 'is practically constant'. This may, however, shed some light on his obsession with a constant marginal utility of money: he presumably posited that universal possession of money would make it a constant-valued measure of utility.

The altercation with Edgeworth which ensued was described by Marshall's editor and nephew by marriage, Claude Guillebaud, in the following terms in an editorial appendix to Appendix F:

> In an article in the *Giornale degli Economisti* for March 1891, entitled

'Osservationi sulla teoria matematica dell' economia politica con riguardo speciale agli Principi di Economia de Alfreda Marshall', Edgeworth had contended that the uncertainty of the ultimate position of equilibrium under barter was due, not as Marshall said in his *Principles*, to the fact that we must regard the marginal utilities of both commodities exchanged as varying, but rather to the absence of competition.... He further went on to discuss the possibility that some of those in the market, who had done badly in the earlier stages of bargaining, might be able to improve their position by making further contracts with others whose disadvantage had been of the opposite nature: hence there might be a series of recontracts, and the ultimate equilibrium of the amounts exchanged would not be known until these had all been carried out.

(Guillebaud 1961, v. 2, 791–2)

Guillebaud misunderstood Edgeworth's blocking argument for the property of core convergence, mistaking it with a process of successive recontracting. However, when he addressed Edgeworth's contention that equilibrium in a two-person endowment economy is indeterminate even when the marginal utility of one good is constant, Guillebaud unerringly followed Berry's (1891) argument that Edgeworth was incorrect on this point, a relatively trivial matter.

The results of the controversy were two: Marshall added a brief Note XII *bis* to the *Principles* justifying his analysis while including an Edgeworthian diagram, and Edgeworth represented himself as one 'who has already burnt his fingers and fears the fire of controversy' (quoted by Newman 1990, 273). This may have had an influence on his later evaluation of Marshall's trade theory, including trade offer curves.

As Pigou (1908) and Newman (1990) note, Edgeworth and Marshall were talking about two different causes of indeterminacy: numbers of agents, and hence market power, and successive trading at false prices. In an extremely unpleasant exchange of journal articles and private letters, Edgeworth and Marshall disagreed on spurious grounds largely because they did not explicitly recognize what 'rules of the game' they assumed agents operated under, as in many of the controversies surrounding duopoly theory.

Pigou (1908, 1912, 1948) agreed that equilibrium in bilateral monopoly is indeterminate, indicating in 1948 that knowledge of the number of agents, of agents' demand curves (including offer curves) and marginal cost schedules (where this is relevant) is not in general sufficient to determine a unique equilibrium. In 1908, presumably following on Marshall's interest in multiple equilibria (for which see the next section), Pigou noted that unstable equilibria might as well not be counted as part of the 'equilibrium locus'. His interest in multiple equilibria was of the same fundamental nature as Edgeworth's: that differing bargaining abilities would result in different outcomes. His 1908 contribution was in considering two *agencies*, rather than two agents:

> It is always to A's advantage to force the exchange index from any initial position along that one of B's indifference curves upon which it lies until it reaches the contract curve. We have, therefore, merely to determine when it is in his power to do this.
>
> It is in his power to do it when B consists either of an individual bargaining upon his own behalf, or of a series of individuals completely insulated from one another and bargaining on behalf of a corporation that pays as a single body for its purchases .... It is possible, indeed, even in these cases, that A may be induced by reasons introduced *ab extra*, such as custom or some incidental convenience, to refrain from use of this power....
>
> If, however, B is an official buying on behalf of persons possessed of independent volition, and subject to the condition that any one of them, to whom the contract agreed upon appears less favourable than no contract at all, will not carry it out, the case is different.
>
> (Pigou 1908, 210)

Bowley (1924) portrayed the problem of an exchange economy in a fashion like that of Pareto. Unlike Edgeworth, he placed considerable emphasis on the offer curves of parties A and B, which he gave that name, and defined as 'the locus of points ... at which [a party] is willing to deal, if he cannot control the price' (1924, 7). Starting from the ingredients of initial endowment, strictly convex indifference maps, and offer curves, Bowley's discussion of the final allocation is a bit curious, and appears to bear a family relationship to Pigou (1908). (Although Pigou's nomenclature was a bit odd, it did not lead him into error.) Bowley's discussion also seems to derive from Marshall's Appendix F, although he began by assuming 'in the first instance that the bargain is made as a whole, not as the result of a series of exchanges'. He stated that

> B will try to take that point on A's offer curve which is most advantageous to him, which will be where A's offer touches [is tangent to] one of B's indifference curves (Q_1). Similarly A will aim at a point Q_2, where B's offer touches one of A's indifference curves.
>
> Let the offer curves intersect at Q. The double curve Q_1QQ_2 is called the *bargaining locus*. If B is the stronger bargainer he may secure a point between Q and Q_1; but if A and B are of equal bargaining strength, they will only both be willing to deal at the exchange rate and amount given by Q.
>
> (Bowley 1924, 8. See Figure 4.4 below)

Given that Bowley had supposed that he will consider only bargains made 'as a whole', this approach is incorrect: points aside from Q on the 'bargaining locus'

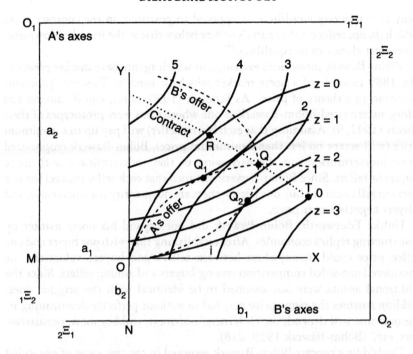

Figure 4.4

are not on the contract curve. At all such points there remain gains from trade. In this type of model, such points will therefore not be final allocations, and can only be intermediate allocations, or temporary equilibria, along a series of bargains. Q_1 and Q_2 are the points on B's and A's offer curves which would yield maximum utility to A and B respectively. In international trade theory, these are allocations that A (B) would seek to achieve by means of an optimal tariff, which would alter the shape of A's (B's) offer curve. However, tariffs are not placed within the rules of the game, and indeed seem irrelevant to an exchange economy. Bowley wrote that

> If the exchange of y for x is not made as a single transaction from the [initial endowment] . . . then temporary equilibrium may be reached wherever a pair of indifference curves touch one another so long as each gains, or at least does not lose, utility. . . . The intersection of the offer curves evidently lies on the contract curve.
>
> (1924, 9)

This pair of assertions suggests that an interest in agents' reaction to prices, which caused Bowley to focus on offer curves, also caused him to assume that any bargaining would take place in terms of successive prices proposed by the parties. In this case, however, points on the 'bargaining locus' other than Q can

73

only be temporary equilibria, as opposed to positions on the contract curve which do not reduce either party's utility below that at the initial endowment. These last alone can be equilibria.[10]

Böhm-Bawerk introduced exchange in which agents have market power in the 1889 example of a horse market which he used to illustrate 'problems confronting a theory of price'. As Schmidt (1990) notes, von Neumann and Morgenstern cited Böhm-Bawerk as one whose ideas were prototypes of their theory (1947, 9). Assuming that each buyer (seller) will pay up to a maximum price (will accept no less than a minimum price), Böhm-Bawerk emphasized price indeterminacy and the narrowing of that indeterminacy with more buyers or sellers. Since Böhm-Bawerk assumed that each seller (buyer) has one horse to sell (wants to buy one horse), there are no quantity considerations, and players negotiate over price.

Unlike Edgeworth, Böhm-Bawerk did not expand his horse market by constructing replica economies. After establishing that with one buyer and one seller, price could lie anywhere between seller's and buyer's valuations, he considered one-sided competition among buyers and among sellers. Since the additional agents were not assumed to be identical with the original ones, bidding narrows the range price may fall in without perfectly determining it: the outcome still depends on 'cleverness, craftiness, stubbornness, persuasiveness, etc.' (Böhm-Bawerk 1959, 218).

The bidding process Böhm-Bawerk assumed in the two cases of one-sided competition is unclear. It would seem, however, to be similar to that in a case with ten buyers and eight sellers. He supposed that buyers as a group make bids which rise until the number of buyers who still want horses equal the number of sellers willing to trade. A single price clears the market and determines who trades. While the maximum number of mutually beneficial trades do not occur, those who are bid out of the market will not trade voluntarily. (Nymeyer (1973) provided an explication of Böhm-Bawerk's analysis.)

From the point of view of core convergence, Böhm-Bawerk's contribution was the analysis of larger economies which were not replica economies. His method, however, more strongly resembles those of bargaining theory, with buyer (seller) valuations functioning as outside options.

TRADE OFFER CURVES

Trade offer curves are most often used for economies characterized by market perfection and full employment. That examinations of economies comprised of many perfectly competitive agents could have been early game-theoretic works might seem laughable. The market reactions of these agents, however, combine into a reaction curve for the economy as a whole, in interacting with other economies. Where the government of the economy does not interfere in international trade, the equilibrium is one of free trade. However, a government with other options can manipulate the economy's offer curve by means of taxes or subsidies to produce different payoffs.

The offer curves used in classical international trade theory are fundamentally similar to those used in the study of endowment economies. Trade offer curves are distinguished by embodying output decisions along with exchange decisions, in general, and by readily permitting an extra degree of strategy to be represented by tariff policy. Like endowment economy offer curves, trade offer curves embody the Cournot–Nash passivity conjecture with respect to prices.

Marshall seems not to have recognized the relationship between trade offer curves and exchange economy offer curves, which he may not have noticed in Edgeworth (1881). Marshall is widely credited with the development of trade offer curves – by Chipman (1965a, b) and in many texts. In his unpublished 'Essay on International Trade' (c. 1872–1874, reprinted 1975) and in 'The theory of foreign trade and other portions of economic science bearing on the principle of *laissez faire*' (1879, reprinted 1975), Marshall stated that he merely quantified the argument of Mill's Great Chapter 18 of Book III, because of the superiority of analytical machinery to numerical example (1975, vol. II, 132–3).

Mill (1871) constructed a $2 \times 2 \times 2$ example with Ricardian production and a particular utility function and derived its equilibrium. Although Mill's discussion does not suggest that he was thinking in terms of offer curves, it was a stunning achievement. Furthermore, he discussed the possibility of a finite number of multiple equilibria, which might be achieved by strategic players. Using Mill's example of English cloth and German linen, Marshall drew what look like the familiar trade offer curves.

Marshall intended to include this matter in the *Principles*, but never did so. 'The theory of foreign trade and other portions of economic science bearing on the principle of *laissez faire*' circulated as a pamphlet.[11] Edgeworth celebrated Marshall's analysis repeatedly. Edgeworth observed that

> There is more than meets the eye in Professor Marshall's foreign trade curves. As it has been said by one who used this sort of curve, a movement along a supply-and-demand curve of international should be considered as attended with rearrangements of internal trade ....
>
> (1905, 143)

However, he went much further:

> It remains only to acknowledge my obligation to Professor Marshall's unpublished chapters on foreign trade. These are the chapters alluded to in the Preface to the *Principles of Economics* as having been printed for private circulation and sent to many economists. Part of their substance is contained in the first volume of the *Principles*; part may be looked for in the second volume. What is written on the subject after a perusal of the

privately circulated chapters, and pending the publication of the second volume, can make no claim to originality or permanence – like the light of the planet which precedes the rising of the sun, borrowed from and destined to be effaced by the prime orb.

(Edgeworth 1894, 46–7)

The simplest geometrical representation of international trade appears to be a construction first used by Professor Marshall and explained by him in the mathematical appendix to his *Principles*.

(1894, 31–2)

The geometrical representation referred to is, of course, Marshall's offer curves (supply-and-demand curves) – interestingly, Edgeworth claimed that they were explained by Marshall in Note XII *bis* to the *Principles*. They were not.

Given Edgeworth's high praise, it is fascinating to find that Marshall derived trade offer curves incorrectly three times, in two different ways. The curves Marshall draws and the axes on which they lie look comfortingly familiar. However, the curves answer the wrong question (1872–1875): Given that England (Germany) will export *n* bolts of cloth (linen), what is the minimum that England (Germany) will charge in linen (cloth) in exchange? His analysis includes nothing, explicitly or implicitly, about England's opportunity cost in the production of cloth. His analysis includes nothing about tastes but the remark that they are given.

Strictures on the shape of offer curves make it clear that Marshall was considering the cost of producing cloth as the determinant of the minimum amount of linen England would take for a quantity of cloth. England's offer curve may intersect a vertical more than once if cloth is inferior in consumption, but England's offer curve cannot intersect any horizontal more than once, because

The only general condition as to the shape of the curves is derived from the fact that no diminution in the cost of production which is directly due to a change in the amount produced, i.e. no diminution which can occur without rendering the curves invalid, can reach so far as to enable an increased amount to be produced at a diminished gross cost. Hence, when the amount of cloth produced in England for exportation to Germany is known, the gross cost of production is known. Hence if the amount of linen which is imported to England is known, and consequently the expense to which England will go in buying it is known, the amount of cloth which she will sell for it is absolutely determined. But if the supply of linen imported to England be increased it may be possible to dispose of it only at a rate diminished in proportion to this increase or even only at a lower rate.

(Marshall n.d. c. 1872–1874, 262–3)

In fact, England's offer curve could be cut by a horizontal line if linen is a Giffen good in some range.

Marshall (1879) derived England's offer curve more explicitly (see Figure 4.5):

Let a curve OE [England's offer curve of exports (valued as cloth) for German imports (valued as linen)] be drawn as follows: – N being any point upon Oy [the linen axis], let it be determined from a knowledge of the circumstances of England's demand for linen, what is the number of yards of cloth, the expenses of producing and exporting which will be covered annually by the proceeds of the sale in England of an amount of linen represented by ON. From Ox [the cloth axis] measure off OM, equal to this number of yards of cloth. Draw lines through M and N at right angles to Ox and Oy respectively, meeting in P; then P is a point on the required curve, OE. If N be moved from O gradually along Oy, P will assume a series of positions, each of which corresponds to one position of N; the continuous string of points thus formed will be the curve OE. (In other words, OE will be the locus of P.) .... We may call OE 'England's demand curve'; and bearing in mind that PM is equal to ON, we may describe it thus:

England's demand curve is such that any point P being taken on it, and PM being drawn perpendicular to Ox; OM represents the amount of cloth which England will be willing to give annually for an amount of linen represented by PM.

(Marshall 1879, vol. 2, 135–6)

Once again, if we do not know where production is on a production possibility frontier, we do not know the cost of producing cloth in linen, or indeed in any other unit. Marshall did not analyse – perhaps did not realize that he ought to analyse – how international price would influence the 'rearrangements of internal trade' mentioned by Edgeworth.

In a letter to Edgeworth dated March 1891, Marshall stated that offer curves 'had perhaps more real applications to industrial groups and employer–employé-questions than to Foreign Trade' (1975, vol. 1, 112). Not only has Marshall's speculation not proven out in practice, but he himself must have come to disbelieve it. In *Money Credit and Commerce* (1923), Marshall presented trade offer curves one last time.

This time, rather than focusing on an undefined production cost, Marshall focused on demand.[12] In discussion of the shape of the trade offer curve, Marshall emphasized the elasticity of demand, and it was this sort of concern which gave rise to what is now called the Marshall–Lerner condition for stability of equilibrium.[13] This stemmed directly from a rather spurious construction of offer curves by means of example, from data in a table in both the body of the text and Appendix J. (Marshall felt that 'The possible relations of demand and value in the exclusive trade between two countries

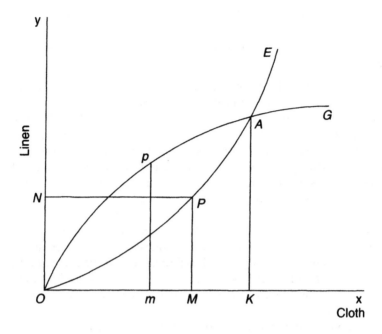

Figure 4.5

are most effectively represented by diagrams. But diagrams are not effectively assimilated by all readers; and they are therefore relegated to Appendix J' (1923, 161). Few would agree.)

In discussing the problem he was to confront, Marshall stated that

> Proceeding on Ricardo's lines, we may suppose that the following tables represent the amounts to which E and G would be severally willing to trade at various 'terms of trade'; or, to use a phrase which is more appropriate in some connections, at various 'rates of interchange'....

> These tables, which may be called E's and G's 'trading schedules', embody the fact that, if G's specialities generally were very scarce in E's markets, they would be bought up at very high costs by wealthy persons who had an urgent desire for them. If their supply increased greatly some of them would need to attract other persons, who were less wealthy, or had a less urgent desire for them; and the purchasing power for which each hundred of them could be sold in E would fall considerably....

> (1923, 161–2)

Marshall's table had a rather curious form. Column (1) listed various numbers of bales that England (E) might export. Column (2) listed 'Number of [German] *G* bales per hundred *E* bales at which *E* will part with those in (1)'. If this was to mean the *minimum* number of bales *E* would accept, this is given not by any reaction to price, but by *E*'s autarkic-equivalent indifference curve. Hence it is not properly a point on *E*'s offer curve.

Column (3) compiles (1) and (2) to arrive at the 'Total number of *G* bales for which *E* is willing to part with those in (1)'. Column (4) is headed 'Number of *G* bales per hundred *E* bales at which *G* will buy those in (1)',[14] and Column (5) compiles (1) and (4) to arrive at the 'Total number of *G* bales which *G* is willing to give for those in (1)'. Marshall combines (1) and (3) to yield England's offer curve, (1) and (5) to arrive at Germany's.

These offer curves are asserted rather than derived: the table is the fundamental datum. Moreover, at the lowest price of cloth at which England is explicitly shown to be willing to export, one bale of linen per ten bales of cloth, Marshall supposes that England will export 10,000 bales. No price at which England would prefer to export linen is indicated to exist, and I suggest that Marshall did not imagine one might exist. Just as in the case of partial equilibrium, a linen dealer would not change to selling cotton. In constructing Columns (2) and (5), Marshall seems to have been imagining the demand curves of a partial equilibrium model. Given that this was the case, consideration of the elasticities of demand and derivation of the condition for equilibrium stability must have been relatively natural.

If Marshall was 'proceeding on Ricardo's lines', and imagining that each country *could* produce both cloth and linen, England's technology must be violently biased in favour of cloth production, and Germany's in favour of linen production. If Marshall presupposed a situation in which England could produce cloth but not linen, and the reverse for Germany, no 'rearrangements of internal trade' are implicit in this case, and the notion of cost of production is problematic if not absent.

Marshall ignored the degree of market power that each country typically has in international trade. His thinking as to what behavioural question an offer curve answers was not only muddy, but inexplicit as to conjectures about trading partner behaviour. And, indeed, Marshall's analysis of tariffs (1923, 342–50) is very much a comparative statics analysis, rather than a strategic analysis.

Mill's Great Chapter marked tremendous progress in trade theory. In adding to Mill's work, Marshall's contributions consisted of the derivation of the condition for the stability of an equilibrium, of the axes on which offer curves should be drawn, and of the *look* of offer curves. His three successive explanations of offer curves, however, were wrong. They were not only bad game theory, but bad trade theory.

That Marshall has continued to be lauded as the originator of offer curves is strange, but it is stranger that Edgeworth praised Marshall's trade theory so highly. Edgeworth was certainly aware of the relationship between endowment economy offer curves and trade offer curves as Marshall seems not to have been:

this awareness colours Edgeworth's remark that Marshall explained offer curves in Note XII *bis* of the *Principles*, which discussed an endowment economy. Similarly, Edgeworth recognized that embedded in a country's trade offer curves were 'rearrangements of [its] internal trade'. It is far from clear that Marshall fully understood this. It seems likely that, having 'burnt his fingers and [fearing] the fire of controversy', Edgeworth attempted to steer readers of Marshall's trade theory aright without explicitly correcting Marshall.

BILATERAL MONOPOLY AS LABOUR–MANAGEMENT NEGOTIATION

With the theory of a wages fund not long dead, it is not surprising that economists interested in bilateral monopoly would attempt to apply the tools used for an endowment economy to a situation of wage bargaining between labour and employer. The interdependent goals of the two sides make this representation of the problem natural, but the framework was too constricting for ultimate usefulness. Zeuthen's analysis, although flawed, turned inquiry into this problem in a more fruitful direction because of its greater generality.

Edgeworth's initial example of an exchange economy was that of Robinson Crusoe, who hires the labour of Friday (1881, 28–9). Moreover, although he stated that 'The *pre-determinateness of the wage-fund*, which has received its *coup de grâce* from Mr Sidgwick, must always, one would think, have appeared untenable from the humblest mathematical point of view...' (1881, 32), Edgeworth felt that the methods he developed to study an exchange economy would be valuable in considering wage negotiation. He felt that the relation was that

> No doubt these latter conditions [first and second derivatives of utility with respect to labour and consumption] are subject to many exceptions, especially in regard to abstinence from capital, and in case of purchase not for consumption, but with a view to resale.... Still, these exceptions, though they destroy the water-tightness of many of the reasonings in this and the companion calculus, are yet perhaps of secondary importance to one taking a general abstract view.
>
> (Edgeworth 1881, 34–5)

As noted above, Marshall wrote to Edgeworth that offer curves 'had perhaps more real applications to industrial groups and employer–employé-questions than to Foreign Trade' (Marshall 1975, vol. 1, 112). Neither Edgeworth nor Marshall, however, did much more than speculate on such applications.

Pigou stated that 'Of bargaining proper there is little to be said' because it results merely in a transfer between the parties (Pigou 1912, II, VII, §13: 169; Pigou 1948, II, ix, §16: 201). In 1905, however, Pigou added a most curious appendix 'On the extent to which wage bargains between industrial combinations are indeterminate', to *The Principles and Methods of Industrial Peace*.

Explicitly attaching his analysis to that of Edgeworth (1881), Pigou began by deriving a variety of offer curve for each of labour and management. His construction, however, was nonsensical.

Zeuthen's doctoral dissertation focused on wage bargaining, and he repeated his analysis in the fourth chapter of *Problems of Monopoly and Economic Warfare* (1930). As Schmidt (1990, 602) notes, Zeuthen introduced the term 'interplay' to economic literature, and remarked on the absence of interpersonally comparable utility in the game. This, says Schmidt, gave 'room to the game'. Brems (1976) provides a very useful summary and critique of this work. As in his analysis of a number of firms with market power, Zeuthen felt that there was a 'right' answer, which would be the outcome of wage negotiation, although

> It is generally maintained in cases where organisations of employers and workers are opposed to each other, that it is possible to fix definite economic limits within which agreements may be obtained, but that the question as to at which point within these settlement will be made, is indeterminate from an economic point of view.
>
> (Zeuthen 1930, 104)

Zeuthen felt that 'The limits of the fighting sphere are determined by the expected cost of a fight plus or minus the expected fighting costs' (Zeuthen 1930, 105). This 'fighting sphere' was the range of wage within which labour and management will argue rather than elect 'conflict' (one party giving up), and may be considered the core of the wage-bargaining problem. Using Brems's notation, the limits are set by c_L, 'the money wage rate after conflict reduced by the costs of conflict' and c_M, 'the money wage after conflict raised by the cost of conflict' (Brems 1976, 401). With conflict a perpetual threat during negotiation which is never realized, the eventual wage settlement $w(t)$ satisfies

$$c_L < w(t) < c_M.$$

In Zeuthen's formulation, when workers (management) do not agree to terms proposed by management (workers), they risk conflict, but

> Surely [workers] would be willing to risk something in order to raise the rate beyond the point at which a settlement was worth no more to them than a conflict, and they would sacrifice something if they could thereby further reduce the claim of the employers. The sacrifice – as we shall see – may be measured in terms of the *probability* of *conflict to which they are willing to expose themselves by maintaining an ultimatum.*
>
> (Zeuthen 1930, 110)

Once again using Brems's notation (and his correction of Zeuthen by the addition of utility functions), labour demanding $w_L(t) > w_M(t)$ offered by management is supposed to take on a probability q of conflict and wage c_L, with probability $1-q$ of achieving $w_L(t)$. The highest probability of conflict which labour will contemplate risking is that which leaves utility from accepting

81

$w_M(t)$ now equal to the expected utility of risking conflict. This probability $q_L(t)$ satisfies

$$q_L(t) = \{U_L[w_L(t)]U_L[w_M(t)]\} \Big/ \{U_L[w_L(t)U_L[c_L]\}.$$

Analogously for management,

$$q_M(t) = \{U_M[w_M(t)]U_M[w_L(t)]\} \Big/ \{U_M[w_M(t)U_M[c_M]\}.$$

The party less willing to take on risk (with the lower q) 'gives in' by initiating a $t+1^{st}$ round with a wage demand (or offer) less favourable to it. This brings $q_L(t+1)$ and $q_M(t+1)$ closer together than $q_L(t)$ and $q_M(t)$ were. Zeuthen assumed that when the two probabilities are eventually equal, agreement on wage takes place.

> Just as in the market of a certain commodity, we shall, where the parties have a correct conception of each other's readiness to fight, have a demand curve and a supply curve in which to each price there corresponds another quantity (probability), which at the point of intersection will be equally great for both parties.
>
> (Zeuthen 1930, 135)

As Brems points out, the initial construction of $q_L(t)$ and $q_M(t)$ assumes that if there is not agreement between labour and management at the tth round, the only possible outcomes are conflict or the other party's proposed wage. Since a failure to agree leads to a $t+1^{st}$ round and an eventual wage equal neither to that under conflict nor either of the initial wages, an element of time inconsistency in the mental processes of labour and management has been introduced.[15]

While Zeuthen's arithmetical formulation of the wage negotiation problem had the imperfections of time-inconsistency and a mechanistic derivation of limit probabilities, Zeuthen's reflections on wage negotiation more generally struck at the heart of what became game theory:

> If either party over-estimates the warlike tendencies of the opposite side, peace will easily be made, so that one or both unexpectedly strike a good bargain. If, on the other hand, both under-estimate each other's readiness to fight, and consequently forward unreasonable claims, a conflict is likely to ensue. If only one party makes a wrong estimate, the result will be the same, whilst if they make wrong estimates each in their own direction, the difference between these will determine the manner in which settlement is made, whereas the common part of the mistake will react directly on the wage.... In cases where the parties entertain wrong conceptions of each other's position, the limits to which either of them will advance their claims, are determined by the point where the risk which they are willing to incur (determined independently of the other

party's supposed decision), coincides with the probability of conflict which they believe the other party is willing to risk.

(Zeuthen 1930, 136–7)

The beliefs of each player on the other's probable behaviour determine the strategy used, and those beliefs may be incorrect. The economics of bilateral monopoly produced the ideas of the core and core convergence, extended reaction functions to the case of offer curves and introduced blocking arguments. But perhaps as great a contribution of this literature was the reiteration of indeterminacy, a 'problem' with which game theory still wrestles.

5

LEWIS CARROLL AND THE GAME OF POLITICS[1]

While a game-theoretic school of political science has existed since Riker's innovation of the 1950s (see Riker 1992), nineteenth-century English writers on methods of election employed arguments which indicated a recognition of the strategic interdependence of voters – and, even more so, parties. Spurred by parliamentary reforms of suffrage and such abuses as rotten boroughs and redistricting, they contemplated substantial changes in geographic representation, seats per district, votes per elector and criteria for winning. The most interesting of this literature is that written by proponents of various forms of proportional representation (PR).

The PR literature is quite different from the better-known and pioneering work of Condorcet and Borda in the eighteenth century, which focused on properties of voting rules by drawing attention to such anomalies of the majority voting rule as vote cycling and tended towards the mathematical and axiomatic. Most of the PR literature is in prose and addresses issues from a perspective of coalition and side payment which has since been codified in cooperative game theory.[2] Although Droop, Baily and J.G. Marshall made relatively systematic observations, Hare, the most famous exponent of proportional representation and founder of the Proportional Representation Society (PRS), was among the least analytic of these writers. In itself, such literature, which is discussed in the first section below, would not merit more than a brief discussion in this book. This literature is important as furnishing the environment from which a most important analysis of strategic interdependence in electoral rules emerged.[3]

The Oxford mathematician Dodgson (better known as Lewis Carroll) published a pamphlet, *The Principles of Parliamentary Representation* (1884g: henceforth *PPR*), which is still a stunning accomplishment. Although the perspective of other advocates of PR resembles that of cooperative game theory, Dodgson's model in which players are two political parties and a rule-maker is non-cooperative. It is in fact very close to being a full-blown mechanism design model. Black has called Dodgson's work 'the most distinguished contribution that has been made to Political Science since the seventeenth century' (Black 1970, 28), and it was Black (1967, 1969) who brought *PPR* and its game-theoretic nature, Droop, Baily and Marshall to our attention. Dodgson's letters and pamphlet on proportional representation are discussed in the second section below.

ANALYSIS IN THE PROPORTIONAL REPRESENTATION MOVEMENT

Background

The Reform Bill of 1832 which extended franchise in England also stimulated thought on the results of the voting system used. From the 1830s on, a number of English voting theorists sought to construct a voting system whereby the party composition of parliament would more closely approximate that of the enfranchised country. Debate quickened with the second Reform Bill of 1867 and with extension of the franchise and redistribution of districts in 1884. This section analyses the growing complexity of analysis employed by Hare, Droop and others and shows their relationship with constructs of cooperative game theory. This relationship has gone largely unnoticed, perhaps because proportional representation (PR) theorists were primarily interested in altering the characteristics of the electoral game.

These thinkers recognized that coalitions of voters select and elect candidates and were concerned with the value to a registered elector of his vote. This led to the desire for some sort of equity for people of differing viewpoints and for increasing the value of a vote so that electors might be more willing to exercise their franchise and to vote more responsibly. These are among the concerns of cooperative game theory, although, unlike Shapley (1953), nineteenth-century theorists were concerned with the value of an elector's vote given his political stance, which effectively limits the coalitions he might enter.[4] In the use of data from past elections to argue their points, which was sufficiently novel to require apology (Hart 1992, 75), and in suggestions that a few districts be used as tests of new voting systems, the nineteenth-century theorists presaged experimental game theory. And although most nineteenth-century analysis was far from rigorous, Droop's analyses are particularly interesting, while Dodgson's PPR (1884g) was genuinely game-theoretic, as Black (1967, 1969) appreciated. It is of interest to examine the literature on which he built.

In examining this material, some background is helpful. Throughout most of the nineteenth century, English electoral districts returned one, two or, in a few much-discussed cases, three Members of Parliament. These last three-cornered districts were felt to present 'problems'. Voters satisfying the necessary qualifications of property (requirements for which declined as reform bills were passed) and maleness[5] were permitted to cast one vote in single-member districts and two in two- or three-member districts. A few wealthy men were qualified in more than one district.[6]

A novelty of nineteenth-century analysis for the contemporary reader is a definition of representation, which, as Tullock (1972, 144) noted, is unlike that of modern political science. Popular phraseology of the time, like that today, called an elector represented if there was a member from his district. As Fawcett noted, though, this is the representation of bricks and mortar, not human beings (Fawcett 1871, 3). The relevant concept of representation for this chapter, as for the English theorists, is that a Member of Parliament is an agent for the preferences of a voter, acting as the voter would wish (subject to constraints to be discussed).[7] Thus a communist MP would not be said to represent a Tory constituent, even if they were of the same district. This gave rise to the principle that 'representation should be a reflex...of the Nation itself, [consisting] of a majority and a minority' (Hill 1860, 86). A stronger notion of representation is involved in the concept of the wasted vote. A vote was deemed wasted if it was not necessary for the election of a representative desired by the elector. Votes above those required to return an MP and those on losing candidates were wasted. An elector, by the strong definition, was represented if his vote helped to elect a member of his choice.

The first Englishman to concern himself with the desirability of PR in a legislative assembly, however, seems to have been Thomas Wright Hill (1763–1851) (Hart 1992, 6–9). According to the *Dictionary of National Biography*, Hill was a somewhat feckless person of wide-ranging thought who taught magnificently, but consistently failed to remain solvent. His work was unpublished until his children issued a memorial of his life and selections from his papers (1860). His representation scheme, however, influenced municipal institutions in Adelaide, South Australia through the agency of his son Rowland (of penny post fame) and was given in evidence before the Commons Special Committee upon the Corporation of London in 1854 by William Hickson.

Hill suggested that, where a district returned n members, the electorate be permitted to form n equal sections, each of which 'equal quorums' would be permitted to return a member to the assembly. 'By this mode of election parties will bear the same relation to each other in the council which they may bear in the elective body, and the minority will be secured of being fairly and fully represented' (Hill 1860, 88). This method would require much time to organize coalitions and secure agreement among coalition members, but would allow electors to be represented by agents they had actively selected. If coalitions selected representatives unanimously, all electors would have a voice in decisions. It would not merely allow one minority to be represented, but several, so long as each was large enough to sway a coalition. The use of the term quota should be noted: a number of the nineteenth-century theorists, including Hare, determined a quota by dividing the electorate by the number of members to be elected. When applied to ordinary voting procedure, this definition was in error, an issue discussed below.

Single-member districts and a limited vote

In 1831, just before the advent of three-cornered districts, when nearly all districts returned two members, Winthrop Mackworth Praed, poet and Tory MP, suggested that the limited vote would allow better minority representation (Hart 1992, 9–11). Under this system, voters from multiple-member districts have fewer votes than there are seats to fill. He recognized that where an elector's votes equal the number of seats, the majority could fill all seats, even if majority barely outnumbered minority. In particular, he felt that the seven districts which were to become three-cornered should hold limited vote elections, a measure which was not introduced until 1867 as an experiment. That experiment would be felt to be a failure, since the majority could use votes which would otherwise give their candidates more votes than needed to win, to choose which minority candidates would be seated.

Fawcett (1871, 3–4) pointed out that, even so, the minority was better represented than they would be without a limited vote. She did not note that the minority was in error in running more candidates than they could secure seats for, although she addressed this issue in another context. Many critics of the limited vote and other measures to safeguard minority representation argued that such efforts actually strengthened the party system, since they were accompanied by increased organizational exertions by Liberals and Conservatives. Increased organization was a sign that the voting measures increased the cost to parties of securing seats from minority voters. The critics' confusion remained virtually unaddressed.

Droop (1869, 4) noted that under the single or cumulative vote the cost of party organization increased, growing still further with constituency size and number of candidates, but did not call this a virtue. Droop (1871, 22) cited increased costs as *limiting* the freedom of electors. Lubbock *et al.* (1885, 318) repeated the objection that 'The single transferable vote [defined below] could not be worked without inordinate wire-pulling, and this would arise and would operate to such an extent as to destroy the independence of the elector'. While the authors responded accurately enough that wire-pulling would be less effective under this system, they did not state that increased attempts at wire-pulling indicated greater organizational costs for parties.

In three articles in the *Edinburgh Review*, Greg introduced several of the central concerns of voting theory and the PR school. An unsuccessful candidate for parliament and frequent contributor to periodical literature (Hart 1992, 16), Greg feared that the extension of electorate to lower income classes would disenfranchise the allegedly more thoughtful and cultured men of higher incomes.

Greg (1852a) argued that the organization of electoral districts to approximately equalize their population made sense only if the number of bodies in a district were to be represented, rather than property, intellect or other voter attributes. He noted that the current system could produce 'numerical anomalies' of representation, in which Parliament's composition differs markedly from that of the popular vote (1852a, 251–2) and, indeed, that in a country of single-member districts a minority could go completely un-represented if political opinions were fairly evenly distributed across consti-tuencies. That is: under some rules of the election game, a planner's criteria for distributional fairness might be ill satisfied. (Dodgson was to consider precisely the rules of seats per district and votes per elector in *PPR*.) Greg's argument for these propositions was conceptual: he posited particular dis-tributions and calculated electoral results. This method, basically one of 'fictitious play', was followed by many nineteenth-century theorists and frequently countered by assertions that such distributions were unlikely and thus need not be provided for.[8]

In 1884, Gladstone argued that a change to single-member districts 'might be termed the representation of minorities, . . . for it would secure a large diversity of representation' (Hart 1992, 114). Greg earlier rejected the notion that differences between districts sufficed for the representation of minorities nationwide (Greg 1852a, 271–2). Fawcett was to say that

> The idea of the minority in one place being represented by the majority in another place is certainly ingenious, but it overlooks the fact of there being any differences between members of the same political party. There are Liberals and Liberals, and it was probably no source of consolation to Mr Mill's supporters in Westminster to know that in Marylebone Mr Harvey Lewis had been returned by a triumphant majority.
>
> (Fawcett 1871, 2–3)

Greg addressed the question of how many votes each elector should have and seats each electoral district should own, but found no satisfactory answer:

> Some have proposed that no elector should vote for more than one member. This, where there are two members, would remedy [minority lack of representation], but would involve unfairness of an opposite kind; since, in that case, the majority and minority might each return one member, and would, therefore, be *equally* represented, unless the majority should exceed two-thirds of the whole.[9] Others suggest that each constituency should have three members, each elector still being restricted to one vote. But this would involve the disfranchisement or amalgamation of many boroughs, or the augmentation of the House of Commons to a most inconvenient extent.
>
> (1852a, 272)

Greg (1852b) explicitly introduced the concept of the wasted vote which later theorists used. Yet Greg (1853) raised the concern that if representation were not proportional, discussion of issues in a representative assembly perhaps should be – a question discussed by Tullock (1972, 155–6).

Greg also seems to be the originator of a version of the median voter theorem on the basis of his observations which, however, he attributed to the wrong cause. He felt that due to the extended franchise,

> The Whigs have become more Radical and the Tories more Whiggish than they were. Indeed, it would be more correct to say that the old boundary lines between the various sections of politicians have been swept away, and that they differ no longer in kind, but only in degree . . . .
>
> (1852a, 215)

It is not clear that Greg had any particular influence on voting theorists or Parliamentary debate, but Marshall (1853), a recent Liberal MP, did.

Marshall and the cumulative vote

Marshall explicitly introduced the notion of proportionality in representation, discussing the rights appropriate to majorities and minorities. In particular, he felt that while a minority had not the right to carry a vote, it should be heard, which could only occur with representation. Marshall advocated the cumulative vote, a rudimentary form of point voting, as a means for minorities to elect members (Marshall 1853, 13). Under this system, each elector has as many votes as there are seats to fill in his district, but may allocate them as he wishes (implicitly subject to an integer constraint). This would permit a minority to stack up its votes on a small number of candidates, while the majority might distribute its votes among a large number of candidates.

Proponents of PR considered a cumulative vote a worthy alternative to other voting schemes throughout the nineteenth century (see Baily 1872, 3–4). Dodgson (1884e, 1884g) rejected it on grounds a modern voting theorist would approve: that in practice it would be used as a single vote by optimizing voters, who would vote insincerely. Droop remarked that

> In its practical operation this method will be found almost identical with single voting [one vote per elector], and its chief recommendation is that, instead of having, like single voting, the false appearance of taking away part of an elector's voting power, its very form shows that it frees the voter from existing restrictions, and thus increases his power.
>
> (1869, 4)

Voters seem not necessarily to have clumped their votes, however. Fawcett (1871, 15–16) said that London School Board elections run under a cumulative vote system produced more representative assemblies and general satisfaction, a point stressed by Droop (1871, 5). She claimed that dissatisfaction with the system arose only in the case of the Birmingham School Board. There a majority of Liberals succeeded in achieving only a minority of seats, which she attributed to their presentation of more candidates than they could elect.

Droop (1871, 5) unfortunately argued that where superior organization or chance resulted in unfair representation in one district, it was likely to be compensated for in other districts.

The issue of how many candidates a party should put up when a given number of seats are at stake was first addressed explicitly by Marshall. He suggested that

> If we suppose the country to be divided between two parties, the smaller being, for example, one-third of the whole, if that minority were to restrict their list of candidates to one-third of the number to be elected, and were to distribute their votes equally amongst them, might thus secure the return of their list of candidates.
>
> (1853, 12)

This principle may seem obvious, but it was clearly sometimes forgotten by political parties, and sometimes by voting theorists (see Dodgson 1884d).

Two other notable points about Marshall's pamphlet were his tabulation in Appendix C of the number of seats minorities of various sizes could obtain in n seat, m candidate races (varying m and n as well) under the one-vote-per-elector majority rule and under sincere cumulative voting. This method illuminated the representational differences of different voting methods, and resembles a technique of Dodgson (1884e, 1884g). In one case examined in his Appendix, Marshall also gave what is now known as the Droop quota, correctly calling it 'the smallest number of votes to secure a candidate' (Marshall 1853, 32). While Greg correctly gave the proportion of minority electors needed to elect one of two members, nineteenth-century theorists (particularly followers of Hare) commonly assumed that one-nth of the voters were needed to elect one of n members.

Hare and the PRS

While Marshall's pamphlet was influential, Hare is generally hailed as the chief thinker of the PR movement. This title is justified by the voting method (and its variations) which he proposed, which was recommended by the Proportional Representation Society (PRS). His writings are unfortunately prolix and of no great theoretical interest. He is mentioned here as one of the originators of what is now known as the Hare system, or the single transferable vote.

The single transferable vote (STV)

Under STV, voters each cast one vote in the form of a list. The candidate named first gets the vote if he needs it – i.e. if he has not yet gained a quota (the number of votes necessary to elect him) and if he has not yet dropped from the race. Otherwise, the elector's vote goes to the candidate named second, and so on. At first scrutiny, candidates with a quota of votes from those listing them first are declared elected. Where seats remain unfilled, votes beyond the quota are transferred from elected candidates to the second choices of voters selecting them first. Thus, any candidate having a quota is elected. This process is repeated as long as possible or until all seats are filled. If seats then remain empty, the candidate with the smallest number of votes is eliminated and his votes given to the next choices of those voting for him. This process is repeated until all seats are filled. Hare argued that, under such a system, locally popular candidates would find it particularly easy to be elected, since they need only achieve their quota to win.

Both Hare's PRS and opponents paid much attention to how votes should be transferred. If A received n votes, more than his quota of votes q, and after q votes were registered for him the last $n - q$ votes were transferred to the elector's second choice, the order of ballots for A first could determine what other candidates won seats. Another concern was the cost of totting up votes. The transfer scheme eventually endorsed along with STV by the PRS (Hart 1992, 72) was that the proportion of A's n ballots which listed B, C, etc. as second choices should determine how many of the $n - q$ excess A votes should be given to B, C, etc. This permits a transfer from A conditional on the expressed sentiments of his supporters.

Hare and his followers argued that, with an STV balloting scheme, 'the elector would know his vote to be effective'[10] (Hart 1992, 28) and more likely exercise it. This, in turn, would draw forth better and more diverse candidates. Moreover, Hare's party argued that bribery for votes and political corruption would decline with institution of STV and a national slate. While Hare's opponents argued that expanded districts and STV would make elections more expensive and thus prohibit workingman candidates from winning, Lubbock *et al.*, officers of the PRS, responded reasonably that

> The great expense of elections lies in the efforts to get at and influence the uncertain votes which must be secured in order to obtain a majority. It is not only corruption but also the chief part of the legitimate expense of publicity and agitation that is directed to this end. Therefore those candidates who are sure of their quotas might be elected at less cost under proportional representation than under the single-member system. And this would be the case with workingmen candidates, wherever they would have much chance under any system.

> (1885, 317)

Responding to Parliamentary inquiry in 1860, Hare gave evidence that voting participation declined with increase in district size, suggesting that the extension of franchise might impose new needs for protection of minorities. Henry Fawcett, Professor of Political Economy at Cambridge, Liberal MP, postmaster-general under Gladstone, member of the PRS and Hare's interpreter, laid more emphasis on this issue than Hare did (Hart 1992, 41), but

Hare's evidence embodied the suggestion that confidence that a vote would be effective might induce more votes.[11]

While Hare's ideas profoundly influenced nineteenth-century thought, he was not his own clearest proponent. Henry Fawcett's articles expounded a simplified version of Hare's system, as did those of his wife, the political economist Millicent Fawcett, whom we quote extensively. These articles cleared up Hare's arguments and many administrative details of his scheme. Other members of Hare's school used arguments more effective than his, corrected some errors, and introduced new concepts which became corner-stones of voting theory. Droop, a mathematician and barrister, was one of the ablest PR theorists. Droop (1868) corrected Hare's use of the term quota, indicating that with n votes and m candidates, candidates securing votes in the amount of the integer above $n/(m+1)$ had secured election. Some, but not all, theorists before Droop had used the correct quota. Baily (1872, 6–7) cited Droop and used the Droop coefficient. Dodgson (1884c, 1884e, 1884g) did so without citation. Fawcett (1871) confusingly used Hare's incorrect quota at times and the Droop coefficient (unattributed) at others. Hare himself seems not to have understood that his quota was wrong, and did not correct it in later editions of his *Treatise*. Droop (1868, 1881) analysed the properties of different voting schemes, using a model of exemplary constituencies with honest voters which has remained popular in voting theory.

Droop and Courtney

Like other theorists, Droop (1869, 3) argued that one vote per elector was preferable to more, as limiting the power of the majority. As noted above, he criticized the cumulative vote as an alternative to empower minorities, although he recognized that it was not a complete failure in practice. (Droop (1871) was less critical of the cumulative vote, apparently because of its success in London School Board elections.) He differentiated the limited vote of three-cornered districts which gave each elector two votes from the single vote which allowed an elector only one vote (1869, 7), whether under majority rule, cumulative voting or a single transferable vote. Droop's (1871, 22) distinction between single vote and cumulative vote was, alas, all wrong. He argued that greater organizational efforts by a party obtained the same results as under the multiple-vote system, ignoring the difference in quota needed to elect representatives.

A remarkable feature of Droop's analysis is an observation which was to become the median voter theorem. He stated that

> . . . the principal cause of [the] apparent preference for commonplace candidates, is the system of majority voting, which obliges the managers of each party, in choosing their candidate, to look, not for the man who

would make the best member of Parliament, but for the one who will get the most votes.

(1869, 11)

Unlike Greg, who noted the same phenomenon, Droop attributed it to the correct cause. While Hare (1859) complained that the current system produced mediocre candidates, he did not analyse the reason this occurred. Courtney (1876, 79) remarked the same phenomenon noted by Droop, referring explicitly to attempts to woo lukewarm electors. Similarly, Droop (1869, 19, 20, 26–7) saw that the two-party system sprang directly from majority rule, and that exceptional opinions would be likelier to secure representation under a PR system. Courtney (1879, 150) suggested that, under PR, the party system would deteriorate. Empirical evidence bears this out: under PR, more than two parties generally flourish (Mueller 1989, 222).

Courtney was another advocate of PR whose arguments were notably clearer than those of Hare himself. Courtney wrote leaders for *The Times* and was Professor of Political Economy at University College London and long-time Liberal MP. Courtney (1876, 75) remarked in passing that a voter could influence only one issue when voting for a representative. This point had been made previously by Droop (1869) who, however, thought that it was a problem only under multiple-vote majority rule. It lies at the basis of one of the fundamental theorems of voting theory: if alternatives can be thought of as occupying positions along a line and if voters have single-peaked preferences, preference aggregation which satisfies the criteria of Arrow (1952) can be performed. If alternatives cannot be represented on a line, such aggregation does not exist, regardless of restrictions on voter preferences. Candidates can always be represented by positions along a line. Platforms, however, generally cannot be when more than one issue is addressed.[12]

Courtney used his appreciation of an assembly's inability to accurately represent electors' views to argue for the greater incentives to research and responsible voting under PR, which would at least allow more than two parties to be represented (1876, 83–4). He also suggested that whenever people 'obtain no share in the representation which constitutes the authority of a country, their political energies die away and disappear' (Courtney 1879, 145). Remarkably, he explicitly included women, who had no franchise, in this class in both his 1876 and 1879 papers.[13]

Experiments in voting

Early proponents of PR invented numerical examples to make their arguments. Hart (1992, 73) argues that this method was used deliberately, in order to avoid any appearance of party bias. As mentioned above, this led to assertions that such constituencies would be unlikely to occur in fact, and that those voting patterns would not occur even in such districts. Eventually PR theorists bolstered their arguments with data from recent elections. While Droop used hypothetical constituencies in his earlier pamphlets, he reproduced vast tables of data in 1881. Hart attributes this change in method to Martin's publication of data on the 1868 and 1874 elections (1874).

In examining and comparing the outcomes of different voting systems, PR theorists were actually examining the ways in which populations played voting games. As is frequently the case with social scientists, they were using information from unplanned experiments and with poor excuses for controls. However, that they made use of the games with which nature provided them to argue about the incentives of voting systems is surprising at that period.[14]

Martin attempted to answer the question of whether the change from a House Liberal majority to a House Tory majority was due to a change of sentiment among voters or to increased franchise – not a question of great interest to PR theorists. Clearly, though, Hare's followers took an interest in this paper. Among comments published were two by Courtney and Droop. A point of interest in Martin's data unstressed by him was that Liberals maintained a popular majority of 1,377,998 to 1,088,532 in 1874, although they won only 301 seats to the Conservatives' 351 (Martin 1874, 194). This lent teeth to earlier contentions by PR theorists that, under the existing system, majorities could attain a House minority (Greg 1852a) and that PR would better represent a majority (Hare 1866b; H.T. Fawcett, quoted by Hart 1992, 63). In the 1880s, MPs urging PR on Parliament made frequent use of electoral statistics, which apparently brought them a number of allies within the House (Hart 1992, chapter 5).

Advocates of PR had long suggested that its methods be tried in particular districts or in certain types of election. After the mid-1870s, pressure for a trial of PR increased. The experiment with cumulative voting for London School Boards was unfortunately misinterpreted by many, as noted above. Recommendations to experiment and analyse experiments' outcomes are of interest in foreshadowing experimental game theory, whose focus is discovering how individuals actually play games rather than how they 'ought' to. Nineteenth-century theorists whose arguments were implicitly based on agent optimization were not *wrong* to argue in this way. They pointed out the abuses a voting system could give rise to and which could be avoided by use of a different rule. An examination of how a particular voting scheme worked in practice, however, added to their artillery and could, with more experiments, have helped more. Data advanced by Martin permitted Lubbock *et al.* (1885) to base many of their replies to Hare's opponents' objections on the fact that the use of local majorities by no means guaranteed that the popular majority would have a majority in Parliament.

A primary objection to the Hare system was that voters would find it impossible to understand. Gladstone stated in 1884 that he did not understand the single transferable vote, which he termed a '*pons asinorum*' (Hart 1992, 87). While the 1884 version of the single transferable vote might have been difficult for MPs to understand, Mill claimed that it was simpler than algebra. More importantly, Viscount Folkestone, Conservative MP and prominent in the PRS, stated that 'at all public meetings where test elections had been held, uneducated people understood what they were required to do both as voters and in counting the votes' (Hart 1992, 115, 118).

A more serious criticism of PR was the argument that a strengthened majority in Parliament was desirable to effect a decisive assembly and a government less likely to fall.[15] Droop (1869) argued that representative assembly was desirable as substituting for the plebiscite assembly of classical Greek democracy or Swiss canton, but his historical argument was really no better than the contention of opponents of PR that plurality rule was sanctified by tradition. Courtney's (1879, 141) argument that, since each person is affected by the government elected, each should have some influence on its selection dominates on rather heuristic grounds of justice. He also stated that 'no party can be trusted to exercise justice to an excluded party' (Courtney 1879, 145). Lubbock *et al.* argued that the composition of Parliament was less likely to fluctuate under PR,

> because the people who fluctuate will affect only their own quotas, instead of affecting the representation of those who are staunch, by turning the majorities in a large number of districts. Now, a steady pressure is not less potent for progressive legislation, and is more likely to be wisely applied, than an occasional rush. The majorities obtained by large turnovers are in truth too insecure in themselves to afford steady support to a Minister.
>
> (Lubbock *et al.* 1885, 313)

In fact, coalition governments elected under PR have had significantly shorter lives than those selected by majority rule (Mueller 1989, 224–5). This criticism of PR stands, if one's objective for a government is the power to act.

Conclusion

Proportional representation (PR) theorists of the nineteenth century, concerned with an individual elector's ability to be heard in Parliament, pioneered a number of the concepts of voting theory and cooperative game theory. Some, such as a concept of the value of an individual's vote subject to the rules of the voting game, appear in implicit or primitive form. A cooperative interpretation of voting and recognition that the size of an effective coalition depends on the rules was better developed. Mathematical theorists such as Droop and Courtney expressed these ideas rather formally. While Dodgson's work constitutes a fully blown game-theoretic model sixty years before von Neumann and Morgenstern, his contemporaries also merit study.

DODGSON'S MODEL

Dodgson (Lewis Carroll), a staunch Conservative and able mathematician, not only proposed a form of PR differing from that advocated by Hare and the PRS, but used a form of analysis very different from theirs. They were literary and often discursive: his methods were explicitly mathematical. Much earlier discussion, starting from voters, has about it the flavour of cooperative game theory: Dodgson began with political parties, and used non-cooperative analysis to determine the success voters experienced in getting themselves represented. Dodgson developed a two-stage game in which political parties use maximin strategy in a two-person zero-sum game, after the government's choice of electoral method to minimize the maximum number of voters left unrepresented. The model has gone largely unnoticed. This may be because Dodgson was primarily interested in PR, which has not been a fashionable topic in North America, the cradle of public choice theory. Dodgson's work on PR remains an important, though neglected, landmark in the field.

While modern public choice theorists have analysed various voting schemes by determining their properties under various voter preferences and Riker has used game theory to discuss strategic voting and coalition formation,[16] PR schemes have been relatively neglected. Mueller (1989) analyses the scheme most frequently associated with Hare and includes a section on empirical outcomes of PR, but does not examine the nineteenth-century literature. Similarly, Tullock's (1972) discussion of PR does not address the early literature. Hart (1992) indicates that interest in proportional representation has not been constant, but has mushroomed periodically. Debate is currently active in the UK and the USA.

Since Black's (1958) clear explication of their pioneering achievements, the importance of Dodgson's 1873, 1874, and 1876 pamphlets on the concepts of vote cycling and 'disequity' is widely appreciated. Yet although Black (1967, 1969, 1970) discussed Dodgson's later letters and pamphlet on PR, and Grofman (1987) largely follows Black, the later publications are scarcely known even to choice theorists. They embody the use of a game-theoretic model before von Neumann and Morgenstern (1944), as Black (1969) noted.[17] Moreover, in the first stage of the game Dodgson modelled, he used PR criteria to derive the appropriate number of seats per district and votes per elector. Although nineteenth-century PR theorists had discussed the appropriate number of votes per elector and initiated limited experiments with limiting votes to less than the number of seats to be filled, their arguments were relatively heuristic.

In letters to the *St James Gazette*, Dodgson examined the version of the Hare scheme advocated by the PRS and raised other issues about the voting process. Most of these concerns were embodied in his last known work on voting theory, *PPR* (1884g; with a second edition in 1885). Black (1970) gave an excellent account of Dodgson's activities and diary entries as related to his theory of voting and its motivation.[18]

Letters to the *St James Gazette*

Dodgson took his public letters quite seriously. He sent copies of a letter on 'Purity of elections' (*St James Gazette*, 4 May 1881; largely reprinted in Collingwood 1899, 233–4) 'to Gladstone, Lord Salisbury, etc.'. In this letter, he suggested that the desire to be on the winning side was a normal human motivation. To prevent it from influencing general elections which took several days, districts with polls closing early should have their ballot boxes sealed to preclude any announcement until all districts had returned. Salisbury replied that others had suggested a one-day election for the same purpose – Dodgson's plan had the advantage of not partially disenfranchising voters with votes in more than one district. In discussing the purity problem in *PPR*, Dodgson specifically argued against 'pluralists' ('like Cerberus, three gentlemen at once') (Dodgson 1884f, 35–6). Parliament adopted sealed ballot boxes in 1917 (Dodgson 1979, 429).

Dodgson (1884a) used the grounds of Hare's disciples to advance an objection to the single transferable vote. The PRS suggested a single transferable vote: list voting by electors, with second, then third and up to nth choices being transferred to those candidates as preferred candidates were declared elected. Dodgson instanced a constituency with 11,999 voters, two seats and three candidates. If the votes were as follows,

5,000 for A, then B;
3,000 for A, then C;
1,400 for B; and
2,599 for C,

then using the PRS's transfer scheme, A and C would be returned. Since 6,400 voters prefer B to C and only 5,599 prefer C to B, an injustice would have been perpetrated. Two replies, by Cohen on the following day and Sidgwick on the next, claimed that Dodgson had merely strengthened the PRS's arguments by showing that the minority would be represented. Dodgson (1884b) specialized his example, supposing that there were

5,000 votes for A, then B;
3,000 votes for A, then C;
1,400 votes for B, then A; and
2,599 votes for C, then A,

A and C would still be returned, but 6,400 voters want to elect A and B while only 5,599 prefer A and C. There was no reply to this letter.

Dodgson (1884c) suggested a more restrictive and somewhat confusing version of criteria for transfer which would eliminate this problem. He noted that this method might not serve to fill all of a constituency's seats. In this case, he stated blithely, another method would have to be used.

Dodgson (1884d) advanced another instance of the failure of the single transferable vote, less successfully. He posited a 39,999 elector constituency with three seats and four candidates, Liberals A, B, C and D and Conservative Z and supposed that there were

21,840 votes for A B D;
10,160 votes for A C B; and
7,999 votes for Z.

In this case A, B and Z would be elected under single transferable vote, although there is 'no shadow of doubt A B C should be returned', as the minority for Z is not a quota. The next day Sidgwick responded that he did not

> think to practical politicians that it will seem a great grievance that it should be possible for a minority of one-fifth to return one member out of three when the majority are so foolish as to get four out of three.

Even with no parties posited, this example too would instance the failure of the single transferable vote to achieve its ends.

Axioms for a system of voting

Despite cavilling at the PRS, Dodgson believed in the principle of PR, though he thought the single transferable vote unlikely to achieve it. Dodgson (1884e, 1884f) set forth the models he would use virtually unaltered in the *PPR* (1884g). Dodgson (1884e) offered axioms which he would rely upon and which he repeated with some amplification in *PPR*.

These, which function as a sort of objective function for the voting system designer, were

1 that the numbers of electors per MP should be nearly equal across constituencies;
2 that the minority should be adequately represented;
3 that wasted votes should be avoided;
4 that the ballot should be simple to mark; and
5 that ballots should be simple to tot up.

Axioms 1 and 3 are goals for the outcomes of electoral rules: so, subject to some definition, is 2. Axiom 3 depends on Dodgson's definition of representation which, like that of many of the theorists discussed above, is that of a vote not wasted.[19] Borcherding (1969) felt that *PPR* was not of great value, largely because this concept of representation is not the contemporary one. However, if a voter knew his most favoured candidate would be elected without his ballot, he would rationally prefer to vote for his second favourite. Axioms 4 and 5 are more mechanical, goals for the implementation of the system chosen.

Axioms 2 and 3 led to a calculation in a two-party country of the percentage of voters unrepresented (votes wasted) under varied numbers of members returned when the number of votes electors have vary from one to the number of seats. This and the second model discussed below were the first explicit analyses of the optimal number of members per district. Dodgson assumed two political parties, Reds and Blues, with 6/11 of the House Red and 5/11 Blue after an election, with a uniform distribution of Red and Blue electors in each district. Under these suppositions, he gave what he thought were the number of electors nationwide represented by Red members, by Blue and not at all, but which was the expectation of such representation (Dodgson 1884g, 23–7; Black 1969, 209, noted that this is an expectation).

Dodgson's two-stage game

Dodgson's model was a game in the first stage of which the government sets number of seats per district, m, and v, the number of votes each elector may cast, and in the second of which a two-party election occurs. Black (1967, 1969) recognized that the election is worked out as a two-person zero-sum game (which he claimed, strangely, was 'isomorphic' to the problem of personal choice). Dodgson's criterion of minimizing the expected percentage unrepresented functions as a minimax criterion, as Black observed, though Black did not note that it was a criterion Dodgson gave the government. Black acutely noted two assumptions underlying this model, which he did not mention were implicit rather than explicit in Dodgson's work. These are that Reds and Blues know their supporters (ergo, their number) and can make them vote to party programme. Otherwise, Reds might all vote for candidate A in a four-member district, while B, C and D are elected by Blues even if Reds could have filled all seats. Thus, he assumed that agents, in this case party organizers, optimize.[20]

Dodgson drew the conclusion that the government should find multiple seats preferable to singleton districts and give voters one vote each. Black's brilliant analysis of Dodgson (1884g) neglected the fact that both partyless and two-party models yield the same results.

As Black (1969) stated, Dodgson's approach employed criteria equivalent to minimax. Dodgson analysed a game between two parties which seek to maximize the number of seats they can fill in a district regardless of the other party's strategy. Strategy consists of a vector [number of candidates, distribution of votes]. Dodgson assumed that parties put up a number of candidates equal to the number of seats the party desires to fill. Given that number of candidates, distribution of votes should always be as even as possible, subject to an integer constraint, which is optimal. (Despite this constraint, a pure strategy equilibrium always exists. As Black (1969) remarked, a mixed strategy is not meaningful in the context of an election.)

Dodgson modelled the m-seat, v-vote constituency, and gave criteria which would indicate to a party which knows its support how many seats it should attempt to fill. Given the strategic behaviour of the parties in the subgame, Dodgson analysed a game in which a benevolent authority determines m and v with the objective of minimizing the number of electors unrepresented. Dodgson's work used subgame perfect equilibrium in analysing this problem and the one discussed below, with the sets of players changing between problems.

The remaining question, not stated directly by Dodgson, was whether the percentage of voters unrepresented could be reduced further than by instituting one-vote multiple-seat districts. That is, could the game yield better results for the benevolent authority if its strategy could be expanded beyond choosing (m, v) for each district? Dodgson's axiom 3 was the principle that as few votes as possible be 'wasted' by being cast for a candidate who was to receive more than the Droop quota out of votes cast. Dodgson suggested that all candidates with more than the Droop quota be declared elected directly by the returning-officer. If any seats remained to be filled, all candidates would be called together by the returning-officer. At this meeting, those with extra votes and those with votes insufficient to elect them would be permitted to assign them to candidates not yet elected (Dodgson 1884f, 36–40). Dodgson thought that, under these circumstances, all those whose votes (whether transferred or not) were used to seat a member would be represented. Dodgson suggested this to keep each ballot simple and because most voters probably had very incomplete preference lists, knowing only their most-favoured candidate. It might not seem as equitable as the single transferable vote, the weakness of which Dodgson had already shown in his letters to the *St James Gazette*. However, Dodgson's system adhered to axioms 4 and 5. Dodgson discussed candidates' transfer of votes in the context of the party system, but it would have been as reasonable in a no-party race. It nonetheless looks to a modern reader as though Dodgson assumed that an elector who voted Conservative would prefer any Conservative candidate to any Liberal one.

Black (1969) described two other approaches by Dodgson to the problem of further decreasing the percentage of the population unrepresented which he said he found in the Supplement and Postscript to the Supplement of Dodgson (1884g), reprinted in the second edition. One of these (the 'conceptual approach') suggests that an equilibrium set of coalitions among re-contracting electors to fill various numbers of seats would produce an optimum set of members, were it not for high transactions costs. The other (the 'operational approach') was an attempt by Dodgson (doomed to frustration) to guess on the basis of electoral preference schedules what coalitions they might make.

These approaches do not appear in the Supplement or Postscript to the Supplement, nor have I found them elsewhere in Dodgson's work. The first ('conceptual') approach cited by Black seems to derive from Hill's scheme, in which electors form coalitions of Droop quota size and these coalitions select representatives. Black suggested that the 'conceptual approach' he mentioned was a predecessor in 'what we know today as the coalition games with ordinal utilities' (Black 1969, 210). Any voting game in which side payments are possible is such a game. The closest Dodgson came to such an approach was to indicate that vote-packing was a way of avoiding 'wasted votes',

> ... needing the constant supervision of a 'caucus' and also a very docile body of Electors, each willing to vote for *any* man on the 'right' side – is a way, but a very clumsy one, for doing this.

(Dodgson 1884e, 5)

Black's 'operational approach' is more nearly present in Dodgson's pamphlet and letters. In the Supplement and Postscript, and in the letters of 15 May, 19 May and 6 June 1884 (1884a, b, d), Dodgson gave examples of populations with different distributions of preference schedule. He used them, however, to illustrate the aberrations he believed might occur under the voting-systems proposed by the PRS, and how his schemes would differ. He did not suggest that he was attempting to divine what coalitions voters would form.

Dodgson's second model, which neither Grofman (1987) nor Black discussed (Black stated this explicitly: 1967, 1), took the numbers of districts, seats and electors in the country as given, and used the Droop quota Q. Where e is the number of electors in a district and m the numbers of members to be elected by the district, $Q = e/(m+1)$, which is approximately equal to $e/(m+1)$ rounded up to the next integer. Given m, Q is the number of electors each member represents. Dodgson's axiom 1 was that each member should represent approximately the same number of electors, regardless of district. If each district i of n districts has m_i seats and e_i electors, then ideally $(m_i + 1)Q = e_i$ for all i. This yields n equations: by adding them we arrive at $(M + D)Q = E$, where M is the number of members in the House and D the number of districts. On Dodgson's equity of representation principle, then, $Q = E/(M+D)$ and $m_i = e_i(M+D)/E - 1$ (Dodgson 1884g, 8–10).

Given Q, M and D, Dodgson compared his method for assigning a district's number of seats with the 'rough and ready' method (based on a more standard notion of representation) by which $m = (eM)/E$ with respect to districts of different sizes, given M and D. He found that the 'rough and ready' method assigned too many members to small districts and too few to large ones by his criterion (Dodgson 1884g, 11–13). He then considered a system based on employing the nation's population P, rather than its number of electors, to compute $Q' = P/(M+D)$. Dodgson gave $m' = e/Q' - 1$, rather than $m' = p/Q' - 1$, where p is the district's population, but this must be a typo (Dodgson 1884g, 13–15). Dodgson justified this procedure as preferable on the eve of the Franchise-Bill, when he wrote, because it would be difficult to estimate the eventual number of electors in each district. He was nonetheless aware that it would give different results unless the proportion of electors to population was nearly the same across districts.

Dodgson next considered what number of votes each elector should be permitted in an m seat race. Dodgson developed a more sophisticated version of the Droop quota which depends on the number of votes each elector can give to m and the number of seats a coalition wishes to fill (Dodgson 1884g, 16–20). Dodgson used this to draw up a table (Dodgson 1884g, 21) for the percentage of electors needed to fill s seats out of m, where each elector has v votes to cast to separate candidates, $m \in [1,6]$, $v \in [1,m]$ and $s \in [1,m]$. This table indicated that where $v = m$, 51 per cent of electors are needed to fill any one seat. As m rises and v approaches 1, it takes fewer electors to fill one seat (or more seats, as long as s is not too close to m). Each entry on the table gave the percentage of the electors who must be in a coalition for the coalition to command s seats, given that each had v votes. The table does not assume that formal coalitions exist, however, and the percentages can be interpreted as the proportion of electors in agreement, whether they know it or not. Dodgson favoured a large number of members per district, with one vote per elector, so that people with minority opinions might nonetheless fill a seat.

Conclusion

While Black (1967, 1) felt that Dodgson's pamphlet was 'the most interesting contribution to Political Science that has ever been made',[21] he noted that it had been little noticed and less understood. The neglect of Dodgson compared with Hare has nothing to do with the acuity of his reasoning, which was well in advance of its time. Among political scientists and public choice theorists, obliviousness of Dodgson is probably due to his isolation from the PRS and to his publication outlets: letters to the *St James Gazette*, a pamphlet, and letters to the Tory leader Lord Salisbury.[22] Such neglect holds *a fortiori* among game theorists who have read little public choice.

Although only Dodgson's pamphlets from the 1870s on voting are at all well known, his later work on voting is of considerable interest. In letters to the *St James Gazette* and in *PPR*, Dodgson rigorously analysed the ideal number of seats per district and votes per elector, and introduced a game-theoretic form of reasoning. Dodgson's method was implicitly one of maximin. Moreover, his analysis includes what we can recognize as a two-stage sub-game perfect equilibrium. A government attempts to maximize voter welfare according to Dodgson's axioms subject to non-cooperative party behaviour in the second stage.

Most nineteenth-century English PR theorists, starting with their concern for the ability of constituents to gain representation, cast their thinking in a form at least partially cooperative. Their work was centred on permitting the payoff to non-majority coalitions to be positive and to valuing votes. It is of interest as an early approach to coalition problems and as a backdrop to

Dodgson's pamphlets. Unlike the work of most PR theorists, Dodgson's was cast in a non-cooperative style in which parties exercise strategy in a game of competition for a fixed number of parliamentary seats. Not only did he break from the paradigms of his predecessors, but he originated a rigorous mathematical model. It is an astonishing *tour de force*.

6

EARLY MATHEMATICAL MODELS OF CONFLICT[1]

Game theory deals with the mathematical modelling of conflict and cooperation. Formal mathematical analysis of conflict emerged from World War I in the writings of Frederick Lanchester (1868–1946) and Lewis Richardson (1881–1953). Their concerns were sharply distinct – those of war and of peace. Lanchester's *Aircraft in Warfare* (1916) examined how to win battles by choice of appropriate strategy such as concentration of forces. Richardson was a pacifist Quaker who, from his *Mathematical Psychology of War* (1919) onward, attempted to understand the dynamics of arms races and the statistics of outbreaks of war as aids to preventing war.

Lanchester's and Richardson's work is of particular interest. While strategic and tactical manuals for military commanders have been plentiful from a very early period, formal models in this area are lacking. Such manuals typically focus on peace if it is a peace that comes with victory, but not the prevention of conflict *per se*. Even chess, a 'war game' sometimes said to have been invented to produce peace, accomplishes this only when a leader playing with a potential opponent exhibits overwhelmingly superior strategic ability.

This makes Richardson's work especially surprising. Not only did he analyse conflict in order to produce peace, but his proposed methods of propagating peace included education in general and wider education in foreign languages. He constructed mathematical models aimed to persuade readers of factors which favour relatively prompt conflict and of the disastrous consequences of conflict.

The second feature of particular interest in the work of Lanchester and Richardson is their common modelling method: one in which they constructed what might now be called differential games.[2] While chess and most other war games are games of attrition, no previous analysis of strategic interdependence had focused on factor flows as decision variables or determinants of 'success'. Lanchester and Richardson innovated this new approach.

In the first section, we discuss the early and celebrated war manual of Sun Tzu, *The Art of War*. The second addresses Lanchester's models and the third, Richardson's.

104

SUN TZU

Martin Shubik has counselled us to include discussion of Sun Tzu's *The Art of War*, which he cited in Shubik (1987). Advice from as expert a reader as Shubik (who brought Cournot to public notice as a genuine precursor to the theory of games) is to be ignored at considerable peril. Therefore, while we feel that this work falls into the category of treatises which bear game-theoretic interpretation rather than of game theory, we include it here. Those readers interested in specific game-theoretic interpretations of Sun Tzu are referred to Niou and Ordeshook (1990), who credit Sun Tzu with anticipations of dominant and mixed strategies and, with weaker textual support, understanding of minimax strategy.

An editor and translator states that

> *The Art of War (Sunzi bingfa/Sun-tzu ping-fa)*, compiled well over two thousand years ago by a mysterious Chinese warrior-philosopher, is still perhaps the most prestigious and influential book of strategy in the world today, as eagerly studied in Asia by modern politicians and executives as it has been by military leaders and strategists for the last two millennia and more .... *The Art of War* is ... a book not only of war but also of peace, above all a tool for understanding the very roots of conflict and resolution
>
> (Cleary 1988, vii–viii)

because

> Taking a rational rather than an emotional approach to the problem of conflict, Sun Tzu showed how understanding conflict can lead not only to its resolution, but even to its avoidance altogether.
>
> (1988, 2)

The Art of War is addressed to those military leaders (and, implicitly, to the states they fight for) who wish to become 'master warriors'

> who [know] the psychology and mechanics of conflict so intimately that every move of an opponent is seen through at once, and one who is able to act in precise accord with situations, riding on their natural patterns with a minimum of effort.
>
> (1988, 3)

In the context of game theory, this suggests that the study of Sun Tzu's manual forms a sort of first-mover advantage for a Taoist general. In turn, this suggests comparison with a conventional or naive reading of Machiavelli's *The Prince*[3] – also with gaming manuals such as those of Arbuthnot, discussed on pp. 7–9. Considered in this way, these works also hint at one of the enduring problems of non-experimental game theory: is this literature positive, describing and predicting the behaviour of rational agents, or is it normative, making recommendations for their strategic conduct?

Sun Tzu was deeply concerned with the advantages of gaining and concealing information. He wrote that leaders should assess their opponents '... to find out their plans, both the successful ones and the failures'. Even more interestingly, he indicated that actions by opponents were valuable as sources of information: 'Incite them to action in order to find out the patterns of their movement and rest' (Sun Tzu 1988, Book 6, 109–10). Sun Tzu's Book 13 focuses on the varied roles which simple spies, spies furnishing disinformation to opponents, and double agents play.

He advised military leaders:

Be extremely subtle, even to the point of formlessness. Be extremely mysterious, even to the point of soundlessness. Thereby you can be the director of the opponent's fate.

(Sun Tzu 1988, Book 6, 104)

Cleary adds an editorial clarification, setting this in a Taoist framework:

Inscrutability in this context is not purely passive, does not simply mean being withdrawn or concealed from others; more important, it means perception of what is invisible to others and response to possibilities not yet discerned by those who look only at the obvious. By seeing opportunities before they are visible to others and being quick to act, the uncanny warrior can take situations by the throat before matters get out of hand.

(1988, 20–1)

Far from suggesting passive inscrutability, Sun Tzu's recommendation suggests a randomization strategy which is, in fact, optimal in games without a pure strategy equilibrium. The exhortation of subtlety 'even to the point of formlessness', however, suggests something further: the problem of policy neutrality in some macroeconomic problems set up as games. Where an analyst assumes a form of the economic game in which the first mover can affect second-stage outcomes only by fooling second-stage players, rational second-stage players can be manipulated only by completely random policy, which cannot achieve any systematic second-stage result! This, as well as Sun Tzu's dearth of specific 'rules of the game' in the form of strategy sets and payoffs, militates against viewing *The Art of War* as early game theory, as does the suggestion, embedded in Cleary's gloss, that the 'master warrior' is distinguished from others by a recognition of the *true* rules of the game.

Sun Tzu's recommendations spring very largely from an *ex ante* perspective on battle and war:

The first book of *The Art of War* is devoted to the importance of strategy. As the classic *I Ching* says, 'Leaders plan in the beginning when they do things', and 'Leaders consider problems and prevent them'. In terms of military operations, *The Art of War* brings up five things that are to be assessed before undertaking any action: the Way,[4] the weather, the terrain, the military leadership and discipline.

(Cleary 1988, 17)

Sun Tzu admonishes leaders to consider these five factors from the outset, and to

Therefore use these assessments for comparison, to find out what the conditions are. That is to say, which political leadership has the Way? Which general has ability? Who has the better climate and terrain? Whose discipline is effective? Whose troops are the stronger? Whose officers and soldiers are the better trained? Whose system of rewards and punishments is clearer? This is how you can know who will win.

(1988, Book 1, 46)

Moreover,

... there are five ways of knowing who will win. Those who know when to fight and when not to fight are victorious. Those who discern when to use many or few troops are victorious. Those whose upper and lower ranks have the same desire are victorious. Those who face the unprepared with preparation are victorious. Those whose generals are able and are not constrained by their governments are victorious. These five are the ways to know who will win.

(1988, Book 3, 80–1)

Not only will this enable the military analyst to 'know who will win', but Sun Tzu's emphasis on the *prevention* of outright conflict strongly suggests a parallel with Morgenstern's remarks on Holmes and Moriarty. When all parties know who will win, there is no need for them to actually play the game. Both works relate as well to a curious point noted by critics of game theory: equilibrium is often characterized by strategy profiles which give rise to situations in which all parties are indifferent about which strategy they play.

In another passage, Sun Tzu suggests that learning the art of war can give the warrior a sort of first mover advantage:

In ancient times skilful warriors first made themselves invincible, and then watched for vulnerability in their opponents. Therefore skilful warriors are able to be invincible, but they cannot cause opponents to be vulnerable.

(1988, Book 4, 84–5)

Furthermore, this passage hints at the results of Zermelo (1913), who formulated and proved what is sometimes called the first theorem of game theory: in a finite game, there exists a strategy whereby a first mover (such as Sun Tzu's 'skilful warrior') cannot *lose*, but it is not clear whether there is a strategy whereby the first mover can *win*. A 'skilful warrior' playing such a strategy may be able to win only if their opponents are not similarly invulnerable.

Sun Tzu's Book 2, largely on questions of depletion of one's own and opponents' forces, offers a strong parallel with later differential military games: winners are those whose forces survive longer in a game characterized by attrition. Book 3 on sieges is similar. In several passages, Sun Tzu offers hints of what were to become Colonel Blotto games.[5] In such games the players distribute a fixed number of troops over a set of sites, while an opponent does the same: more troops at a battle-site give a player an advantage in that battle.

> When you are concentrated into one while the opponent is divided into ten, you are attacking at a concentration of ten to one, so you outnumber the opponent.
>
> (1988, Book 6, 107)

However, while a number of Sun Tzu's themes *suggest* game theory or game-theoretic reasoning, we think it, as a work, something which game theory interprets rather than game-theoretic analysis in itself.

It seems worth mentioning that not only did military theorists read analyses of strategy and tactics – they also often played war games with dice, boards and mock forces. Chess, a simple example mentioned above, was also the paradigm for Zermelo's Theorem (1913).

Sometimes these games were played as simulations, in order to help formulate strategy in ongoing wars and battles. A reported example from World War II is of particular interest:

> The United States won the pivotal battle of Midway in World War II thanks to a roll of the dice, according to Imperial Japanese Navy officers Captain Mitsuo Fuchida and Commander Masatake Okumiya.
>
> Following its attack on Pearl Harbor on December 7, 1941, Japan hatched a plan to finish off the crippled US Pacific Fleet. Japanese aircraft carriers would launch a massive assault on the US outpost at Midway Island in the central Pacific. Japan's inevitable and overwhelming victory would intimidate the United States into negotiating a peace.
>
> To prepare for the operation, Japan's top naval officers assembled at the combined-fleet headquarters for four days of elaborate war games, played with dice and diagrams on large sheets of paper. Masatake Okumiya, acting as umpire, threw the dice to determine the number of Japanese aircraft carriers hit by American bombers. He rolled a nine, but Rear Admiral Matome Ugaki, the presiding officer, arbitrarily reduced the number of hits to three. Ugaki's subordinates swallowed their objections, and the admiral kept up his flagrant cheating throughout the games, thus making it seem as if the battle of Midway would be a piece of cake for the Japanese.
>
> It wasn't. By the time Japan attacked on June 4, 1942, the US military

had decoded Japanese communications and was ready for action. Allied observers attributed Japan's defeat in the crucial Midway battle to more than an unheeded roll of the dice, however. As historian B. H. Liddell Hart says, 'Japanese troubles were multiplied by a string of tactical errors.... Most of these faults could be traced to a complacent overconfidence'. With the heavy losses at Midway, Japan forfeited its edge in the war, never to regain it.

(Wallace *et al.* 1983, 166)

That this example stems from simulation to guide one of the Pacific naval battles is especially interesting. Haywood (1954) produced famous game-theoretic analyses of specific battles, along with the claim that US military decisions were made on a basically game-theoretic basis, subject to a stochastic environment.

Indeed, the US government began to hire mathematicians to study war during World War II. Operations research, a branch of decision theory intimately related to game theory by both its subject matter and its mathematical methods, was developed in response to military demand. Morse and Kimball's *Methods of Operations Research* (1951), originally a classified manuscript, was written while Morse was the director of the United States Navy Operations Research Group. Rees (1980) and Owens (1989) trace the development of operations research as a field back to US research groups in World War II. Moreover, the US military establishment was to become the first major source of funding for research in game theory after the war. Mirowski (1991) argues that this relationship between game theory and a demand for military applications influenced, and possibly tainted, the field. Similarly, operational research in Britain was pioneered by A. V. Hill's group studying anti-aircraft warfare at the Ministry of Munitions in World War I, and P. M. S. Blackett's section studying anti-submarine warfare at the Admiralty in World War II.

Military leaders read strategic advice and played strategic games for centuries. Many excellent strategic and tactical decisions can be interpreted game theoretically.[6] The formal mathematical analysis of military issues, however, began with Lanchester and Richardson.

LANCHESTER

Lanchester, an English engineer, built an experimental automobile engine as early as 1895 and began producing the Lanchester automobile in 1900. The Physical Society of London declined in 1897 to print a Lanchester paper on the inherent stability of model airplanes, for which 30 years later the Royal Aeronautical Society awarded Lanchester a gold medal (Newman 1956, 2136n.). His interest in aircraft extended beyond their physical properties to their effect on military strategy, which he expounded in 1914 in a series of articles in *Engineering*, which were the basis for his book two years later.[7]

In the course of examining the role of aircraft in warfare, Lanchester essayed a mathematical analysis of the relationship between opposing forces in battle to determine the conditions under which a smaller force could defeat a larger force. Neither Lanchester nor Richardson used an explicit payoff function. Implicitly, the payoffs in Lanchester's analysis were victory or failure to achieve victory, without consideration of the cost of winning a battle in one way rather than another. Lanchester's payoffs would thus be of the form (-1, 1), so that he was analysing a two-person zero-sum game. Considering two armies, with b the numerical strength of the Blue army and r the numerical strength of the Red army, Lanchester represented the time derivatives of the size of the two forces as

$$db/dt = -Nr \times \text{constant} \tag{1}$$

$$dr/dt = -Mb \times \text{constant} \tag{2}$$

where N and M are positive and represent the fighting value of the individual units on each side. The fighting values would reflect differences in armament. The attrition of each force's numbers thus depended on the number of opponents shooting at it. This formulation led directly to Lanchester's recommendation of concentration rather than division of forces, so that a larger force would be shooting at a given enemy force.

If the Blue and Red forces were equal in fighting strength, then

$$\frac{db}{b\,dt} = \frac{dr}{r\,dt} \tag{3}$$

which, together with (1) and (2), implied

$$-Nr/b = -Mb/r \tag{4}$$

and

$$Nr^2 = Mb^2 \tag{5}$$

'In other words, the fighting strengths of the two forces are equal when the *square of the numerical strength multiplied by the fighting value of the individual units are equal*' (Lanchester 1956, 2145). From this result, which depended for its validity on the assumed equality of fighting strength of the two sides, Lanchester concluded too hastily that the fighting strength of a force would depend on the square of its numerical strength, according to his 'n-square law'. He gave several illustrations, with application for example to Nelson's strategy before and at Trafalgar, but took the foundations of his law as established.

Lanchester allocated a role for strategy, both in concentration of forces (maximizing the initial value of b or r) and in increasing M or N through improved training or armament. He also considered the possibility that long-range weapons might nullify the advantages of superior number and indicated that closing the distance between two numerically disparate forces to reduce the value of the smaller's long-range weapons could benefit the larger force.

> ... let us imagine a 'Blue' force of 100 men armed with the machine gun opposed by a 'Red' 1,200 men armed with the ordinary service rifle. Our first assumption will be that both forces are spread over a front of given length and at long range. Then the 'Red' force will lose 16 men to the 'Blue' force loss of one, and, if the combat is continued under these conditions, the 'Reds' must lose. If, however, the 'Reds' advance, and get with short range, where each man and gunner is an individual mark, the tables are turned..., and, even if 'Reds' lose half their effective [sic] in gaining the new position, with 600 men remaining they are masters of the situation; their strength is $600^2 \times 1$ against the 'Blue' $100^2 \times 16$.
>
> (Lanchester 1956, 2148)

Lanchester's suggestion was that, with long-range weapons, a force's power might no longer be proportional to the square of its number. The Reds could return the 'rules of the game' to their former state by changing tactics. In Lanchester's illustration, the fighting power coefficients of the forces did not change, but the larger force could square its effectiveness by approaching the enemy.

The precise way in which effectiveness depended on weaponry, proximity and other factors was not modelled. Lanchester considered formally only the strategies of division versus concentration of forces. Such strategies as 'run away' or 'burn a village' were not on his palette. He did not formally consider the choice of an optimal strategy from among a set of possible strategies (other than the choice of concentration over division of forces) to maximize the probability of victory (equivalent to maximizing expected payoff in Lanchester's framework). His mathematical analysis of two-person zero-sum conflict with regard to strategic choice, though limited, is a clear precursor of the mathematical theory of strategic games although, like Lanchester's work on aerodynamics, it had little immediate impact.

Lanchester's contribution has been recognized by the establishment of the Frederick W. Lanchester Prize of the Operations Research Society of America. The Lanchester equations are the basis for much later work in military operations research (see Shubik 1982, 404, for references on Lanchester games, Taylor 1979 for a survey, and Schmidt and Blackaby 1987 for pervasive references to Lanchester's work) and were cited extensively in Morse and Kimball (1951), a pioneering wartime work on operations research emphasizing anti-submarine warfare. The then novel military use of aircraft which inspired Lanchester's analysis was also the occasion for the first operational research group, the Anti-Aircraft Experimental Section of the British Ministry of Munitions led by A. V. Hill, brother-in-law of J. M. Keynes, and later Nobel laureate in physiology (Hill 1960, 265–6, 307–8). Another novel feature of World War I, submarine warfare, led Thomas Edison in 1915 to devise a war game to simulate 'zigzagging' as a way for merchant ships to evade submarines (see Whitmore 1953) and William (later Lord) Beveridge, then Assistant General Secretary of the British Ministry of Munitions, to develop 'Swish', a submarine war game, in 1916. Ardzrooni (1934, ix) also reports that 'There was a memorandum on a practicable method of fighting submarines written by [Thorstein] Veblen and presented by him before a group of military officials at the time, but unfortunately no trace of this memorandum has been found in spite of painstaking and diligent inquiry'. While Lanchester hoped to win battles by concentration of air power and Hill to shoot down the aircraft, Richardson wished to prevent wars by learning how arms races provoked them.

RICHARDSON

Lewis Richardson took first-class honours in Part I of the Natural Sciences Tripos at Cambridge in 1903, but his first degree was the D.Sc. in physics awarded him by the University of London for his published work on meteorology in 1926, the same year that he was elected a Fellow of the Royal Society. He also took second-class honours in the London special B.Sc. examination in psychology as an external student in 1929. His meteorological research, which led to his work on approximation methods for differential equations, provided the background to his use of differential equations to represent arms races. According to Richardson's son, 'calculations took longer to complete than did the predicted weather to arrive. Richardson undertook one of these enormous computations and included the results in [*Weather Prediction by Numerical Process*], even though they did not agree with the facts' (Richardson 1957, 300). This policy also provides a backdrop to his work on arms races.

As a conscientious objector in World War I, Richardson served with the Friends' Ambulance Unit in France and, after the war, he resigned from the meteorological office when it was transferred to the Air Ministry. 'Despite his achievements in meteorology and their recognition in the 1920s, he was not offered any positions in British universities, largely because of his stand as a conscientious objector which disqualified him according to the then prevalent ideas.' He was finally offered a professorship in 1940, but chose instead to retire after 11 years as principal of Paisley Technical College in Scotland at the early age of 59, to devote himself to studying the causes of war (Richardson 1957, 300–2).

Richardson wrote his first study on the *Mathematical Psychology of War* while serving with the Friends' Ambulance Unit in France. 'There was no learned society to which I dared to offer so unconventional a work. Therefore I had 300 copies made by multigraph, at a cost of about 35 pounds, and gave them nearly all away. It was little noticed. Some of my friends thought it funny. But for me it was quite serious, and was the beginning of the investigations on the causes of war which now occupy me in my retirement' (Richardson 1960b, xxix). Sixteen years later, Richardson (1935a, 830n.) announced that the last few copies were still available from the Geneva Research Center in Switzerland. This monograph is now scarce, available in British copyright libraries (Richardson 1957, 305), but the core of the work is available in extracts that Richardson published in 1935 in *Nature*, the prestigious weekly British scientific journal.

The approach of another world war provided Richardson with the scientific audience he had lacked: in 1938 he presented a paper on 'Generalized Foreign Politics', summarizing his three *Nature* contributions (1935a, b, 1938) in Cambridge to Section J of the British Association for the Advancement of Science, and in June 1939 the *British Journal of Psychology* published a monograph supplement by Richardson with the same title as his British Association paper (eventually revised and enlarged as Richardson 1960a). *Nature* remained the main forum for Richardson's research on the causes and frequency of wars, printing contributions by him on those topics in 1941, 1944, 1945, 1946 and 1951. After the war, his studies on war and peace appeared in a great variety of scholarly periodicals: *British Journal of Medical Psychology, British Journal of Sociology, British Journal of Statistical Psychology, Eugenics Review* (on the pacifying effect of intermarriage), *Journal of the American Statistical Association, Journal of the Royal Statistical Society, Psychometrika* and *Sankhya, the Indian Statistical Journal* (see Richardson 1957, 306–7 for references).

Not all journal editors, however, accepted Richardson's opinion of the importance of his work. 'In 1939, when the clouds of the Second World War were ominously gathering over Europe, an American journal received for publication a paper from Lewis F. Richardson. The paper contained the essentials of chapters ii and iii of the present book, as well as fractions of other chapters. In his letter of transmittal Richardson urged that the paper be published immediately because its publication might avert an impending war. The editors of the journal not only did not rush the paper but rejected it' (Rashevsky and Trucco, preface to Richardson 1960a, ix: a 'story, for the authenticity of which the editor cannot vouch but which he heard from a responsible source and has every reason to believe to be true').[8]

Richardson's model was based on a system of differential equations strikingly similar to those of Lanchester. Richardson viewed arms races as the interaction of fear and threat. 'It was asserted in the years 1912–14 that their [Germany's and Austria–Hungary's] motives were fixed and independent of our behaviour, whereas our motives were a response to their behaviour and varied accordingly. In 1914 Bertrand Russell put forward the contrary view that the motives of the two sides were essentially the same, for each was afraid of the other; and it was this fear which caused each side to increase its armaments as a defence against the other' (Richardson 1950a, 1244). Taking x and y as the preparedness for war of two groups of nations, Richardson (1935b) stated the equations

$$dx/dt = ky - ax + g \tag{6}$$

$$dy/dt = lx - by + h \tag{7}$$

where a and b are positive constants representing resistance to armament costs, k and l are positive 'defence coefficients' and g and h are positive or negative constant grievances, modified by friendly feelings or treaties. He took annual defence budgets as representing x and y. In this formulation, even complete disarmament, setting $x = y = 0$, could not prevent the restarting of an arms race if the grievance variables g and h were positive. Since defence budgets could not be negative, no equilibrium level of defence spending would exist as long as g and h were positive.

Richardson (1938) amended this model by redefining x and y as 'threats minus co-operation', $x = U - U_0$, $y = V - V_0$, where threats U and V were measured by annual defence budgets and cooperation U_0 and V_0 in the form of trade, travel and correspondence was taken to have been constant through the 1909–1913 arms race of France and Russia against Germany and Austria–Hungary. Here g and h represented gross rather than net grievances. Setting $k = l$ and $a = b$ on the grounds that 'These two pairs of nations were very roughly equal', Richardson derived the equations

$$d(x + y)/dt = (k - a)(x + y) + g + h \tag{8}$$

and

$$d(U + V)/dt = (k - a)(U + V) + \{g + h - (k - a)(U_0 + V_0)\}. \tag{9}$$

The rate of change of defence spending, $d(U+V)/dt$, would be a linear function of the level of defence spending, $U + V$, with a slope of $k - a$. Using annual data for the years 1909–1910 to 1912–1913 so that he had only four data points, Richardson confirmed that the relationship between $U + V$ and the rate of change of $U + V$ appeared to be linear, with a slope of 0.73 per year. He found that the line cut the axis at 194, so that $d(U + V)/dt = 0$ when $U + V = £194$ million per year (Richardson 1919, analysis without diagram; with diagram 1938, 793; 1950a, 1246; 1960a, 33). 'This 194 million sterling is the amount of defence expenditure, by the four nations concerned, that would just have been mutually forgiven in view of the amount of goodwill then existing. It is, to say the least, a remarkable coincidence that the trade between these opposing pairs of nations was on the average 206 millions sterling, close to 194' (1938, 793). Any level of defence spending less than 194 would lead to a stable equilibrium defence spending of 0 in this model. Defence spending of 194 is an unstable equilibrium, but any deviation of $U + V$ above 194 would start a spiralling arms race.

As Bellany (1975, 119) noted, Richardson used the flow of defence spending rather than the stock of armaments to represent military preparedness and sometimes wrote as if the two formulations were equivalent. In later work (Richardson 1950a, 1951, 1960a) he represented war-like preparations by 'warfinpersal' (war-finance per salary or 'warlike worktime'), annual defence expenditure divided by the annual earnings of a semi-skilled engineer, which he related to Keynes' wage-unit (Richardson 1960a, 132–3, where he also cites Hawtrey). The alternative stock formulation has been the basis for at least one successful forecast. Lorie Tarshis (personal communication) recalls that at the American Economic Association Annual Meeting in December 1936, Wassily Leontief predicted that the risk of a European war would be greatest in August or September 1939, when the German lead over Britain and France in stock of armaments would be at its peak. In general, in line with the theory developed in capital accumulation games, we would expect that only investments in war-use *stocks* would have deterrence value, although some of these stocks might be composed of human capital. 'There have been only three great arms-races. The first two of them ended in wars in 1914 and 1939; the third is still going on', wrote Richardson (1951, 567). Could the third great arms race end without actual contest? Incorporating measures of 'submissiveness' and of objection to the cost of rearmament into his equations, Richardson concluded that the arms race could end without war.

One aspect of Richardson's later work that was ahead of his time was the application of chaos theory, which he had elsewhere applied to the probability of encounters between gas molecules, to the number of nations on each side of a war which he modelled as a chaos, restricted by geography and modified by the infectiousness of fighting (1946, 1960b, 247–87).

Richardson was aware of the limitations of his specific models: 'It is instructive to regard large groups as deterministic, and to represent their behaviour by differential equations, provided that we remember that such a treatment is a caricature' (1951, 567). Even those writers who have most praised Richardson for applying mathematics to the analysis of conflict have expressed reservations about the details of formulations, such as using the flow of defence spending rather than the stock of armaments. Boulding (1962, and quoted by Rashevsky and Trucco in preface to Richardson 1960a, vii–viii) demurred at Richardson's use of the volume of trade as a measure of cooperation, suggesting instead the difference between actual trade and what trade would be if there were no restrictive tariffs or quotas.

Although the motivation for Richardson's studies was the prevention of war, he provided no explicit discussion of what nations should do to halt an arms race. He stated that his 'equations are merely a description of what people would do if they did not stop to think . . . . It is what *would occur if instinct and tradition were allowed to act uncontrolled*' (Richardson 1960a, 12). Implicitly, intervention to halt the process by actors who understood the model would mean changing the game, a parallel with Lanchester. Unlike Lanchester's, however, Richardson's formulation included a simple mechanism for such change: the cooperation, or net grievance, parameters. He did not discuss alternative strategies using trade, treaties or intermarriages when using the 1919 arms escalation model, but later articles make it clear that he envisioned such policies as military deterrents. In his n nation model, Richardson explicitly supposed that 'When an alliance is formed, the defense coefficients between allies sink to zero' (1960a, 170).

Richardson's model differed sharply from later game theory by not starting from the optimizing actions of rational agents. Indeed, he did not give an explicit payoff function. The context in which Richardson worked, and what he said about his system, indicates that he felt that the lower the probability of war or the smaller the stock of armaments, the higher the joint payoff. For Richardson, however, 'peace or war' was not a binary zero-sum payoff alternative. In his statistical studies of conflicts (1950b, 1960b), his concern with the number of people killed is evident. He may also have been concerned that arms competed with civilian expenditures in government budgets, but this is much less clear. (By contrast, Lanchester's concern with the mere winning of a conflict as opposed to losing it is transparent.) It is as though Richardson bypassed discussion of the game being played and considered only the Cournot-type reaction functions of the player-nations to some unstated game (see Boulding 1962 for interpretation of the Richardson equations as reaction functions). Richardson (1960a) gave what are basically phase diagrams to show the areas of stability and instability of his system depending on the values of the coefficients of defence and net grievance. Presumably, the wise government would alter its coefficients and initial position accordingly.

As considering Richardson's equations as reaction functions makes evident, a Richardson equilibrium is a Nash equilibrium: neither player can better its status by its individual actions. Just as in the case of rival oligopolistic firms, however, the players in this model would seem to forgo potential gains from collusion. If they could agree not to attack each other, they would have both security and no need for stockpiling arms.

Richardson (1960a) also considered extending the number of players beyond two and analysing his approach at this point becomes much more difficult. Richardson assumed that the behavioural function of the ith of n players was

$$dx_i/dt = g_i + \sum_{ij} x_j \qquad (i,j = i) \quad \text{(Richardson 1960a, 146)},$$

where g_i was the ith country's net grievance. If the behavioural equations are to be viewed as reaction functions, this means that all players play Nash strategies regardless of the number of their potential allies. Richardson's analysis went on to consider the stability of a three-player system and concluded that even if all pairs of nations would be stable in two-player versions of the game, the triplet may not have a stable equilibrium (Richardson 1960a, 154–6).

It is surprising, given Richardson's modelling strategy, that his representation of a three-player arms race with Nash players bears this striking resemblance to the three-player transferable utility log-rolling game. When he considered alliances between countries explicitly in the theory of n nations,

Richardson assumed that alliances changed the defence coefficients between the two allies, rather than changing the behavioural equations in any more fundamental way. While he considered the effect of differing degrees of information on other nations' stocks of arms, Richardson modelled perfect information by a nation's concern with the difference between its own stocks and those of each other nation, rather than by any bargaining process connected with alliance formation (Richardson 1960a, 160–2, 170–6).

Although Richardson did not model agent choice explicitly, Brito (1972) and Simaan and Cruz (1975a, b) have shown that the Richardson model and more general Richardson-type models can be derived from goal-oriented rational calculations. Simaan and Cruz (1975a) also demonstrated that Richardson's model can be reformulated in the language of the modern theory of differential games.

Richardson's influence on the area of game theory known as conflict resolution (Boulding's term) or peace science (Walter Isard's term) can be seen most clearly in *Fights, Games, and Debates* by Rapoport, who acknowledges 'the methods exemplified in the work of Rashevsky and specifically of Richardson, which dominate Part I of this book' (Rapoport 1960, xi), and in the discussion of Richardson-process models by Boulding (1962, 25–40). Wright (1942) gave an early discussion of Richardson's work, and he and the pioneering mathematical social scientist Nicholas Rashevsky edited Richardson's manuscripts (1960a, b) for posthumous publication. Richardson's analysis is the starting point for modelling of arms races in the *Journal of Conflict Resolution*, of which Rapoport is gaming editor and whose editorial board includes the noted game theorists Harsanyi, Selten and Shubik.

Empirical application of the Richardson model has been disappointing. Majeski and Jones (1981) suggest that this is because the form in which the model has usually been applied, converted to difference equations because budget data is discrete, is overly restrictive – relating arms spending in one country only to last year's arm spending in another country, rather than to a distributed lag of past expenditure. Even using the more general distributed lag model, Granger causality testing by Majeski and Jones found independence (no arms race) for seven of twelve pairs of arms expenditures commonly proposed as arms races. While this is plausible for the five (out of six) South American pairs, where animosity was unaccompanied by recent or prospective military conflict, it is surprising for USA–USSR (1949–1975) and India–Pakistan (1948–1975). The only instance of two-way causality as predicted by Richardson was between Israel and the Arabs (Egypt, Syria and Jordan). Contrary to the Richardson model, in this case it was instantaneous causality with only current spending mattering – not even last year's spending by the other side. Iraqui spending affected Iranian spending, and Peruvian spending affected Brazilian spending, but there was no influence in the opposite direction, either instantaneous or lagged. Greek and Warsaw Pact spending depended on current and lagged Turkish and NATO spending, respectively, but Turkey and NATO responded only to current, not lagged, Greek and Warsaw Pact spending. Majeski and Jones (1981, 281) concluded that 'we have found *no evidence to support the classic Richardson discrete arms race model*'.

Great activity in building upon Richardson's foundations does not necessarily imply satisfaction with the results. Anderton observes that

> We have over one hundred Richardson-process (differential equations-type) arms race models in the literature. We have considered dozens of variables in these models under deterministic and stochastic conditions. One could argue that this reflects the popularity and success of Richardson-type models. I believe, however, that the search for bigger and better differential equations is a reflection of frustration over the limited applicability of Richardson-type models. This is a sign, not of a successful research program, but of a degenerating one . . . .
>
> I am *not* arguing that Richardson's *work* on arms races is theoretically weak. Richardson offers an extensive and plausible verbal justification in *Arms and Insecurity* and *Mathematical Psychology of War* that provides a theory, understanding, and explanation of the arms race process. What I am arguing is that the Richardson *model* and Richardson-process models in general do *not* add much to the understanding already given in the verbal justification. Modelling efforts that take account of gross behaviour and strategy from the start are attempts to push the arms race modelling enterprise to a deeper level than Richardson and other Richardson-process modellers have pushed it . . . . This is a noble effort and Richardson was the first to attempt the application of mathematics in the analysis of arms races. This was his genius, not the models that he developed.
>
> (1989, 349, 356–7)

It may be taken as a testimonial to the vitality of Richardson's work that 70 years after his first, barely-noticed monograph, and after the publication of over a hundred Richardson-type models, a researcher finds it necessary to argue the case for going beyond the specifics of Richardson's mathematics while highly praising his contribution.

CONCLUSION

Lanchester and Richardson built mathematical models of conflict which can now be seen as differential games. Their basic differential equations resembled each other in assuming linear feedback between two players. Their approaches, however, were diametrically opposed: Lanchester's concern was that battles be won, with no apparent concern for human cost, while Richardson's work was motivated by pacifism. Curiously enough, a nation exercising Lanchester-type consideration would wish to build up its forces in order that it could produce good concentrations at a number of locations, thus producing a Richardson arms-race. While each author's analysis concerned the competitive behaviour of two players, neither modelled available strategies explicitly or was fully conscious of any payoff function involved. Nonetheless, the work of each has had a lasting influence on writers in the now more mature fields of game theory and operations research. In addition, that Lanchester and Richardson formulated such models before the formal innovation of game theory indicates the aptness of game theoretic analysis for the military establishment. Recognizing this, the US military was long the major funding source for research in this branch of applied mathematics.

7

THE MINIMAX APPROACH TO NON-COOPERATIVE STRATEGIC GAMES FROM WALDEGRAVE TO BOREL

As previous chapters have shown, writers before von Neumann and Morgenstern's epochal 1944 publication did a good deal of work on the analysis of strategic interdependence – the stuff of game theory. While economists such as Stackelberg (see Chapter 3) gave considerable thought to the nature of equilibrium in such situations, relatively little formal work on the definition and existence of equilibrium for games in general was written before 1944, among the most important of which was von Neumann (1928a, b). Most writers employed a notion of equilibrium 'natural' to the situation modelled. Strategic games, whose outcome depends on the skill of the participants in choosing a strategy of play, received widespread attention among mathematicians and economists only with the publication in 1944 of the first edition of von Neumann and Morgenstern's *Theory of Games and Economic Behavior*. The book marked an important advance, but it built upon an existing literature on strategic games, to which both its authors had contributed.

This chapter examines the pre-1944 literature on formalizing equilibrium conditions and on the minimax theorem, which holds that two-person zero-sum games with finitely many pure strategies (or a continuum of pure strategies and continuous convex payoffs) have solutions (equilibria) under maximin and minimax strategies which are identical. An agent A whose choices are governed by a maximin criterion looks at each strategy she might follow and, in each case, considers the lowest payoff she can receive by following this strategy. She then chooses to play the strategy whose minimum payoff is the highest. This is an extremely conservative and pessimistic approach: it assumes that B's ability to deliver to A her lowest payoff possible, given her choice of strategy, is the paramount element in A's choice of strategy. Player A ensures her minimal payoff by taking this approach. A player C taking the minimax approach, on the other hand, looks at the payoffs her opponent D can achieve given each strategy of C. C then chooses to play the strategy which will give D the lowest payoff, if D would always play so as to maximize his payoff subject to C's strategy. While the maximin approach presumes a player who wishes to guarantee her own minimum payoff, minimax conjectures a player who wants to guarantee her opponent's maximum payoff. While the maximin player is conservatively greedy, the minimax player is conservatively aggressive.[1]

Aumann (1989, 6–7) stresses the importance of the minimax solution of such games as a 'vital cornerstone' for the development of game theory, noting that 'the most fundamental concepts of the general theory – extensive form, pure strategies, strategic form, randomization, utility theory – were spawned in connection with the minimax theorem' and that the Cournot–Nash concept of strategic equilibrium in non-cooperative n-person game theory is an outgrowth of minimax. We focus on the contributions made by the eminent French probabilist Borel (1871–1956) in a series of papers from 1921 to 1927, in particular because of the claims of priority which Fréchet (1953) has made for him. We place his work on minimax solution of games of strategy in the context of later papers by von Neumann (1928) and Ville (1938) and of earlier work.

BEFORE BOREL

The earliest minimax solution of a game was proposed more than two centuries before Borel's 1921 paper. It is of particular interest because of the formality of the solution – a formality emphasized by the fact that the equilibrium strategy is a mixed one.[2] De Montmort wrote to Bernoulli, in November 1713, in a letter translated in Baumol and Goldfeld (1968, 7–9), quoting a solution to a two-person version of the card game *le Her* proposed in a letter to Bernoulli on 13 November 1713, by Waldegrave, then Baron Waldegrave of Chewton and later first Earl Waldegrave (1684–1741). In this game,

> Peter holds a common pack of cards; he gives a card at random to Paul and takes one himself; the main object is for each to obtain a higher card than his adversary. The order of value is *ace, two, three, . . . ten, Knave, Queen, King*. Now if Paul is not content with his card he may compel Peter to change with him; but if Peter has a *King* he is allowed to retain it. If Peter is not content with the card which he at first obtained, or which he has been compelled to receive from Paul, he is allowed to change it for another taken out of the deck at random; but if the card he then draws is a *King* he is not allowed to have it, and must retain the card with which he was dissatisfied. If Paul and Peter finally have cards of the same value Paul is considered to lose.
>
> (Todhunter 1865, 106)

Paul would change any card lower than seven and hold any card higher than seven, while Peter would change any card lower than eight and hold any card higher than eight. If Paul always changed a seven, Peter would gain by adopting a rule of changing eight. However, if Peter always changed an eight, Paul would gain by always holding a seven instead of changing it. That is, in the doubtful cases (eight for Peter, seven for Paul), Peter would wish to follow the same rule (always hold or always change) as Paul, while Paul would wish to follow a rule opposite to that of Peter. Bernoulli thought that both players should change cards in the doubtful cases, while de Montmort concluded that no rule could be established.

Waldegrave considered the problem of choosing a strategy that maximizes a player's probability of winning, whatever strategy may be chosen by his opponent. (The probability of winning is the appropriate goal of each player when the implicit payoff of winning is fixed at the beginning of the game and is not renegotiated during subsequent play.) The resulting matrix of probabilities for a win by Peter, given the mixed strategy chosen, persuaded Waldegrave that a player could select a strategy assuring him of a certain outcome, while the other player could prevent him from doing better. Waldegrave concluded that Peter should hold cards of eight and over (and change lower cards) with probability 5/8, and should change cards of eight and under, holding higher cards, with probability 3/8. Paul should hold seven and over with probability 3/8, and change seven and under with probability 5/8 (see Kuhn in Baumol and Goldfeld 1968, 4–6; de Montmort in Baumol and Goldfeld 1968, 7–9; Todhunter 1865, 106–10). N. W. Rives, Jr. (1975, 554) states incorrectly that Waldegrave derived a *matrix* of probabilities of winning from optimal *mixed* strategies. Rives also indicates that Waldegrave's solution involved the dealer always holding on seven and over and the other player always changing on eight and under, but this would mean that each player followed a pure rather than a mixed strategy and would result in a scalar probability of winning. Waldegrave's solution of *le Her* was a minimax solution, but he made no extension of his result to other games, and expressed concern that a mixed strategy 'does not seem to be in the usual rules of play' of games of chance. He abandoned mathematics for diplomacy after leaving France for England in 1721. Although his mother was the natural daughter of the last Stuart king, James II, by Arabella Churchill (the sister of the first duke of Marlborough), and his brother, the Jacobite duke of Berwick, defeated the British at the battle of Almanza in the War of the Spanish Succession, Waldegrave served the House of Hanover as British ambassador to Vienna and to Versailles.

De Montmort published his correspondence with Jean and Nicolas Bernoulli, including his letter about *le Her*, as an appendix to the second edition of his *Essai d'Analyse sur les Jeux d'Hasard* (1713, 283–414; cf. Todhunter 1865, 113–34). This appendix became renowned for a letter from Nicolas Bernoulli to de Montmort stating the St Petersburg paradox (see Daniel Bernoulli 1738). Despite this, Waldegrave's minimax solution of *le Her* was largely unnoticed. The notions of a minimax solution, first used by Waldegrave, and of maximization of expected utility, diminishing marginal utility and risk aversion put forward by Daniel Bernoulli (1738) in his analysis of the St Petersburg Paradox,[3] lie at the core of game theory. These elements were not assembled until von Neumann and Morgenstern (1944), who noted in an appendix on axiomatic utility theory in their second edition (1947, 629) that

Bernoulli's moral expectation, which equated utility to the logarithm of wealth, satisfied their conditions for rationality. The two elements were not combined by Borel, the rediscoverer of minimax solutions, even though he wrote extensively on the St Petersburg paradox (see Jorland 1987, 177–8, 189 for references). Waldegrave's players attempt to maximize their probability of winning rather than their expected monetary gain on each play, let alone the 'moral expectation' (expected utility) of such gains. In a fixed-pot game of *le Her* all these are equivalent, so examination of this game would not have led Waldegrave to formulate a different objective function.

One writer did notice the correspondence between de Montmort and Bernoulli about *le Her*. Todhunter reported it in his compendious *History of the Mathematical Theory of Probability* (1865, 106–10), although he also reported, without taking sides, the views of those who 'asserted that it was impossible to say on which rule Paul should *uniformly act*' (1865, 429). Todhunter's book was recognized as the standard authority on its subject for nearly a century, so it might be expected that his discussion of *le Her* would attract notice or that Todhunter's lengthy presentation of the work of Condorcet, Borda and Laplace on the mathematical theory of elections (1865, 351–92, 432–4, 546–8, 618) would have been an early stimulus to social choice theory. Unfortunately, Todhunter's book, in the words of an admirer of it, Kendall (1963, 204–5), 'is just about as dull as any book on probability could be . . . . [Todhunter was] so unlike the colourful authors of whom he wrote, so meticulous in his attention to detail and so blind to the broad currents of his subject' that his book was widely known rather than widely read. Literary style can make a difference to the development of a subject. If Todhunter had been a livelier writer and had given a fuller account of de Montmort's letter, probabilists might have been thinking about minimax solutions of games of strategy and about voting theory in the late nineteenth century.

Waldegrave's solution of *le Her* was replicated, without mention of Waldegrave, by Fisher in 'Randomisation, and an old enigma of card play' (1934). Although Kuhn (in Baumol and Goldfeld 1968, 4n.) states that Fisher was 'unaware of Waldegrave's work', Fisher discussed the views of de Montmort and Nicolas Bernoulli on *le Her*, dismissing de Montmort's conclusion as 'unsatisfactory to common sense'. Fisher's second sentence (1934, 294) refers to precisely those pages of Todhunter (1865, 106–10) which discussed de Montmort's correspondence about *le Her*. Walker and Osborne have pointed out that we erred, in Dimand and Dimand (1992), in stating that Waldegrave's solution was available to Fisher in Todhunter's book. While Todhunter included a section on the de Montmort letter in which de Montmort gave Waldegrave's minimax solution to *le Her*, Todhunter did not present Waldegrave's solution.

Bertrand is best known to economists for his 1883 review of Cournot (1838) and Walras, often cited as the first review of Cournot (but see Dimand 1988, for an 1857 review by the Canadian mathematician Cherriman). Bertrand analysed the game of baccarat in 1889.[4] He considered whether a punter should draw another card when holding a count of five. He noted that the problem was psychological as well as mathematical, with the punter's decision on whether to draw for five depending on whether the banker expected him to do so. Bertrand examined, however, only the strategies of always drawing for five or never drawing for five, and not a strategy of drawing for five on some fraction of plays (Bertrand 1924, cited by Borel 1924, 101). This serves as some indication of how impressive Waldegrave's solution was.

While Borel did not know of Waldegrave, he had two results about strategic games to build on when he began publishing on the topic in the proceedings of the French Academy of Sciences in 1921 – the year he was elected to the Academy. Zermelo[5] (1913) proved that the game of chess is determinate, a result that has since been found to hold for other two-person zero-sum games of perfect information such as checkers, Chinese checkers and Go,[2] but not for such games as bridge or poker in which players have private information (Aumann 1989, 4). It is not, however, known what the optimal strategy is for a chess player, nor what the result would be if the optimal strategies were followed, an ignorance for which chess players must be grateful.

According to Leonard (1995, 733–4), following Zermelo, chess became a standard topic in Viennese mathematical circles. Kalmar (1928–9) of the University of Szeged, writing in German in his university's mathematical journal, noted that Zermelo

> had shown that for games like chess where v, the number of possible positions, is finite, that among other things, when player A stands to win in position q, there exists a strategy by which he will win in v moves. The proof of this rests primarily on the fact that if A stands to win in position q, then A can follow an appropriate strategy 'without repetition'. That is, be able to win so that regardless of how the opponent plays, there will be no match in which a position is repeated . Zermelo did not prove this last nontrivial fact, thus, as König has noted, a hole appears in Zermelo's proof. Therefore König, inspired by a verbal comment from von Neumann, rather than proving the aforementioned statement of Zermelo, proved a statement which covers not just finite games, but all games in which only a finite number of new positions $\mu = \mu(q)$ can be reached via an acceptable move from position q.
>
> (Kalmar 1928–9, translated by Zantke)

That von Neumann made a relevant suggestion to König before publication of his 1928 paper is of interest in itself. Kalmar improved on Zermelo's proof by following on 'Zermelo's original thought processes' as König had not. Drawing extensively on von Neumann's writing on the axiomatization of set theory, Kalmar attempted to show that a game of perfect information has a solution by giving a more general proof of non-repetition which, unlike König's, did not depend on any finiteness assumptions. The original thought process followed by Kalmar was, in fact, backwards induction.[6]

Kalmar's proof of non-repetition by backward induction (a concept which in itself makes non-repetition intuitive) rested on defining the types of positions which could be reached in play as winning, non-losing or losing. Unfortunately, Kalmar did not show that the types of positions he defined must appear on every branch of the potentially infinitely long and thus infinitely branched game tree. Without this sort of spanning argument for the types of nodes defined, Kalmar's proof was not valid. Interesting features of Kalmar's approach were his definition of the 'script game' (what we call a subgame)[7] and his definition of strategy. Kalmar thought of a strategy as a restriction of the game, as indeed it is, but while his definition of strategy was equivalent to ours, the mental processes involved would seem very different. A strategy (i.e. a complete plan as to how to react to opponent play under every possible circumstance) does indeed restrict a player to less than the full set of moves, hence of paths down the tree, allowed by the rules of the game.

BOREL

Borel published four notes on strategic games and an erratum to one of them between 1921 and 1927. Three of these notes were translated by Savage (1953) in *Econometrica*. Rives (1975, 559n.) follows Fréchet (1953, 95n.) in crediting Borel with seven notes on game theory in this period. However, the sixth and seventh items by Borel in Fréchet's bibliography (1953, 126) are the 1938 volume by Borel and collaborators in which Ville (1938) appeared and a chapter by Borel in that volume, while one of the two untranslated notes is a 1923 article with the same title as a chapter that Savage translated from a 1924 volume by Borel. Borel was already an eminent probabilist when he turned his attention to strategic games, having stated the strong law of large numbers in 1909, and also had a prominent public career which brought him the *Croix de Guerre* in World War I and the Medal of the Resistance in World War II, the portfolio of Minister of the Navy in 1925, and the Grand Cross of the Legion of Honour. His scientific honours included the presidency of the Institut de France and, in 1955, the first gold medal of the Centre National de la Recherche Scientifique (Fréchet 1965; Knobloch 1987; Kramer 1981, 248–9).

Borel (1921) considered a two-person game of chance and strategy that was symmetric in the sense that if the two players adopted the same strategy, their chances of winning would be equal. The number of possible pure strategies was assumed to be finite. If A chooses method of play (pure strategy) C_i and B chooses method C_k, the probability of A winning is $a = 1/2 + \alpha_{ik}$ and the probability of B winning, $b = 1 - a$, is $b = 1/2 + \alpha_{ki}$, where $\alpha_{ik} + \alpha_{ki} = 0$, $\alpha_{ii} = 0$, and α_{ik} and α_{ki} are contained between -1/2 and +1/2. Borel assumed that each player maximizes his probability of winning. As long as the payoffs are zero-sum and symmetric, this is equivalent to maximizing expected gains. Borel eliminated as 'bad' those strategies C_i for which α_{ih} is negative or zero for every strategy C_h not already excluded as bad. Borel's criterion for the elimination of a bad strategy was, in the case of symmetry such as was assumed in Borel (1921), equivalent to the criterion in current game theory for elimination of a weak strategy. A weak strategy is one which has a payoff less than or equal to that of some other strategy, no matter what the other player does. Borel therefore both anticipated the later criterion of elimination of weak strategies and notes that with such elimination, new pure strategies are likely to become weak.

If a strategy C_h existed such that α_{hk} was positive or zero for all k, that would be the best strategy. Borel noted that such a best pure strategy may not exist, and then it would be advantageous to adopt a mixed strategy of varying one's play across the n pure strategies remaining after the elimination of bad strategies. At any moment, the probability of player A playing strategy C_k is p_k, and the probability of player B playing strategy C_k is q_k. The probability of A winning is $a = 1/2 + \alpha$, where α is the summation across all i and k of $\alpha_{ik}p_iq_k$.

For the case of three strategies, Borel noted that it is possible to select positive values for the p's such that α is zero, whatever q's may be chosen by the other player, and that the other player faces a symmetric problem of choosing q's.

Borel's 1921 solution of the choice of a mixed strategy when only three pure strategies are left after elimination of bad strategies is a minimax solution. However, Borel (1921, 98–9) went on: 'But it is easy to see that, once n exceeds 7, this circumstance [existence of a minimax solution] will occur only for particular values of the α_{ik}. In general, whatever the p's may be, it will be possible to choose the q's . . . in such a manner that α has any sign determined in advance.' Borel argued that, in the case of n greater than 7, as soon as one player has chosen a mixed strategy and his choice has been observed, the other player 'may vary his play in such a manner as to have an advantage'. Borel presented no explanation or argument for this incorrect conjecture about the limitation of the minimax solution beyond the assertion that the result was easy to see.

Borel added that 'It is easy to extend the preceding considerations to the case where the manners of playing form an infinite continuum', but did not explain how extension from three strategies to an infinite number of pure strategies would be easy when extension to finite numbers greater than seven was not. He observed (1921, 100) that 'The problems of probability and analysis that one might raise concerning the art of war or of economic and financial speculation are not without analogy to the problems concerning games, but they generally have a much higher degree of complexity'. This complexity would include asymmetry and more than two players as well as more than seven possible pure strategies. In keeping with his belief that a player who knows his opponent's mixed strategy has an advantage when there are a finite number of strategies greater than seven, Borel concluded that 'The only advice the mathematician could give, in the absence of all psychological information, to a player A whose adversary B seeks to utilize the preceding remarks, is that he should so vary his plans that the probabilities attributed by an outside observer to his different manners of playing shall never be defined.... It seems that, to follow [this advice] to the letter, a complete incoherence of mind would be needed, combined, of course, with the intelligence necessary to eliminate those methods we have called bad.'

Borel began his 1924 paper, 'On games that involve chance and the skill of the players', by noting the origin of the calculus of probabilities in the study of the simplest games of chance, and suggested that the study of games involving the skill of players (choice of strategies) as well as chance should also begin with the simplest cases. He discussed Bertrand's analysis of baccarat, indicating the complexity of even baccarat when compared to a very simple two-player symmetric game such as paper, scissors and stone ('Paper covers the stone, scissors cut the paper, stone grinds the scissors'), which Borel had chosen to study. Borel did not define the concept of symmetry he used in this paper, merely remarking 'that neither player has a privileged position relative to the other. Further, it is evident, by reason of the same symmetry, that it is not possible to formulate advice permitting one of the players to win for sure; because if his adversary followed this same advice, he must also win for sure' (1924, 102). In this game, 'Each player chooses at will, in an independent and secret manner, one of the three letters A, B, C. If the two players have chosen the same letter, the game is tied; otherwise it is agreed that A beats B, B beats C, and C beats A.' Borel solved the game by maximizing the expected return for each player. If J chooses A, B and C with probabilities x, y and z, respectively, $x + y + z = 1$, and J' chooses A, B and C with probabilities x', y' and $z', x' + y' + z' = 1$, then J has an expected return $E = x(y' - z') + y(z' - x') + z(x' - y')$ and J' has an expected return of $-E$. For any x, y, z, J' can be sure of not losing systematically by adopting $x' = y' = z' = 1/3$, which sets the value of the game $E = -E = 0$, and similarly J can avoid systematic loss by choosing $x = y = z = 1/3$. Borel then solved the game for the case where J is the proprietor of a gambling house with an advantage over the punter J' in that, when J has A and J' has B, J receives the sum s, which is greater than 1. Borel extended his analysis to an asymmetric game in this instance and gave a good intuitive explanation of the house playing A less often than B or C: if the banker chose $x = y = z = 1/3$, 'it would suffice for the punter never to play B in order that the advantage of the banker should be zero' (1924, 106). Borel also solved a symmetric two-person game with five possible pure strategies, showing that G, the mathematical expectations of the first player's winnings, would be zero, where

$$G = \sum \sum x_i y_k \alpha_{ik} = \sum x_i Y_i,$$

with x_i being the probability that the first player plays A_i and y_i the probability that the second player plays A_i.

However, Borel (1924, 114) went on to state that 'I will assume the hypothesis that, for n sufficiently larger, it is possible to so choose the constants that it is not possible to find positive non-zero values of the y's in such fashion that all the Y's should be all positive or zero (or else all negative and zero). Under these conditions, whatever the y's may be, once they are determined, the x's can be chosen in such fashion that G will be positive.' As in his previous paper, Borel held, without offering any justification, that the minimax solution would not hold for large numbers of possible pure strategies, although he no longer asserted that the breakdown of the solution would occur as soon as n exceeded seven. This surprising claim does not follow from the analysis in his paper. It led Borel to conclude incorrectly that 'The player who does not observe the psychology of his partner and does not modify his manner of playing must necessarily lose against an adversary whose mind is sufficiently flexible to vary his play while taking account of that of the adversary' (1924, 115). His analysis of symmetric games with $n = 3$ and $n = 5$ had shown, on the contrary, that in those games the first player has a mixed strategy to achieve $G = 0$ regardless of what his opponent does, and his opponent has a mixed strategy to prevent him achieving $G > 0$ no matter what the first player does.

Borel (1927) is very brief. Borel again defined the concepts of the symmetric game and the 'tactic' or strategy. His previous definition of optimal play was a method 'that gives the player who adopts it a superiority over every player who does not adopt it' (1921, 97). He now stated that the central question of game theory is whether B can choose a tactic 'so that player A if he knew that tactic, would nonetheless be unable to adopt a tactic of his own making G positive' (1927, 117). Borel's 1921 quest for a strategy which gives 'superiority', which happened to coincide with a minimax strategy for the game he chose to examine, was replaced in 1927 by a search for a minimax strategy.

Borel concluded by indicating that he now believed that such a strategy exists for games which have as many as seven pure strategies, and might exist more generally:

> The problem that arises is thus the following: *Determine the α_{ik} such that for all nonnegative y_i there are Y_i nonzero and not all of the same sign*. In this case player A can, by suitably choosing the x_i, give G the sign he wishes; i.e. win for certain on the average. This problem, unsolvable for $n = 3$ and $n = 5$, seems to me unsolvable also for $n = 7$. It would be interesting either to demonstrate that it is unsolvable in general or to give a particular solution.
>
> (1927, 117)

As von Neumann (1953) states, Borel has certainly not proved the minimax theorem. He may not even have stated it. Part of the minimax theorem is the statement that $\max_x \min_y G = \min_y \max_x G$. It is not clear that such equality occurred to Borel as necessary for equilibrium, although his definition of optimality yields equality in the case of the class of games he examines. In a symmetric zero-sum game, Borel's equilibrium gives B the ability to prevent A from making G positive and A the ability to prevent B from making G negative. This automatically implies that equilibrium strategies by both parties set their expected payoff to zero. Borel had, however, correctly solved a non-symmetric game for minimax strategy in Borel (1924).

Steinhaus, a professor at the University of Lwów (then in Poland, now in the Ukraine), contributed a short paper on 'Definitions for a theory of games and pursuit' to the December 1925 inaugural issue of a Lwów student journal that expired with its second issue. Steinhaus discussed a payoff function with strategies (which he called modes of play) as independent variables and defined the best mode of play as that which maximized the minimum expected payoff, including cases with a continuum of choices. He did not distinguish between pure and mixed strategies, as Borel had done. As Steinhaus recalled in his 1959 letter approving publication of an English translation of his 1925 paper, 'After having found the concepts of minimax and maximin I was well aware that the minimax time of the pursuer is longer or equal to the maximin time of the pursued, but I did not know whether they are equal in all similar games' (1925, 108).

VON NEUMANN

The first proof of the minimax theorem for two-person games of chance and skill with any finite number of pure strategies was given by von Neumann (1928b) in a paper presented to the Göttingen Mathematical Society on 7 December 1926, three weeks before von Neumann's twenty-third birthday. Von Neumann had received both a Ph.D. in mathematics with highest honours from the University of Budapest and a simultaneously-pursued undergraduate degree in chemical engineering in Zurich that year. His first mathematical paper had been published in 1922, submitted when he was a 17-year-old gymnasium student. By the end of 1927, before his first game theory papers appeared, von Neumann had published 17 major mathematical articles, notably on quantum mechanics and on the axiomatization of set theory, and was the youngest *privatdozent* (lecturer) ever appointed in any subject at the University of Berlin (Macrae 1992). Von Neumann's proof was a complicated one, combining elementary and topological concepts in a manner not easy for the reader to follow, but it was a valid proof. In a footnote, von Neumann (1928b, 25n.) remarked that 'While this paper was put into its final form, I learned of the note of E. Borel in the *Comptes Rendus* of Jan. 10, 1927. Borel formulates the question of bilinear forms for a symmetric two-person game and states that no examples for MaxMin < MinMax are known. Our result above answers his question.' As Leonard (1992) relates, von Neumann sent Borel a note on his result, which Borel presented to the Académie des Sciences in June 1928 (von Neumann 1928a).

In his 1937 paper (initially presented to a Princeton seminar in 1932), von Neumann gave an entirely topological proof of the existence of general competitive equilibrium, using Brouwer's fixed point theorem to provide a much clearer and more elegant proof than his 1928 proof of the minimax theorem. The first elementary (non-topological) proof of the minimax theorem, using convexity arguments and the concept of a supporting hyperplane, is due to Ville[8] in a 1938 contribution to Borel's *Traité du calcul des probabilités et de ses applications*. Ville (1938) also gave the first proof of the minimax theorem for the case of a continuum of possible pure strategies. The proof of the minimax theorem in von Neumann and Morgenstern (1944) is a non-topological one, based on the proof in Ville (1938) rather than on the one in von Neumann (1928). Weyl (1950) gave a simpler elementary proof of the minimax theorem, based on earlier work on convex polyhedra in a paper (Weyl 1935) that he had given at Göttingen in 1933 just before leaving to become a colleague of von Neumann at the Institute for Advanced Study in Princeton (having been a professor in Zurich while von Neumann was a student there).

The subject of priority in scientific discovery is a prickly one, since original scientific contributions are prized and multiple independent discoveries do occur. Samuelson (1989, 120–1) refers to the instance of von Neumann's proof of the weak ergodic theorem in the early 1930s, shortly before Birkhoff proved the strong ergodic theorem: 'According to reliable legend, Birkhoff pulled strings so that von Neumann did not even get to publish his result before it would be eclipsed by the greater one.' Although Borel (1927) is mentioned in a footnote in von Neumann (1928), none of Borel's papers on strategic games were cited by von Neumann and Morgenstern (1944), in which Borel's name appears only in footnotes referring to the 1938 volume in which Ville's paper appeared (von Neumann and Morgenstern 1947, 154n., 186n., 219n.). Von Neumann (1953) responded to Fréchet's commentary on the Borel notes by stressing that his 1928 paper gave the first proof of the minimax theorem and that Borel had believed the theorem to be false when the number of possible strategies is large.

Von Neumann deserves the credit for the first general proof of the minimax theorem. Waldegrave provided the first minimax, mixed strategy solution of a two-person game of strategy more than two centuries before Borel and von Neumann, but his contribution was isolated and ignored. It was also an implicit application of definitions and propositions made only later. Waldegrave aside, Borel gave the first modern formulation of a mixed strategy in 1921, since Bertrand and Zermelo had dealt with pure strategies only. Borel found the minimax solution for two-person games of chance and skill with three or five possible strategies. While he initially held that games with more possible strategies would not have minimax solutions, by 1927 he considered this to be an open question, as he had not found a counterexample. Ville, writing as a collaborator of Borel in 1938, provided the first elementary proof of the minimax theorem, and extended the theorem to cases of infinitely many (continuous) strategies. Borel has received relatively little attention in the literature of game theory, e.g. a single sentence in Aumann (1989, 6). His achievement in formulating mixed strategies, eliminating bad strategies and finding minimax solutions of particular cases was a substantial contribution.

8

FROM GAMES OF PURE CHANCE
TO STRATEGIC GAMES
French probabilists and early game theory[1]

That the study of gambling was central to the development of probability theory is indicated in the title of David's history of the subject, *Games, Gods, and Gambling* (1962).[2] Initially, there was no true dichotomy between the more analytical gaming manuals and mathematical work on probability. Early probabilists studied games of pure chance, using simple and widely known gambling games as a starting point and to introduce readers to thinking in probabilistic terms. For example, Louis Bachelier (1901) used simple games of pure chance to make his novel contributions to probability theory more accessible to readers.

For probabilists used to pondering games, it was a short step from games of pure chance such as roulette or craps to contemplation of baccarat, blackjack or poker, where the probability of winning depends on the strategy chosen by the player. (The relationship between the analysis of specific games, probability theory and game theory was discussed at greater length in the first chapter.) Such a step was taken in the early twentieth century by Borel and his associates, notably Ville, working within the French tradition of probability theory, the tradition of Laplace, Poisson, Cournot, Bertrand and Poincaré. Starting from Bertrand's analysis of baccarat, Borel (1921, 1924, 1927) found minimax solutions to several two-person zero-sum strategic games and failed to find a counterexample of such a game without a minimax solution (see Chapter 7). This preceded von Neumann's proof of the minimax theorem, which Borel communicated to the Académie des Sciences (von Neumann 1928a, b; Leonard 1992). Borel papers of 1921, 1924 and 1927 attracted attention when translated by Savage in *Econometrica* in 1953. Von Neumann and Morgenstern (1944) made no mention of Borel's early minimax papers, one of which von Neumann had cited in 1928, but acknowledged (1944, 154n.) that their proof of the minimax theorem was based on the first largely elementary proof by Ville (1938),[3] rather than on von Neumann's intricate topological proof of 1928.

Apart from mention of Ville's 1938 proof, and from a footnote by von Neumann and Morgenstern (1944, 186–7n.) on a 1938 treatment of poker by Borel and Ville, the literature of game theory has ignored the study of strategic games by French probabilists between 1928 and 1944. This paper proposes to show that Borel and his associates produced a substantial and interesting body of work on strategic games in the 1930s, a development interrupted by World War II. Although Borel and Ville analysed games of chance, Borel was alive to the promise of their methods for military and economic problems. He suggested that problems of a type now known as Colonel Blotto problems,[4] as well as pricing problems for multiproduct merchants, could be approached by similar methods (Borel 1938, 86–7). Borel's interest in proper economic application of probability had earlier been demonstrated in such papers as 'Un paradoxe économique: le sophisme du tas de blé et les vérités statistiques' (1907, *Revue du mois* vol. 4, 688–99). Moreover, Borel's emphasis on the role of information in games which are not played in a simultaneous coup makes it clear that his analysis of games was an approach to investigation of such problems.

The career of the eminent mathematician and public figure Borel has been discussed by Fréchet (1965), and his contributions to probability treated by Knobloch (1987). Borel's *magnum opus* was the *Traité du calcul des probabilités et de ses applications*, whose four volumes were published in eighteen parts from 1925 to 1939. Tome IV, Fascicule II, 'Rédigé par Jean Ville, d'après un Cours d'Emile Borel', published in 1938, was 122 pages on 'Applications aux jeux de hasard'. In addition to five chapters compiled by Ville from Borel's lectures, Fascicule II also included Ville's note on the minimax theorem, Borel's comments on Ville's note, and a note by Borel. Tome IV, Fascicule III, 'Valeur pratique et philosophie des probabilités', which completed the work in 1939, included Chapter III on 'L'incompréhension des joueurs et des esprits super-stitieux' and reprinted (from *Mercure de France*, Tome 75, Fascicule IV, 1937) Borel's 'Eloge du jeu'.

Théorie mathématique du bridge à la portée de tous, by Borel and Chéron, appeared in 1940 in a series of monographs on probability edited by Borel, with a preface by Borel attributing the origin of the 424-page monograph to the interest taken by bridge specialists in some pages of Tome IV, Fascicule II, of the *Traité*. Borel (1950, 155–64) included an appendix recapitulating his earlier work on psychological games in an elementary book on probability. Borel and his collaborators wrote extensively on strategic games such as poker and bridge in the 1930s, but these writings have been neglected in the post-von Neumann and Morgenstern literature.

BERTRAND ON BACCARAT

As Borel (1924, 101) noted, the starting-point for his investigation of strategic games was the analysis of baccarat by Bertrand ([1889]; the date of 1899 given in Knobloch 1987, and, alas, Dimand and Dimand 1992 is contradicted by the title page. Borel cited the posthumous third edition of 1924). Bertrand is known to economists for his critical 1883 review of Cournot and Walras (translated into English by Magnan de Bornier 1992, who shows that what most economists think that Bertrand wrote in that review bears only a limited resemblance to what he actually did write).

Bertrand ([1889] 1924, 38–42) considered the punter's choice of whether to draw another card when holding a count of five in baccarat. Since the punter's choice of drawing or standing precedes the dealer's (where neither has won immediately), the dealer has a little information on the punter's hand in formulating a decision. The punter's object is to obtain a higher count than the dealer without going over nine.

Bertrand argued that the punter's choice should depend on whether the punter believed that the dealer would stand or draw on a count of five. However, the dealer's decision whether always to stand or always to draw in such a situation should depend in turn on the dealer's belief about the punter's strategy, which affects the dealer's priors on the punter's hand and thus the dealer's expectation of gain from drawing. Bertrand showed that if the punter's pure strategy must be revealed, the punter should choose a revealed strategy of always drawing on five. If the punter can make the dealer believe in a pure draw-on-five strategy without having committed to it, the punter should stand on five. Thus Bertrand's analysis of optimal play stressed the same sorts of expectational issues on which Zeuthen and Stackelberg focused (see Chapter 3). Having introduced psychological considerations and the desire to select the strategy with the highest expected gain, Bertrand's resolution of the problem was incomplete, since he did not consider a mixed strategy of standing on some percentage of plays and drawing on the others as a possible solution.[5] Such an optimal solution would give no additional edge to even a dealer with perfect knowledge of the punter's habits. His approach to the problem is nonetheless of interest in its emphasis on the dealer's extra information and in his use of backward induction.

BOREL ON GAMES OF CHANCE

Although Borel intended the *Traité* as 'the missing comprehensive presentation of probability theory and its applications' and 'rightly foresaw that this publication would be a landmark in the history of science' (Knobloch 1987, 217), accessibility was emphasized as well as rigour and comprehensiveness. The portion on games of chance compiled by Ville from Borel's lectures (Tome IV, Fascicule II) is notably easy to read and did not assume that probabilistic reasoning was well known even to mathematicians. Borel distinguished games of pure chance from 'psychological games' whose result depends on the ability or behaviour of the players. He predicted that methods stemming from psychological games would be useful in analysing economic questions (Borel 1938, x–xi).

Throughout the book, Borel and Ville stressed the importance of who has what information when. In some asymmetric games, the player who moves first has an advantage (as in Stackelberg's analysis a few years before), while in other asymmetric games the first mover is disadvantaged by revealing information (Borel 1938, 23). Borel discussed the updating of information during the game of '*écarté*' and mentioned the possibility of gaining information from a player's manner (1938, 52–3, 58). Discards at five-card draw give information to the opposing players, just as does the first bet in five-card draw without discards, so who bets first should rotate among the players (1938, 101, 97). For games with sufficiently complex information structures, the minimax approach is not useful (1938, 115–17).

The second chapter, 'Problème des partis' (the 'Problem of points' in Todhunter's terminology), examined a problem posed by Pascal: how should a pot be divided among two players if a game (such as getting n wins at heads or tails) is halted before its end?[6] The question is analogous to finding a measure such as the Shapley value for the power of players in 'psychological games' (but only games of pure chance were considered in that chapter). The analysis is illustrated with a matrix similar to that for a two-person zero-sum matrix game, except that instead of strategies, the rows and columns represent the number of heads (or tails) achieved out of the number needed to win (1938, 10). Independence of plays, which is necessary to construct such a simple table, is assumed implicitly, being made explicit only at the beginning of the next chapter, when the assumption is dropped. Under the assumption of a coin with equal probabilities of heads or tails, Borel examined the advantage of playing first, and the effect on this advantage of alternating the order of play on subsequent rounds.

The third chapter of Borel (1938) considered what generalizations could be made about the mathematics of card games, in which successive coups or tricks are not independent because they reveal information. His section on 'les jeux de coïncidences' shows the strong degree of interdependence in even a trivial game. Borel considered the study of card games of applied, rather than pure, mathematics, since it depended on the actual sequence of revealed tricks. He cited Poincaré as holding that chess is not truly mathematical because the large number of possible sequences prevents any generalized statement of the problem facing a player. This view is noteworthy in light of Zermelo's 1913 proof that a solution (an optimal strategy guaranteeing a certain result to the white player) must exist for chess. It is not known whether the solution is a draw or a win for the first-mover white, let alone how to determine the sequence of moves to achieve this result. Simon (1982, 413) has estimated that, with thirty legal moves possible from a typical position and with forty moves as a reasonable estimate of the average length of a chess game, 'there would be perhaps 10^{120} possible games of chess'.

Borel emphasized the probability distribution of possible hands for the players and the way in which information received by a player alters the prior probability distribution the player should use in making decisions. Borel's stress on the incorrectness of naive calculations as compared to those employing Bayesian calculation suggests that use of Bayesian inference was still something of a novelty. Borel recognized, but set aside, '*les subtilités du jeu*' in which a partner's or opponent's manner as well as show of cards affects a player's probability distribution. In his work on bridge, Borel was to note that these factors made players' expectations subjective. In doing this, he avoided two complications. He implicitly excluded consideration of card games as the second stage of a game in which players' 'types', including preferences for risk and bluffing, affect their payoffs. Since payoff structures affect play, in that situation, play would give information not only on players' hands but on the players' type and hence strategy. (Similarly, a rational player's trick-by-trick strategy would be affected by the knowledge that each revealed card gave information on type as well as hand.) Games of this sort were not analysed until the 1970s, when Harsanyi introduced the idea of modelling player type as endowed by nature at a first stage of the game. Borel also assumed away the possibility that players could reduce the complexity of the game by encoding signals in bids or cards played which called for a particular response.

Both player type and encoded signals are substantial features of card games in life. Some players are bold, some cautious, some inveterate bluffers. Knowledge of a player's type is useful to an opponent or a partner. Encoded signals are a major point of the 'conventions' which make the intricate game of bridge more manageable.

Despite Borel's substantial simplification, analysing card games remained difficult (Borel 1938, 58–60). He was able to arrive at a mathematical expectation of the number of points a player could expect from a given hand immediately after a deal, based on a prior probability distribution for the opponent's discarding. The rational player then discards only if the expected value of the new hand exceeds the expected value of the one currently held. An additional problem was that the value of a point to a player in a game which is won by the first to gain n points depends on the number of points currently held by each player. Borel underscored this by printing a *problème des partis* table for a five point game with independent coups (Borel 1938, 60). Yet for most card games, he stated, this approach becomes hopelessly complicated, necessitating the construction of a sequence of tables depending on the coups which have occurred. Worse yet, such tables have limited value in any case, since they cannot incorporate information from players' behaviour, which in turn is influenced by the current point total.

Borel concluded his third chapter with a sketch of a theory of finessing. Although this section is not very satisfactory and no refinements on the idea occur in subsequent chapters, it is perhaps this part of the fascicule which attracted the attention of bridge players. Borel and Chéron were to write extensively on the finesse in their work on bridge.

PSYCHOLOGICAL GAMES

The fourth chapter considered psychological games '*où le hasard mécanique se trouve remplacé par une sorte de hasard psychologique*'. Borel began the chapter with a minimax solution of the two-person zero-sum game of odd/even, analysed in terms of the advantage or disadvantage to a player of deviating from the mixed strategy of playing odd and even with probabilities 1/2, 1/2 (1938, 71). From this simple game where the optimal mixed strategy is constructed by randomizing over only two discrete pure strategies, Borel moved to continuous variable games. His examples involved choice of a point on the unit circle (1938, 73–4) and on an equilateral triangle – i.e. a simplex (1938, 79–86). He resorted to geometric presentation of such continuous variable games for schematic purposes but relied on integral evaluation for precise analysis of the games. The optimal strategy was a probability distribution over the unit circle in the first game and over the simplex (with a portion having zero probability) in the second. These games bear a strong relation to the Hotelling problem of locating a business.[7]

In Borel's first work on strategic games, he conjectured that no minimax solution could be found when the number of possible pure strategies exceeded seven, but paradoxically added that 'It is easy to extend the preceding considerations [of a mixed strategy as a minimax solution] to the case where the manners of playing form an infinite continuum' (Borel 1921, 99; and as we noted in the previous chapter). Borel (1921) did not make the supposedly easy extension, nor explain why an infinity of pure strategies presented no problem if finite numbers of strategies greater than seven did. Von Neumann's 1928 proof of the existence of a minimax solution was applicable to continuous as well as discrete pure strategies, but he gave no examples of specific games. The games for which minimax solutions were found in the fourth chapter of Borel (1938) were the first examples constructed with a continuum of strategies.

Borel's section 'Relations entre les problèmes économiques et le jeu de stratégie' (1938, 86–87) discussed the relation of the psychological games considered in the chapter to other problems. He outlined, without solving, a pricing game between merchants each of whom sells a number of goods. The fourth chapter also provided the first presentation (without solution) of the class of military deployment games now known as Colonel Blotto, in which opposing generals with fixed forces distribute them at a number of locations, winning the battle at each site where their force is superior. Military application of his mathematical ideas was a natural interest for Borel, who won the *Croix de Guerre* in World War I and was Minister of Marine when the first part of the *Traité* was published in 1925. In Borel's example, the two generals have the same number of soldiers to deploy. Borel remarked that, while such a problem was different from those discussed in the body of the chapter, the same methods would work.

Borel's example of a pricing game between two merchants, analogous to the

136

military problem, looks odder to present readers. He posited that each merchant has the same stock S_i of item i of each of n articles to sell. Each stock S_i has the common value V_i calculated at a unit price p_i which is given and common to both merchants. The merchants separately choose rebates on each good i, which reduce the cost to consumers of the goods. Each merchant's object is to have the lower consumer cost on the majority of goods, subject to a fixed 'sacrifice' D which is common to both merchants. In Borel's formulation, the two merchants choose vectors of rebates subject to the constraint that, where r_i indicates the first player's rebate on good i and r_i indicates the second's,

$$\sum_{i=1}^{n} V_i \frac{p_i - r_i}{p_i} = \sum_{i=1}^{n} V_i \frac{p_i - r_i\prime}{p_i} \equiv \sum_{i=1}^{n} V_i - D$$

and thus

$$D = \sum_{i=1}^{n} \frac{V_i r_i}{p_i} = \sum_{i=1}^{n} \frac{V_i r_i\prime}{p_i} \equiv \sum_{i=1}^{n} \rho_i \equiv \sum_{i=1}^{n} \rho_i\prime$$

It is interesting to compare Borel's two-merchant problem to Cournot's duopoly problem. Like Cournot's duopolists, Borel's merchants are strategically interdependent. Their objective, however, is far more obscure than that of Cournot duopolists. Rather than desiring to maximize one period profit, each attempts to offer a higher rebate than the other on most items. It is not clear why the merchants would wish to compete in this way, since each apparently expects to sell an entire stock. We might consider the merchants to be operating side-by-side discount stores, and thus to be concerned to attract customers by representing their prices as generally lower than their competitor's. Still, since the game sketched by Borel is a one-shot game, no longer run effects due to reputation or customer loyalty which might be gained by such a policy can operate. Moreover, the rationale behind a constraint which sets each merchant's 'sacrifice' at an identical value D is puzzling.

Consequently Borel's two-merchant game is less compelling than a Cournot or 'Bertrand' market game. Nonetheless, Borel's suggestion that economic and strategic problems are appropriate domains for the use of game theory was prescient.

FIVE CARD DRAW

The fifth chapter of Borel (1938) examined a two-player variant of five-card draw poker. Particular attention was focused on the question of whether to raise and whether to accept or reject the raise, with rejecting the raise not implying folding one's hand (1938, 91–7). Borel's variant of five-card draw also differed from the standard version in ranking suits, so that hands are fully ordered with no ties. This assumption allows the hands received by the two players to be represented on the unit square, with each hand given a value between 0 and 1.

Borel calculated the number of ways of getting different sorts of hands from a 52-card deck, and converted these into probabilities of getting each type of hand (1938, 89–90). These probabilities are known to the players.

Player A will raise the bet by an amount α if A's hand has a value of at least a. Player B will accept the raise if B's hand has a value of at least b. α is assumed to be exogenous, but the players decide on a and b. This value b will be a function of a, $b = fn(a)$, since by raising (or not raising) by α, A has informed B that A's hand has a value of at least (less than) a. Knowledge of a and of B's own hand allows B to calculate the probability that A's hand is stronger than B's. Similarly, $a = fn'\,(\alpha, b)$, the minimum value of A's hand that will induce A to raise will depend on the amount of the raise and on the threshold value of B's hand for B to accept the bet, since A will win if B accepts the bet and A's hand has a higher value. Hence, $a = fn'(\alpha, b) = fn';(\alpha, fn\,(a)) = fn'(\alpha)$. B presumably forms an estimate of a by observing A's behaviour on successive plays.

The discussion of five-card draw (1938, 91–7) was followed by consideration of particular cases of poker with discarding (1938, 97–103). These cases are much more complex unless extreme simplifying assumptions are made, because the information content of discarding is inconsistent with the independence of successive plays. Borel (1938, 99) noted that in practice players follow more intuitive rules of thumb than those suggested by his analysis. This raised the issue of whether game theory is positive or normative well before the critiques of Ellsberg or the advent of experimental game theory. His discussion of gamblers' fallacies in the next fascicule is also relevant.

MATHEMATICS OF BRIDGE

Stimulated by the interest of bridge players in Tome IV, Fascicule II, Borel went on to recruit a newspaper bridge editor, André Chéron, as co-author for a work on the theory of bridge, *La théorie mathématique du bridge à la portée de tous*. Proofreading of the book was interrupted by the outbreak of World War II: Borel, who had hoped to check the proofs himself, had to cede this task to Chéron. Borel was later to receive the Medaille de la Résistance. The authors' approach to bridge, like that of Borel 1938, was based primarily on classical probability. The meticulous application of this method to the uncertainties of the shuffle and to deals with a perfectly randomized pack was perhaps related to Borel's and Chéron's desire that all interested bridge players might benefit from the application of probability theory to bridge. Appendices on basic concepts of probability and a reading schedule for the book and its appendices were intended to make the book truly accessible to all. The authors advertised 134 probability tables on their title page. Not only does Borel's preface stress the fastidious checking of each entry in each table, but the book includes a chapter on the operation of mechanical computing machines and the degree of importance of rounding errors.

Despite their evangelical intention of bringing formal probability theory to card-playing barbarians, the authors' *'Plan de l'ouvrage'* (Borel and Chéron 1940, 1–3) makes clear their interest in the updating of players' probability distributions over hands held and over points to be won after the deal, after the bids and during the course of play. Borel and Chéron recognized that, during the round of bidding, probability distributions become subjective, depending on a player's analysis of information received. Probability distributions were used to form expectations of numbers of tricks to be gained in a rubber. They made assumptions which considerably simplified the structure of bridge in order to analyse a game in which *'La meilleure ligne de jeu est celle qui rend maximum . . . l'espérance mathématique de chaque joueur dans les diverses éventualités'* (Borel and Chéron 1940, 2, phrases reversed).

PARIS AND PRINCETON

Since the establishment of game theory as a distinct field stems from the path-breaking book by von Neumann and Morgenstern, it is of interest how Borel and his collaborators interacted with von Neumann and his collaborator. Leonard has argued that the work on strategic games by French probabilists in the 1930s was entirely isolated from the developments leading to von Neumann and Morgenstern (1944). Commenting on the work of Borel, Ville and de Possel in the 1930s, Leonard (1992, 45) states that *'all this went by, it appears, unbeknownst to von Neumann'* (Leonard's emphasis). He subsequently noted that 'in December 1941, Morgenstern *accidentally* discovered Borel's volume (1938) containing the elementary minimax proof by Ville' (1992, 58, Leonard's emphasis; see Morgenstern 1976a, 811, and an excerpt from Morgenstern's diary in Rellstab 1992, 87). Given the war in Europe and the German occupation of France, December 1941 is not an exceptionally late date for a 1938 French book to be noticed in Princeton, accidentally or otherwise, and is well before the completion of von Neumann and Morgenstern (1944), the preface to which is dated January 1943. The proof of the minimax theorem used by von Neumann and Morgenstern is not the topological proof of von Neumann (1928a, b) but one that they stated carried further the elementarization of the proof by Ville (von Neumann and Morgenstern 1944, 154n). Von Neumann and Morgenstern (1944, 198n.) also credited Ville with '[a]n interesting step in this direction' towards a theory of games with continuous parameters. Von Neumann and Morgenstern (1944, 186–7n.) referred to the 'very instructive' consideration of poker by Borel (1938, 91–7) and indicated the relation of their notation to his. Like Borel, they treated a variant of poker in which all hands can be strictly ranked. They claimed, however, rather unfairly, that Borel's analysis of poker was 'mainly evaluations of probabilities applied to Poker in a more or less heuristic way, without a systematic use of any underlying general theory of games' (1944, 186n.). It is true that Borel had no general theory of games: he seems to have tended to consider games one case at a time and thus was greatly struck by phenomena such as differing numbers of pure strategies and differences in informational structure. Nonetheless, Borel's analysis was a valuable approach to many of the issues of what became game theory, and he was, as Fréchet (1965) claims, the first to define psychological games. Although von Neumann (1928b) cited Borel (1927), Borel's papers of the 1920s were unmentioned by von Neumann and Morgenstern (1944). von Neumann and Morgenstern's limited citation of Borel, while it provided the minimum necessary, was hardly generous.

A condensed version of von Neumann's 1928 proof of the minimax theorem was communicated to the French Academy of Sciences by Borel (von Neumann 1928a). A 40-page booklet on popular games by the French mathematician de Possel (1936) (which followed Borel (1924) in classifying games as strategic, based on pure chance) or involving bluff, hailed von Neumann's theorem and proof as fundamental to the theory of games (see Leonard 1992, 45–6). Leonard (1992, 46) states that 'no such credit [as that given by de Possel] is afforded von Neumann in Borel's work of the same period . . . . Remarkably, however, *no* mention is made of what became, for de Possel at least, the "théorème fondamental", that of von Neumann (1928b)' (Leonard's emphasis). Two pages later, however, Leonard quotes Borel's reference to von Neumann's 'important theorem' (Borel 1938, 115) in Borel's comments on Ville's note providing an elementary minimax proof. That is, discussion of von Neumann and the minimax theorem in Borel (1938) was restricted to Ville's note (1938, 105–13) and Borel's observations on that note (1938, 115–17), which Borel began *'Je tiens à remercier M. Jean Ville d'avoir bien voulu exposer pour les lecteurs de ce Livre, le théorème important de M. von Neumann; il a su en simplifier la démonstration et l'étendre au cas des variables continues'*. Confining von Neumann's minimax theorem to a dozen pages at the back of the book does not make it as central to the book as one might wish, but that is not the same as making no mention whatsoever of it.

Mathematicians in inter-war Continental Europe constituted a community whose members were in frequent contact with each other. In Menger's mathematical colloquium in Vienna, Jean Ville presented a paper on work which he published in 1939 in the same monograph series edited by Borel in which Borel and Chéron (1940) appeared (Popper 1976, 217). The papers by von Neumann and Wald on proving the existence of general economic equilibrium were published in the proceedings of that colloquium, and Wald, a regular participant in the Menger colloquium, applied the minimax theorem of von Neumann (1928b) to statistical decision functions. Lwów, where Steinhaus wrote an early paper on pursuit games and where Kurtatowski (of the 1929 Knaster–Kurtatowski–Mazurkiewicz paper on fixed points for an n-dimensional simplex) taught, might seem much more isolated than Paris or Vienna. Such isolation is contradicted by *The 'Scottish Book'* (Mauldin 1981) of problems posed at informal sessions of the Lwów branch of the Polish Mathematical Society, which includes problems posed by Fréchet, who contributed a fascicule to Borel's *Traité* (Problems 117, 118), and von

Neumann (Problem 163, offering a bottle of whiskey of measure strictly greater than zero as the prize for a solution, and an addendum to Ulam's Problem 139). Such notable French mathematicians as Lebesgue visited the Lwów of Steinhaus, Banach, Kurtatowski, Kac and Ulam. Such international communication ended with the German *anschluss* with Austria, the German occupation of Paris, and the successive Soviet occupation, German occupation and Soviet annexation of Lwów. (See Chapter 1 for more information on the problems of *The Scottish Book*.)

CONCLUSION

Emile Borel and his associates remained active in considering strategic games after 1928. Borel taught a course on the application of probability to games of chance at the Faculty of Sciences in Paris in 1936–1937 – notes of his lectures were compiled into a book by Ville. Noteworthy features of that book were an emphasis on information, the introduction of Colonel Blotto games in both military and economic contexts, a discussion of raising strategies in two-person poker, and Ville's elementary proof of von Neumann's minimax theorem and extension of minimax to continuous variables. The book led to collaboration between Borel and a newspaper bridge editor, Chéron, on a long book on a particularly intricate game of information: bridge. The outbreak of World War II disrupted Borel's research until after von Neumann and Morgenstern's 1944 volume had surpassed Borel's pre-war work on games. The Paris and Princeton writers on strategic games acknowledged each other's contributions, even if rather sparingly. The minimax proof contributed by Ville to Borel (1938) was the basis for the still clearer and more elementary proof of von Neumann and Morgenstern (1944).

9

VON NEUMANN AND MORGENSTERN IN HISTORICAL PERSPECTIVE[1]

Von Neumann and Morgenstern's *Theory of Games and Economic Behavior* (1944) made great advances in the analysis of strategic games and in the axiomatization of measurable utility theory and drew the attention of economists and other social scientists to these subjects. In the inter-war period, several papers and monographs on strategic games had been published, including work by von Neumann (1928) and Morgenstern (1935), as well as by Borel (1921, 1924, 1927, 1938), Ville (1938), de Possel (1936) and Steinhaus (1925), but these were known only to a small community of Continental European mathematicians. Von Neumann and Morgenstern thrust strategic games above the horizon of the economics profession. Their work was the basis for post-war research in game theory, initially a specialized field with applications to military strategy and statistical decision theory, but eventually permeating industrial organization and public choice and influencing macroeconomics and international trade.

The initial impact of the *Theory of Games* was not based on direct readership of the work. The mathematical training of the typical, or even fairly extraordinary, economist of the time was no preparation for comprehending over 600 pages of formal reasoning by an economist of the calibre of von Neumann, even though von Neumann and Morgenstern provided much more narration of the analysis than von Neumann would have offered to an audience of mathematicians. Apart from its effect on Wald and a few other contributors to *Annals of Mathematics*, the impact of the *Theory of Games* was mediated through the efforts of a small group of eminent and soon-to-be-eminent scholars who read and digested the work and wrote major review articles. The amount of space accorded these reviews and review articles by journal editors was extraordinary, recalling the controversy following the publication of Keynes' *General Theory*, but there was an important difference. Economists might find the *General Theory* a difficult book, but they read it (until recent years). Apart from the handful of young mathematicians and mathematically-inclined economists specializing in the new field of game theory, most economists had to rely on Hurwicz or Simon, Stone or Wald, or another reviewer for a sense of what von Neumann and Morgenstern had achieved and proposed.

THE BACKGROUND

Preceding chapters of this book have discussed the early literature of strategic games or war, commerce and politics, as well as cards and chess. The historical setting for von Neumann and Morgenstern's *Theory of Games and Economic Behavior* consisted of two sets of writings closer to them in time and place. Several economists, notably Cournot, Edgeworth, Böhm-Bawerk and Zeuthen, had considered the strategic interaction of market participants (see Schmidt 1990). Between the two world wars, a number of Continental European mathematicians interested in probability theory took the step from games of pure chance to games of strategy. The mathematical models of war and peace devised by Lanchester (1916) and Richardson (1919), and those of politics such as Dodgson's (1884g), remained apart until the 1950s.

Borel (1924) started from Bertrand's 1889 discussion of the difficulty of finding an optimal pure strategy for the game of *chemin de fer*. As discussed in Chapter 7, Borel (1921, 1924, 1927) formulated the concepts of randomization through mixed strategies (which were also defined), elimination of bad (dominated) strategies and the solution of a strategic game. He found minimax mixed strategy solutions for specific games with finite numbers of pure strategies. He did not, however, prove that two-person zero-sum games would have minimax solutions in general. He initially conjectured that games with larger finite numbers of possible pure strategies would not have minimax solutions, not noticing that this contradicted his conjecture that games with a continuum of strategies would have minimax solutions. Borel expressed his belief that the theory of psychological games would have economic and military applications.

Von Neumann (1928b) stated the minimax theorem for two-person zero-sum games with finite numbers of pure strategies and constructed the first valid proof of the theorem, using a topological approach based on Brouwer's fixed point theorem. He noted in his paper that his theorem and proof solved a problem posed by Borel, to whom he sent a copy of the paper. Borel published a communication of von Neumann's result in the proceedings of the Academie des Sciences (von Neumann 1928a). Von Neumann learned of Borel's work on the subject after completing a preliminary version, but he already knew Zermelo's 1913 proof that the game of chess has a solution, having corrected an error in the Zermelo paper in correspondence in 1927 (Kuhn and Tucker 1958, 105).

Von Neumann's 1928 minimax paper was acclaimed by de Possel (1936). Borel explored psychological games further in one number of his vast treatise on probability (Borel 1938). In this work, he analysed a military allocation game of the type now known as Colonel Blotto and his student and collaborator, Ville, citing von Neumann, provided the first elementary, non-topological proof of the minimax theorem and extended the theorem to games with a continuum of strategies (see Dimand and Dimand 1992). Von Neumann and Morgenstern (1944) referred to Borel's 1938 discussion of poker and bluffing and to Ville's minimax proof, which they revised to make it more elementary. Their book did not cite Borel's earlier papers.

Von Neumann continued to display an occasional interest in the mathematics of games during the 1930s. In April 1937, the mathematics section of the *Science News Letter* reported a talk given by von Neumann at Princeton about such games as stone–scissors–paper and a simplified version of poker. In November 1939 he listed the 'Theory of Games' as a possible topic for his lectures as a visiting professor at the University of Washington the following summer, and mentioned having unpublished material on poker (Leonard 1992, 50; Rellstab in Weintraub 1992, 90). Most importantly, he cited his 1928a article in his famous paper on general economic equilibrium, published in 1937 in the 1935–1936 proceedings of Menger's seminar, noting that 'The question whether our problem has a solution is oddly connected with that of a problem occurring in the Theory of Games dealt with elsewhere' (Baumol and Goldfeld 1968, 302n.). Even before meeting Morgenstern in Princeton, von Neumann was aware that his minimax theorem was relevant to economic theory.

Morgenstern brought to the *Theory of Games* the other stream of work recognised in retrospect as analysis of games: the economic contributions of Cournot on duopoly and especially Böhm-Bawerk on bargaining in a horse market. Böhm-Bawerk was cited five times in von Neumann and Morgenstern (1944), more often than anyone else except the mathematician Birkhoff.

The treatment of Morgenstern in the literature has been rather curious. He has been credited with encouraging von Neumann to write on game theory, with the Holmes–Moriarty example of Morgenstern (1928, 1935b) and with having '*accidentally* discovered Borel's volume (1938) containing the elementary minimax proof by Ville' (Leonard 1992, 58; Leonard's emphasis). To Mirowski (1992, 130), 'the early Oskar Morgenstern looked more or less like a typical Austrian economist of the fourth generation', while Leonard (1992, 52) noted that Morgenstern 'remained personally incapable of taking the theoretical steps that he himself envisioned ... in his continuous agitation for mathematical rigor, he was ultimately calling for a theoretical approach in which thinkers of his own kind would have increasingly little place'. These remarks occur in a conference volume (Weintraub 1992) on the occasion of the donation of the Morgenstern papers to the Duke University Library. (Leonard (1995, 753–4) views Morgenstern's contribution as more serviceable, but he still seems to us to undervalue the critical work of an economist who was less able at constructive work.) They do not do justice to the economist who was co-author not only to von Neumann on game theory, but also to Granger on the spectral analysis of stock prices (two articles in Schotter 1976, 329–86; and a book, Granger and Morgenstern 1970) and Kemeny and Thompson on mathematical models of expanding von Neumann economies (three papers in Schotter 1976, 73–133; and a book, Morgenstern and Thompson 1976) – contributions not cited in the 1992 conference volume.

One early work in particular identifies Morgenstern as a most atypical Austrian economist. The *Encyclopedia of Social Sciences*, commissioning articles by the outstanding experts in their fields, such as Mitchell on business cycles, Bloch on the feudal system and Kuznets on national income, reached Vienna to assign a long article on mathematical economics (within the article on economics) to Morgenstern (1931). This article is listed in the bibliography of Morgenstern's writings in Schotter (1976), but has otherwise been neglected. Although Morgenstern was an economist, not a mathematician, and was very conscious of the contrast between his mathematical training and ability and that of von Neumann and Wald, he was well acquainted with the existing body of mathematical economics and his mathematical knowledge was distinguished for economics profession of his time.

Morgenstern (1931, 366) offered a strikingly heretical reinterpretation of Austrian economics and its founder Menger: 'Although Menger did not employ mathematical symbols he is listed by Irving Fisher in his bibliography of mathematical economics and quite properly so, for Menger resorts to mathematical methods of reasoning. This is true also of many later representatives of the Austrian school.'[2] He rejected objections to the use of mathematics in economics that 'tend to identify mathematics with infinitesimal calculus and overlook the existence of such branches of mathematics as are adapted to dealing with qualities and discrete quantities; moreover mathematics is no more to be identified with the "mechanical" than ordinary logic' (1931, 364). The application of discrete mathematics to economics is not the only development anticipated by Morgenstern in 1931, for he also criticised Cassel, who 'took over Walras' equations in a simplified form, but in his presentation there are more equations than unknowns; that is, the conditions of equilibrium are overdetermined' (1931, 367). This preceded similar criticisms of Cassel by Neisser in 1932, by Stackelberg and by Zeuthen, the last two in 1933 in the *Zeitschrift für Nationalökonomie* edited by Morgenstern. Interesting for his knowledge of earlier work are Morgenstern's brief discussions of Cournot (1838), 'even at present considered a masterpiece of mathematical economic reasoning'[3] and of Edgeworth, who 'originated the idea of the contract curve, which presents the indeterminateness of conditions of exchange between two individuals;[4] it should be said, however, that Menger before him treated the same notion in a non-mathematical form' (1931, 365, 368). This point about the contract curve was also made in Morgenstern's 1927 obituary of his acquaintance Edgeworth, in which he made the unkept promise that 'The substance of Edgeworth's work will be analyzed at another occasion' (Schotter 1976, 478, 480).

What is noteworthy about these early articles by Morgenstern is his eye for what would be of lasting interest in the application of mathematics to economics: Edgeworth's contract curve, the inadequacy of Cassel's attempted proof of existence of general equilibrium, discrete mathematics. Morgenstern was not attracted by more chimerical approaches to economics dressed up in mathematical garb such as business cycle forecasting based on fixed periodicities, Major Douglas' A + B theorem of Social Credit, or Creedy's 1934 *Econometrica* paper explaining economic fluctuations by rigid analogy to Newton's laws of mechanics (assuming, for example, that at constant times the rate of acceleration of spending equals the unspent balance of income, in analogy with Newton's Third Law). Morgenstern's first book was an attack on mechanical business cycle forecasts (Morgenstern 1928).

In the 1930s, Morgenstern attended the mathematical colloquium of Karl Menger (son of the economist) and was tutored in mathematics by Wald, whom Morgenstern, on Menger's recommendation, had hired at the Austrian Institute for Business Cycle Research. Such an attempt at keeping up with the frontier in mathematical economics was highly unusual for an economist of the time. Morgenstern presented his paper on 'Perfect foresight and economic equilibrium' (1935b), expounding the problem of strategic interaction, illustrated by Moriarty's pursuit of Holmes (1928, 98; 1935b, 173–4; von Neumann and Morgenstern 1953, 176–8) and citing articles by Menger and Wald, in Menger's colloquium. At the presentation, the Czech mathematician, Eduard Cech, drew Morgenstern's attention to von Neumann (1928a) on game theory (Morgenstern 1976, 806). Morgenstern did not, however, meet von Neumann in Vienna, because Menger and Wald accepted von Neumann's paper on general equilibrium (in Baumol and Goldfeld 1968) for the proceedings without von Neumann presenting it in the seminar.

Morgenstern took a particular interest in the work of Schlesinger, Wald and von Neumann on the existence of general equilibrium with non-negative prices (the Walrasian method of counting equations and unknowns failed to count the non-negativity constraints). After Wald presented his two technical papers on the subject (translated in Baumol and Goldfeld 1968), 'In view of the significance of this work and the restricted character of the publication, I persuaded Wald to write an expository article' (Morgenstern 1951, 494). A translation of Wald's expository article was published in *Econometrica* in 1951 as a companion piece to Morgenstern's memorial article. Morgenstern's review article on Hicks extensively cited the Wald and von Neumann papers from Menger's colloquium in attacking Hicks for attempting to prove the existence of equilibrium by counting equations and unknowns (Morgenstern 1941, 192–9), the first presentation of this research in English, although carrying the once-again unfulfilled promise that 'The discussion of the work done by the two mathematicians, J. von Neumann and A. Wald, will be reserved for another occasion when more space is available for a presentation of the fundamental principles involved' (1941, 197n.).

After meeting von Neumann at Princeton, Morgenstern engaged him in the long and fruitful conversation about games that initially was expected to produce a long paper of up to 50 pages for submission to the *Journal of Political Economy*, then a pamphlet of perhaps a hundred pages, then a short book, and finally a book of well over 600 pages (see Morgenstern 1976). The extended conversation busied von Neumann, who did not lack other interests from quantum mechanics to computing, with careful exposition and the exploration of many cases and conditions. The resulting long book full of mathematical notation was not regarded as a commercial proposition by the publisher. Just as Fisher's *Making of Index Numbers* (1922) required the financial support of the monetary heretics Foster and Catchings to be published, the *Theory of Games and Economic Behavior* required a subsidy to the Princeton University Press of $4,000 of Rockefeller money. This source of funding may be related to Morgenstern having directed one of the European business cycle institutes supported by the Rockefeller Foundation. Mirowski (1991, 240) finds another motivation for the subsidy, but his claim that 'J. D. Rockefeller . . . at that time happened to be Chief of Naval Operations' is mistaken (and would have surprised Admiral King). Without the extended conversation between Morgenstern and von Neumann, there would have been no *Theory of Games and Economic Behavior*.

THE ACHIEVEMENT

To examine psychological games as exhaustively as possible, von Neumann and Morgenstern elected to use a method of axiom, definition and successive refinement. This, a novel approach in economics, led them to deal more carefully and explicitly with such issues as the definition of 'solution' and a game's information structure and timing than had previous authors. It also led them, aware as they were of the St Petersburg Paradox, to consider how to model a player's payoff – another question which had previously been finessed rather than pondered. This motivated their demarcation of conditions under which a von Neumann–Morgenstern utility function exists, a subsidiary innovation which captured the economics profession earlier than game theory *per se*.

Borel, von Neumann (1928a, b) and Ville had not questioned whether minimax strategy gave 'the' solution to a game. Early game-theoretic writers blithely employed solution concepts which seemed appropriate to the problems they analysed, whether the issue was card games (Waldegrave, Bertrand, Borel) or the outcomes of voting rules (most notably Dodgson). Writers of works in economics, on the other hand, often tended (and tend) to equate solution with competitive market clearance, although models of monopoly, oligopoly and collusion had been discussed frequently, informally since Adam Smith, and more formally beginning with Cournot.

Von Neumann and Morgenstern were the first writers to define a concept of static economic equilibrium that did not depend on limiting the form of interaction being modelled to perfect competition or, indeed, to markets. Von Neumann and Morgenstern specified that

> A set S of elements (imputations) is a solution when it possesses these two properties:
> No y contained in S is dominated by an x contained in S.
> Every y not contained in S is dominated by some x contained in S.
> (von Neumann and Morgenstern 1947, 40)

Unlike previous treatments of equilibrium, such as the general competitive equilibrium of Walras, Pareto and Fisher, von Neumann and Morgenstern's definition of equilibrium did not depend on any particular 'rules of the game', although the application of the concept is model-dependent. When bidding was not part of the strategy space he considered, Borel assumed that a game had been solved when players maximized their minimum probability of winning. For Walras, an equilibrium allocation was feasible and such that consumers maximized utility subject to their budget constraints and producers' profit maximized. Von Neumann and Morgenstern's 'solution' depended on dominance – on players ruling out strategies which would definitely disadvantage them. The application of 'dominance' depends on the objectives of players and the rules of the game played: this definition of solution applies to problems of individual optimization, cooperative games, games of tiddlywinks and games of politics.

Von Neumann and Morgenstern stressed that, where the game permitted and where individuals could benefit from it, coalition formation was crucial to the concept of a solution. Hurwicz (1945, 517) noted that Stackelberg had remarked in 1932 on the possibility of coalition formation between duopolists, '[b]ut no rigorous theory is developed for such situations (although an outline of possible developments is given). This is where the *Theory of Games* has made real progress.' Similarly, Cournot (1838) had noted the difference between joint and 'independent' profit-maximization for duopolists and this was also discussed by Zeuthen. Moreover, considering coalition as a possible strategy in a game was analogous to the concerns of Coase (1937) in considering that the formation of coalitions (organizations) might be more efficient than market contracts, although there is little reason to believe either author had read Coase's article. They stated explicitly that their concept of solution was in no sense an optimum and that it was not, in general, unique.

Their explicit consideration of information partitions in games (i.e. possibly imperfect information), combined with a definition of solution which did not depend on optimality and in which various coalitions might form, delivered multiple equilibria in most games. While writers on market structure such as Stackelberg were interested in explaining and rationalizing multiple equilibria, and Edgeworth emphasized the indeterminacy of bilateral exchange, recognition of the possibility of multiple equilibria was rare among economists in general. Keynes' *General Theory*, which was general in the sense of considering all states from which there was no tendency for agents to move, had examined multiple equilibria, though in a less systematic form than *The Theory of Games*. Keynes argued that the classical full employment equilibrium was only the limiting case of a range of possible equilibrium levels of employment. It has been observed that, unlike many current game theorists, von Neumann and Morgenstern were attracted rather than disturbed by a multiplicity of equilibria (Shubik 1992; Mirowski 1992).

Minimax strategies as player objectives stemmed naturally from von Neumann and Morgenstern's emphasis on zero-sum games, which arose from the concern with gambling by precursors in game-theory. In such games A's loss is B's gain, the situation is one of complete conflict and maximizing the minimum payoff one can achieve if one's opponent plays in a hostile fashion is quite reasonable. Solutions derived from a minimax objective were a subset of solutions as defined by von Neumann and Morgenstern. These sorts of equilibria, used for much of a book which concentrated on normal form representation and one time play, was brilliantly critiqued by Ellsberg (1956). Why, asked Ellsberg, wouldn't a player be willing to take a little more risk for the chance of greater gain? What if a player had some priors on how her opponent was likely to play which indicated the possibility of greater gains by a strategy other than minimax?

Among other things, Ellsberg was implicitly targeting a concept tacit in von Neumann and Morgenstern's book: the assumption of large numbers as a way to deal with behaviour under uncertainty. Von Neumann and Morgenstern meticulously confined themselves to the consideration of games to be played once when they specified that their analysis was static. But in a game of imperfect information to be played once, where players are not obliged to divulge their strategies, it is not clear why they would use a maximin strategy unless they were facing a large pool of potential opponents who might behave in all sorts of ways. In particular, where a mixed strategy is part of an equilibrium, the idea of random play in a one-time game is a problem. It is easy enough to interpret random play by one's opponents on the basis of each opponent coming from a large pool of potential players of different types. It is less easy, however, to rationalize a player's decision to play a mixed strategy in a one-time game unless one assumes the player wishes to tell her opponent her strategy before using it. Harsanyi (1973), however, suggested in defence of mixed strategy that each player might know her own intended pure strategy exactly for a given coup, but not those of the other players. In such a case, a mixed strategy might be a player's estimate, subject to 'psychological uncertainty', of what others will do.

A game of imperfect information, such as those in which players move simultaneously, partakes of an uncertainty (noted by Borel) which depends on the play of one's opponents. Indeed, there is such psychological uncertainty about any game which does not have a unique equilibrium in pure strategies. Von Neumann and Morgenstern, whose emphasis was on choice problems with a high degree of interdependence between agents, were chiefly concerned with games in which there was uncertainty. Unlike their predecessors, they were worried about simply taking an expectation of monetary payoffs (in the case of gambling games) or probabilities of winning (in the case of elections). Aware of the St Petersburg paradox, but aware of the advantages of using expected money payoffs, they discussed the conditions legitimizing a von Neumann–Morgenstern utility function as an apologia for using expected (utility) payoff in a player's criterion. In so doing, they both acknowledged and finessed the problems of measurability and observability which have remained bugbears of experimental games.

A source of uncertainty to the player of a game is that *he cannot know how an opponent values money payoffs* – whether an opponent takes satisfaction in altruism or in revenge, apart from her valuation of augmented income. Shubik's (1992) description of 'McCarthy's revenge rule' is an amusing example. This is, at least, equally a problem to an experimental game theorist, whether an academic or a Williamsonian entrepreneur. It is potentially a great problem in analysing games, one which von Neumann and Morgenstern assumed away by positing that individual choice obeyed the axioms which allow the use of expected utility. Game theorists have differed about the importance of the axiomatization of (individually) measurable utility in the *Theory of Games and Economic Behavior*. Some have seen it as essential, others as a desideratum. In a way, it was both. Von Neumann and Morgenstern, in effect, said: 'There is a chasm in our sidewalk; under the following circumstances it does not exist' and stepped over it.

Although a number of thinkers had analysed problems in a style which would later become game theory, von Neumann and Morgenstern originally systematized the questions being asked in this branch of choice theory. It was they who first described games as a class, who first delimited a game's information structure, drew a game tree and defined a solution to a game. Whatever one might think of the von Neumann–Morgenstern utility function and its role in their book, it must be acknowledged that they looked a substantial difficulty in the face before ignoring it.

THE IMPACT

Journal editors allocated surprising amounts of space to reviews of the *Theory of Games*. Marschak (1946) took 19 pages in the *Journal of Political Economy*, Hurwicz (1945) 17 pages in the *American Economic Review*, Stone (1948) 17 pages in the *Economic Journal*, Justman (1949) 18 pages in the *Revue d'Economie Politique*, Chacko (1950) 17 pages in the *Indian Journal of Economics*, while Kaysen's more sceptical account of 'A Revolution in Economic Theory?' (1946) not only occupied 15 pages of the *Review of Economic Studies*, but began on page 1 of the journal's 1946–1947 volume, unusual prominence for a review article. Guilbaud's review in *Economique appliquée* (1949) was longer still, taking 45 journal pages (29 in translation). Shorter reviews of four to eight pages appeared in economics journals in Switzerland (Anderson 1949), Denmark (Leunbach 1948), and Sweden (Ruist 1949). Given normal publishing lags and the need for the reviewers to master 625 pages of technical prose, reviews began to appear quite soon after publication. The first review, in the *American Journal of Sociology*, was by Simon (1945), who heard about the *Theory of Games* before its publication and within weeks of its appearance 'spent most of my 1944 Christmas vacation (days and some nights) reading it' (Simon 1991, 108, 114). Simon (1995) relates that, having read von Neumann (1928), he had some idea of what to expect and that he had been concerned that 'all that was new and important in Chapters 4 and 5 of *Administrative Behavior*', then being prepared for publication, might have been 'scooped'.

The length of the review articles and the tone of most of them expressed excitement and enthusiasm. They introduced such concepts as pure and mixed strategies, randomization, the solution to a game and the minimax theorem to an audience of economists uneasy with mathematical reasoning and used to thinking about competitive equilibrium rather than strategic interaction. Simon (1991, 326) recalls that 'In 1950, it was still difficult to get a paper published in the *American Economic Review* if it contained equations (diagrams were more acceptable)'. Simon, who championed mathematics as a tool for the social sciences, wrote an enthusiastic review despite a number of concerns about game theory, which he expressed to Morgenstern in a private letter. Like Ellsberg, Simon was concerned at von Neumann and Morgenstern's stress on an extremely defensive style of play by agents and, furthermore, he was dubious about von Neumann and Morgenstern's definitions of 'solution' and 'stability'.[5] More than anything else, Simon felt that 'economics is an empirical science that should be empirically grounded', and that a mathematical theory which did not predict observed behaviour was not the most useful of tools. He writes: 'It seems that, at age 29, I was more interested in spreading the gospel of mathematics for the social sciences than I was in challenging *The Theory of Games* publicly. I wonder if, having become considerably older and more crotchety, I would make the same decision today' (Simon 1995).

Hurwicz's review article, reprinted in the American Economic Association *Readings in Price Theory* and in Newman's *The World of Mathematics* (1956), eschewed equations, as did the other reviews. This was necessary to make the work accessible to the bulk of the economics profession at a time when a calculus course was not generally required for a doctorate in economics in the USA and even Keynes' *General Theory* had recently been dismissed as unreadably mathematical by G. D. H. Cole, Reader in Economics at Oxford (M. Cole 1971), and Leacock, Dow Professor of Economics and Political Science at McGill: Leacock 'opened the book but, unfortunately, at one of the few pages with algebraic equations. He thereupon threw it down and, in disgust, as he walked away, said: "Goldenberg, this is the end of John Maynard Keynes" ' (Goldenberg, in Collard 1975, 49).

The barrier to comprehension by economists of the time presented by mathematical expression is illustrated by the response to von Neumann's paper on general equilibrium in the proceedings of the Menger colloquium. Kaldor (1989, viii), to whom von Neumann sent an offprint, recalled that 'Unfortunately the paper was quite beyond me except for the beginning', while Goodwin (1989, 125) remarked 'alas, reported back to Schumpeter that it was no more than a piece of mathematical ingenuity'. Hicks (1966, 80n.) recalled 'from personal recollection, that [von Neumann] had these things in mind in September 1933, when I met him with Kaldor in Budapest. Of course I did not understand what he was saying!'

The prominence and enthusiasm of this wave of major review articles achieved little in stimulating work on game theory among economists. The economics profession as a whole displayed nothing comparable to the interest and activity generated among mathematics and economics graduate students at Princeton. Even the reviewers themselves wrote little more on game theory, apart from Wald, whose links with von Neumann and Morgenstern and work extending game theory to statistical decisions predated his review, and Guilbaud (1952, 1960, 1968). Kaysen wrote a paper in 1952 on choice of strategy under uncertainty, Hurwicz (1953) reflected on 'What has happened to the theory of games?', and Stone discussed his original review article in the Royal Economic Society's centenary volume, but otherwise they pursued other interests.

Morgenstern recorded in his diary (quoted by Mirowski 1991, 239 n.13) both the hostility of economists when he discussed game theory in seminars (in contrast to the praise of most published reviews) and his impression that they had not read the book. 'None of them has read *The Theory of Games*' at Harvard in 1945, 'Allais opposed . . . Nobody has even seen the book' in Paris in June 1947, 'Ropke even said later that game theory was Viennese coffeehouse gossip' in December 1947, and in Rotterdam in 1950 'They had heard of game theory, but Tinbergen, Frisch, etc. wanted to know nothing about it because it disturbs them'.[6] The seminars were at least scheduled and attended, even if without enthusiasm from even the future Nobel laureates Allais, Frisch and Tinbergen, some of the most mathematically-sophisticated economists of the time. Allais was particularly critical of von Neumann and Morgenstern's axiomatization of utility theory and their identification of rational behaviour with maximization of expected utility.

At Princeton, Morgenstern's interests were not shared by his colleagues in the economics department and the view that 'this new mathematical bag of tricks was of little relevance to economics . . . was put forward in particular by Jacob Viner whose favourite comment on the subject was that if game theory could not even solve the game of chess, how could it be of use in the study of economic life, which is considerably more complex than chess' (Shubik 1992, 153). Viner's attitude was especially unfortunate, for his hostility to mathematical formalism blinded him to the closeness of game theory to his own thought on strategy. In a lecture to the American Philosophical Society in November 1945, published in January 1946, Viner analysed 'The implications of the atomic bomb for international relations'. He considered the choice of a strategy on the assumption that the other side will respond by inflicting as much damage as it can: surprise was worthless if the attacked country could still respond with nuclear weapons (Freedman 1981, 28, 42–3; Kaplan 1983, 27). Viner, however, 'never was much of a mathematician' (Kaplan 1983, 14) and appears never to have connected his reflections on military strategy to the game theory that he derided.

Aversion to mathematics and failure to read a long, technical book cannot entirely account for the limited response of economists to the *Theory of Games*. The failure of the *Theory of Games* to affect the mainstream of the discipline in the first decades after its publication is shown most clearly by the Cowles Commission for Research in Economics, located at the University of Chicago from 1939 until it moved to Yale as the Cowles Foundation in 1955. Cowles stood out as the centre of mathematical economics and its research staff would not be disconcerted by the hundreds of pages of mathematical notation used by von Neumann and Morgenstern. The back cover of the paperback edition (von Neumann and Morgenstern 1967) quotes effusive praise from four reviews (identified by journal, not reviewer). Three of these reviews were written by members of Cowles: Hurwicz (then at the University of Illinois), Marschak, who was director of research at Cowles, and Simon, then teaching at the Illinois Institute of Technology where he attended the topology course given by his Illinois Tech colleague, Menger. The Hurwicz and Marschak review articles were reprinted together in 1946 as Cowles Commission Paper no. 13, and were endorsed by von Neumann and Morgenstern, who recommended these reviews to the 'economically interested reader' in the Preface to their second edition. At Cowles, if anywhere, game theory could be expected to be taken up by economists.

The list of Cowles Commission and Foundation Papers (reprints) and Discussion Papers in the *Cowles Fiftieth Anniversary* volume (Arrow *et al.* 1991, 109–84) shows what happened. Cowles Commission Paper no. 40 in 1950 by Arrow *et al.* concerned Bayes and minimax solutions of sequential decision problems, following Wald's investigation of minimax solutions to statistical decision problems. Cowles Commission Paper no. 75 in 1953 was 'Three Papers on Recent Developments in Mathematical Economics and Econometrics' from the *Papers and Proceedings* of the American Economic Association and, together with Koopmans on activity analysis and Strotz on cardinal utility, included Hurwicz's reflections on what had become of game theory. Otherwise, there is nothing related to game theory until Shubik, who had been a graduate student in Morgenstern's seminar at Princeton, began appearing in the list with Cowles Foundation Paper no. 164 in 1961. Similarly, among the discussion papers, the only reference to game theory before Shubik's arrival at Cowles was in 1952, when Beckmann considered

'The problem of musical chairs and an equivalent 2-person game' (Discussion Paper no. 2044) and Tornqvist examined 'Some game theoretic points of view on scientific research' (no. 2056). Mirowski (1991, 239) reports finding no papers on game theory among Cowles Discussion Papers 101 to 151, dated April 1947 to April 1950, but, according to the list in the *Cowles Fiftieth Anniversary* volume, the lowest-numbered discussion paper in those years was no. 201 in 1947 (the numbering of the economics discussion papers jumped from 299 for the last in 1950 to 2001 for the first in 1951 because the statistics series had begun with no. 301 and the mathematics series with no. 401, both in 1947). In the Cowles Monograph series, Monograph no. 13 (a conference volume on activity analysis in 1951) includes a paper on 'Iterative solutions of games by fictitious play' by Brown who, the previous year, had collaborated with von Neumann on 'Solution of games by differential equations' in the first volume of Princeton *Contributions to the Theory of Games* (Kuhn and Tucker 1950).

This prolonged paucity of game theory in the publications and discussion papers of the Cowles staff after the initial laudatory reviews is startling, given that the Cowles Commission held seven seminars on the theory of games from January to April 1949 (Debreu, in Arrow *et al.* 1991, 30). Instead of this seminar series leading the Cowles researchers into game theory, what caught their attention was Marschak's discussion in one of the seminars of von Neumann and Morgenstern's axiomatic version of cardinal utility (unique up to a positive linear transformation), notably in an appendix added to the 1947 second edition. The von Neumann and Morgenstern theory of measurable utility struck a familiar note, following as it did a long history of controversy over ordinal versus cardinal utility. Strategic interaction, reduction of a game-tree to the strategic form of a game, or the stable-set solution of the coalitional form of a game elicited no such response. The Cowles economists were attracted by a new twist to something familiar. The titles of Cowles Commission Discussion Papers nos. 226, 2002, 2012, 2021, 2039, 2083, 2105 and 2106 refer to measurable utility. The axiomatic approach of von Neumann and Morgenstern may also have influenced the axiomatic approach to social choice and general equilibrium theory adopted by such Cowles economists as Arrow and Debreu. Whitehead and Russell had attempted an axiomatization of the foundations of mathematics decades before in their *Principia Mathematica* and Kolmogorov (1933) had axiomatized the mathematical theory of probability, but economists had not followed their example.

Applied mathematicians responded more strongly to game theory. Copeland (1945) considered that 'Posterity may regard [the *Theory of Games*] as one of the major scientific achievements of the first half of the twentieth century'. The early substantive responses and contributions, as distinct from expository and evaluative reviews, appeared in the Princeton-based *Annals of Mathematics* or in the *Proceedings of the National Academy of Sciences*. Despite publication lags, the 1945 volume carried three game theoretic articles. Two of them were by Wald, then at Columbia (initially as Hotelling's research associate) but spending much of his time at the summer home of his wife's family in New Jersey and at nearby Princeton, attending Morgenstern's games seminar and lecturing (Morgenstern 1951, in Schotter 1976, 496–7). Wald (1945a) treated statistical decision as a game against nature, in an examination of statistical decision functions that minimized the maximum risk leading to Wald (1950). The shaping of statistical decision theory, through influence on Wald, was the greatest immediate consequence of the *Theory of Games*. Wald (1947) also provided a non-technical exposition of von Neumann and Morgenstern's book for readers of the *Review of Economic Statistics* (as it was then named) and lectured on game theory in Paris and Rome on the trip on which he died (Morgenstern 1951, in Schotter 1976, 497). Wald (1945b) extended the minimax theorem for zero-sum two-person games to certain cases with a continuum of strategies while Kaplanski (1945) explored the role of pure and mixed strategies in zero-sum two-person games. Between 1950 and 1959, four volumes of *Contributions to the Theory of Games*, edited by Kuhn and Tucker, then by Drescher *et al.* and finally by Luce and Tucker, appeared in the series of *Annals of Mathematics Studies* sponsored by the *Annals* through the Princeton University Press. This series published much of the most important work in game theory in that decade. Nash's paper on 'Noncooperative Games', a cornerstone of the next stage of game theory after von Neumann and Morgenstern (1944), and Robinson's 'An iterative method of solving a game' both appeared in the *Annals of Mathematics* in 1951. Loomis (1946), Dines (1947) and Nash (1950a, b) were published by the National Academy of Sciences. The economics profession, apart from the handful already specialized in game theory, are unlikely to have looked at the *Annals of Mathematics* or the *Naval Research Logistics Review*, founded in 1954 and coedited by Morgenstern, although the more technically-inclined economists would encounter game-theoretic articles by Nash, Shubik and others in *Econometrica*.

As a whole, the economics profession in the late 1940s and the 1950s did not take up the interest in game theory encouraged by the book reviewers and shared by Princeton's mathematics department and the strategists at the RAND Corporation and Office of Naval Research. The sheer size of the *Theory of Games* and the mass of mathematical notation, which turned out on closer study to be much more accessible than, say, von Neumann's 1928 article, impressed the reviewers who had committed themselves to reading the book, rather as readers of other difficult books, such as Keynes' *General Theory* or Marx's *Das Capital*, developing a vested interest in the importance of what they struggled through. Other economists, not bound by promises to any book review editor and hostile to mathematics, were repelled by these same features of the book. Acceptance by mainstream economists was also not helped by the sharply critical and condescending attitude of von Neumann and Morgenstern to such eminent works of more conventional economic theory as Hicks' *Value and Capital* (Morgenstern 1941, in Schotter 1976, 185–217) or Samuelson's *Foundations* (von Neumann quoted in Morgenstern's diary, Mirowski 1991, 239n.; cf. Mirowski 1992, 134 on von Neumann declining to review Samuelson's book). Morgenstern criticized Hicks for ignoring results that had been published only very recently by von Neumann and Wald and which may not have been known to Morgenstern himself when *Value and Capital* appeared in 1939. Economists did not regard eminence in another science as a guarantee of soundness in economics, as with Soddy, the Oxford Nobel laureate in chemistry and monetary heretic. Samuelson (1989, 115–16) pointedly listed great mathematicians whose economic writings were undistinguished or worse. The research staff and associates of the Cowles Commission, the outstanding concentration of economists who would not be put off by mathematical formalism, produced an initial flurry of reviews, but the only aspect of von Neumann and Morgenstern (1944) to capture their lasting attention was the theory of measurable utility.

Writing on 'Price Theory and Oligopoly' in 1947, Rothschild sounds remarkably prescient in discussing the then-current scope of game theory and the developments which he thought it might undergo:

A completely novel and highly ingenious general theoretical apparatus for... solution of the oligopoly problem has been recently created by John von Neumann and Oskar Morgenstern.... Unfortunately, at the time of writing this article I had no opportunity of obtaining a copy of this important book, and I had to rely on the very capable summaries given in the review articles by Leonid Hurwicz and Jacob Marschak....

There is no doubt that Neumann's and Morgenstern's approach surpasses in generality, rigour and elegance of treatment by far anything that could be achieved on the lines suggested in the following section of this article. At the same time, this very generality and rigour set, at the present stage of development of their theory, very serious limitations to the application of their theory to the price problem of the oligopolistic world. Not only are certain assumptions introduced for the sake of obtaining a more deterministic solution rather than for their relevance to the real world (e.g., the introduction of 'mixed strategies,' and the neglect of the influence which *variations* in profits may have on price policy), but it also seems that considerable difficulties present themselves when an attempt is made to deal with cases that involve more than three persons. And, above all, the theory is, at present, exclusively static....

It seems to me, therefore, that while the further development of the 'pure' theory expounded in *The Theory of Games and Economic Behavior* may some day yield a very powerful tool for treating oligopolistic price problems, its present stage justifies the simultaneous exploration of the more modest and pedestrian paths indicated in this article. Their greater concreteness and their allowance for dynamic factors may give them a greater usefulness than a more general, 'purer' theory can at present provide.

(Rothschild 1947, 449, fn.19)

In fact, for practical application, game theory has developed to become an invaluable conceptual tool for studying situations of strategic interdependence, where *ceteris* is not very *paribus* for reasonable agents. While game theory supplied constructive new perspectives for problems of general equilibrium with complete markets, it has been essential for studying choice in situations in which no markets obtain and in which markets are imperfect. Many of the problems noted by early critics of von Neumann and Morgenstern remain, of course: for many games, the definition of equilibrium and ideas of what constitutes reasonable play are still complicated by the issues of conjecturing the play of others which have been issues of much work on strategic interdependence from the beginning. Although experimental game theory has given much useful information about how people actually play, and hence how theorists might model their choices, these still remain interesting – and not yet resolved – questions. Game theorists have also worked backwards, studying how the rules of the game arise through mechanism design. Questions of change in rules of the game have been applied by the 'New Institutionalists'. Game theory has been developed as well through its application in such areas as political science and biology. Biology, in particular, has given rise to a new stream of thought, evolutionary game theory, in which agents are not thoroughly rational and successful strategies are those with the greatest survival value.

The community of scholars who responded to the challenge of game theory most immediately were the applied mathematicians, notably at Princeton. From their work, a later generation of economists would take the game theory that they applied to industrial organization, microeconomic theory, macro-economic policy coordination and international trade negotiations. The initial long, effusive reviews of von Neumann and Morgenstern (1944) in economics journals were followed by prolonged neglect by the bulk of the economics profession, but the long run influence of game theory on the discipline of economics has been great and the modern field of game theory stems from von Neumann and Morgenstern. Some landmark works in economics, such as Cournot (1838), were influential only after long delay. Others, such as Keynes' *Treatise on Money*, received great attention upon publication, but then faded from the discipline's consciousness. The *Theory of Games* is highly unusual in having faded from the mainstream of economics after being greeted by enthusiastic review articles, but eventually having its intellectual descendants reshape economics.

NOTES

1 INTRODUCTION:DEFINING GAME THEORY AND ITS HISTORY

1 Our definition, therefore, bears considerable resemblance to the characterization of John McDonald:

> Like all economic theories, the theory of games is based on the assumption that man seeks gain...[and] that man is rational.... The strategical situation in game theory lies in the interaction between two or more persons, each of whose actions is based on an expectation concerning the actions of others over whom he has no control.
>
> (McDonald 1950, 14–16)

2 While an agent may choose a mixed, or randomized, strategy and use a randomization device, this is simply one alternative in the agent's choice set, broadly understood. Similarly, agents may create a coordination device which uses a random process to yield signals which tell each player which of her strategies she should play, in order to avoid undesirable outcomes which might result from independently optimal strategies. However, the ultimate source of randomness for agent A in a game is B's choice of strategy, one element of which may be the use of a randomization device.

3 This explains, at least in part, the extent to which the analysis of behaviour under risk was tied up with the development of game theory. It was at least *necessary* for game theory to develop very far. While such material will be discussed to some extent, it is not part of our primary focus.

4 This issue, which has contributed a tension to game theory that has propelled a great deal of work, has not been satisfactorily settled despite the accomplishments of experimental game theorists.

5 Shortly before sending this manuscript to the publisher, we found that we are in substantial agreement with Robert J. Leonard (1994) not only on the reading of Cournot, but on the subject of a reading of early sources with an eye to tracking precursors. Our interests are, however, less methodological than his.

6 The maxi-min approach is one in which a player i is assumed to wish to choose a strategy which yields the best possible results if other players choose strategies which will give i the worst possible outcome, given i's choice of strategy. It is discussed further below.

7 A mixed strategy is one in which a positive probability is given to playing each of a number of possible strategies: choosing heads with probability 0.5 and tails with probability 0.5 in matching pennies (perhaps by flipping the coin) is an example.

158

8 One example of such assertions is Mirowski, in the introduction to his volume of
   Edgeworth's essays. Mirowski says that

> A modern orthodox economist reading [Edgeworth on price indetermi-
> nacy] might think it an anticipation of the displacement of Walrasian
> general equilibrium by a species of proto-game theory, but that would
> not be the way Edgeworth saw it. In his view, the only logical rationale
> for the law of one price, and therefore price itself as a rational numerical
> entity, was to be sought in the format of a limit theorem comparable to
> the central limit theorem;
>
> (Mirowski 1994, 42–3)

and that

> Various economists, concerned to tout game theory as the next great white
> hope of orthodox economics ... cite Edgeworth as their precursor. There is
> only minor justification in our narrative for [this] ....
>
> (Mirowski 1994, 60)

We would argue that how a theorist thinks about his work is not the only way
of thinking about it. (Similarly, we doubt that the game theorists Mirowski
(1991) discusses saw the influence of their military funders on the core of their
research, as Mirowski does.) Rather, we think it worthwhile to look at earlier
handling of problems which have subsequently become codified into the area
called game theory.

9 An example might be an event space S which is the point outcome of the roll of
   two dies, which are chosen at random from a set of two five-sided dies (with sides
   numbered from 1 to 5) and two six-sided dies (with sides numbered from 1 to 6),
   with each die falling on any given side with equal probability. Consider S_1 to be
   the event 'two five-sided dies were chosen', and S_2 to be the event 'the total is
   even'. Then $\text{Prob}(S_2|S_1) = (0.13)/(0.25) = 0.52$, while $\text{Prob}(S_2) = 0.505$.

10 Given the example of note 9, the probability that two five-sided dies have been
    rolled (event S_1), given that an even number has resulted (event S_2), is equal to
    $(0.52)(0.25)/(0.505) \approx .257$, as opposed to the unconditioned probability
    $\text{Prob}(S_1) = 0.25$. While, as with note 9 above, the difference between conditioned
    and unconditioned probabilities may seem small, the contribution of condition-
    ing information to an agent's well-being depends greatly on what rides on the
    chance.

11 Depending on the theorem, other properties vary somewhat. Similarly, the
    continuity requirements on the mapping $h(\cdot)$ vary from theorem to theorem.

12 A simplex is a set of all positive real vectors of a particular dimension whose
    elements sum to 1.

13 Problems in probability were also contributed.

14 Problem 43, by Mazur, for solution of which a bottle of wine was offered as a
    prize, is:

> Definition of a certain game. Given is a set E of real numbers. A game
> between two players A and B is defined as follows: A selects an arbitrary
> interval d_1; B then selects an arbitrary segment (interval) d_2 contained in d_1;
> then A in his turn selects an arbitrary segment d_3 contained in d_2 and so on.
> A wins if the intersection $d_1, d_2, \ldots, d_n \ldots$ contains a point of the set E;
> otherwise, he loses. If E is a complement of a set of first category, there exists
> a method through which A can win; if E is a set of first category, there exists
> a method through which B will win.

Problem. It is true that there exists a method of winning for the player A only for those sets E whose complement is, in a certain interval, of first category; similarly, does a method of win exist for B if E is a set of first category? *Addendum*: Mazur's conjecture is true.

S. Banach
4 August, 1935
(Mauldin 1981, 113)

Problem 67, by Banach, is:

(A modification of Mazur's game ....)

We call a half of the set E [in symbols, $(1/2)E$] an arbitrary subset H E such that the sets E, H, $E-H$ are of equal power.

(1) Two players A and B give in turn sets E_i, $i = 1, 2, \ldots$ *ad infinitum* so that $E_i = (1/2)E_{i-1}$ $i = 1, 2, \ldots$ where E_0 is a given abstract set. Player A wins if the product $E_1 E_2 \ldots E_i E_{i+1} \ldots$ is vacuous.

(2) The game, similar to one above, with the assumption that $E_i = 1/2[E_0 - E_1 - \ldots - E_{i-1}]$ $i = 2, 3, \ldots$ *ad infinitum*, and $E_1 = (1/2)E_0$. Player A wins if $E_1 + E_2 + \ldots = E_0$.

Is there a method of win for player A? If E_0 is of power cofinal with $\aleph_0$, then player A has a method of win. Is it only in this case? In particular, solve the problem if E_0 is the set of real numbers.

(Mauldin 1981, 138)

15 Our inclusion of a number of less-analytical works of nineteenth-century voting theory forms, perhaps, something of an exception to this rule. We discuss this literature, mostly on various forms of proportional representation, because of its extreme earliness in considering anything approaching cooperative games, and because we feel that it serves as valuable context for modern readers (especially North Americans) in looking at the model of Dodgson (1884g) *Principles of Parliamentary Representation*. Dodgson's (or Carroll's) model is a very early subgame-perfect consideration of mechanism design which has been little read, and which still has much to offer public choice theorists.

16 In Aumann and Maschler (1985).

17 Braithwaite (1955) would seem to have been the first to publish an application of game theory proper to philosophy.

18 We do not follow Chimenti's analysis, which is more detailed. There has also been a great deal of theological argument about this passage of the *Pensées*, which will remain undiscussed and uncited here.

2 STRATEGIC INTERDEPENDENCE: COURNOT AND DUOPOLY

1 Ekelund and Hébert (1990) and Theocharis (1990) discuss the lag, which *should* give pause to enthusiasts for reading only the latest work on the grounds that all prior discovery has been incorporated in current practice. It has not.

2 Von Neumann and Morgenstern (1944), for example, do not cite Cournot despite repeated remark on duopoly as a situation within the domain of a game-theoretic approach.

We learned that Leonard (1994) stresses the differences between Cournot's work and the employment of similar concepts by modern game theorists only just before this manuscript went to the publisher: we are in fundamental agreement with his analysis.

3 Cournot's demand relation, though posited rather than derived, would seem to be Marshallian in nature, although Cournot's characterization of demand as a function of course preceded Marshall.

4 Magnan de Bornier argues that Cournot thought consistently in terms of price adjustment rather than quantity adjustment:

> only one section out of forty (25 to 65) in the book that deal with price theory (and only one out of seven in the chapter on oligopoly) is written with quantity as the apparent strategic variable.
>
> (1992, 630)

5 The models of mechanism design are, basically, two-stage games about moral hazard or adverse selection. Consider a moral hazard model. In the second stage, agents can engage in a choice of actions (often high or low productivity), and an output desired by the principal ensues. The principal can (usually) observe the output perfectly, but not the effort of the agent(s) directly. The principal pays the agent based on the output.

In the first stage, the principal tenders the agent(s) a contract which associates pay with output. The principal would like to construct a contract which agents will be willing to take on (which satisfies a participation constraint), and which encourages agents to engage in high-productivity behaviour (thus embodying incentive-compatibility). Given information on agent utility functions by type and the distribution of outcomes for high- and low-productivity choices, the principal can do so.

Adverse selection-type mechanism design models are roughly similar, but focus on encouraging high-productivity types to take up contracts, and not to behave like low-productivity types on the job.

6 As in the case of a monopolist, how the price is arrived at in the market once quantity is determined is unspecified. For consistency with Cournot's model(s), this can be thought of in two ways.

1 A sort of partial-equilibrium Walrasian auctioneer clears the market; or
2 knowing the demand curve for the good, the two producers look at the quantity they have jointly produced and set the price accordingly. Neither way of arriving at the price, given output, seems thoroughly satisfactory.

7 Conversely, where what is exchanged for spring water is to some extent indivisible, multiple equilibria result. Suppose the smallest unit of money to be one centime, and call the two price-competing duopolists A and B. There are three types of equilibria:

1 A and B each set a price of zero centimes;
2 A (or B) sets a price of zero centimes, while B (or A) sets some positive price;
3 A and B both set a price of one centime.

8 It is customary to assume (often implicitly) that control of the first move yields greater profits than a simultaneous move game or the position of Stackelberg follower gives. However, moving first and thus obliging an opponent to optimize subject to one's move need not produce higher profit than simultaneous or following moves would. The first mover optimizes subject to the second mover optimizes subject to her first move: this need not be an advantage.

Where first-mover advantage is modelled, it is forced by the functional forms adopted for demand and cost. Amoroso's example merely uses functional forms which result in the opposite phenomenon.

9 The lag in the application of formal game theory to industrial organization is rather interesting as paralleling the lag in widespread reading of Cournot. Shubik's *Strategy and Market Structure: Competition, Oligopoly, and the Theory of Games* (1959b) 'was one of the first books to take an explicitly non-cooperative game theoretic approach to modelling oligopoly' (Walker 1995, 6).

10 Smithies also wrote a much less formal extension of Hotelling (1929), which is discussed in the next chapter.

3 STRATEGIC INTERDEPENDENCE: COURNOT'S HEIRS AND ASYMMETRY

1 In long-run equilibrium, profit for fringe firms must be zero: otherwise entry or exit occurs, so long as entry is free. Potential for this to occur adds another dimension to the dominant firm's strategy. The dominant firm may choose price to arrive at a fringe of the optimal size, typically by setting a lower price (in the short-run) than is given by the one-period model. Early work in this area, which developed into the concept of market contestability, includes Kaldor (1935).

2 While the translated volume appeared later than 1944, its initial appearance in German was in 1943. The only reference to von Neumann or Morgenstern is by the translator, Alan Peacock (xx). This volume, which followed Stackelberg's death in 1946, reproduces much of the matter of Stackelberg (1934).

3 From which the authors of this work unfortunately suffer.

4 Heyward (1941) also illustrated Stackelberg's analyses of situations other than that of 'simple duopoly': near-duopoly, complementary goods, mediate bilateral monopoly (in which monopolist A sells inputs to a competitive market which sells to monopsonist B), and situations in which both players use price as their instrument, and in which one player uses price while the other uses quantity. With the exception of the cases in which the focus is on the instrument, the analysis differs chiefly in the slopes of the reaction curves, and in the interpretation of the (a_1, b_2) position, which sometimes indicates collusion.

5 Though not inevitably. Consider the model of Professor Amoroso, which Edgeworth criticized as an example of why equilibrium is typically non-existent or indeterminate in the case of duopoly (discussed in Chapter 2).

6 Stackelberg, following Bowley (1924), presumed that the output in the case of warfare for the position of leader would produce an output close to the competitive one.

7 This suggests that, while Stackelberg was conscious of the oddity of assuming that players will abide by *some* rules or market situations, he did not generically doubt economic models in which there are incentives for agents to change the assumptions. Thus, his anticipation of mechanism design is partial indeed.

8 Introduced by Zermelo (1913).

9 Its origins shrouded by the fertility of the atmosphere of the game theory group at Princeton, this theorem states that, in an infinite period repeated game, almost any path can be supported as an equilibrium by some set of expectations. Shubik (1959) 'contains an early statement of the Folk Theorem' (Walker 1995, 6).

10 An imputation in game theory is a vector of payoffs.

11 Stigler (1947) furnished an exposition and critique of these papers.

12 Sweezy felt that such conjectures were most likely in a differentiated oligopoly, but recognized that a kinked demand curve with the opposite elasticity characteristics was possible for other conjectures and market forms.

13 It is perhaps not surprising that Stigler, an exemplar of the Chicago-style economics which presumes that deviations from market perfection are trivial,

felt that the kinked demand curve model was less than useful. Stigler (1947) presented data purporting to show the irrelevance of this model.

14 This term was used by other authors to indicate any imperfect competition which fell short of monopoly. Except in quotation, we adhere to the modern terminology.

15 Similarly, transactions costs in transactions-motive money demand models may be equivalently modelled by including money in agents' utility functions. The deceptive component in implementing such a duality-trick is that 'nice' transactions cost functions do not usually result in 'nice' utility functions when one takes the trouble to derive the indirect utility function.

16 Non-atomic means arbitrarily small: where all agents satisfy this condition, the market is truly competitive. As Cournot showed, an increase in the (finite) number of (atomic, because finite in number) agents causes convergence to the competitive price under symmetric market conditions with perfect substitution between products. Cournot's model is discussed in Chapter 2. Edgeworth's partially-proved conjecture (discussed in Chapter 4) of what was later called core convergence exhibits a similar phenomenon.

17 This depends on an implicit assumption that c is 'sufficiently low'.

18 This depends on the implicit assumption that total sales in these markets are invariant to prices.

19 This mathematical peculiarity of Hotelling's model is what later analysts have avoided by assuming that the differentiating characteristic can be represented by a circle rather than by a line segment.

20 Whose work is discussed in Chapter 5.

21 Calculus was avoided by means of heavy use of equilibrium conditions.

22 Again, as mentioned in Chapter 2, this result is reminiscent of Aumann's (1974) notion that player conjectures can function as a coordinating device.

23 Smithies' note 5 is of interest. In this note, Smithies recounted the work of Guy H. Orcutt, who had

> constructed a mechanical model for solving this problem with a greater degree of generality than is possible by analytic methods. The principle of the machine is to represent, for each competitor, price, quantity per unit distance, and distance by voltage drops along linear resistance wires. These resistance wires are included in an electric circuit such that the product of these three voltages, i.e. total profits, can be read off a voltmeter. The machine is operated by varying price and distance for each competitor, in accordance with the assumptions of the problem, until a simultaneous maximum is achieved.

Orcutt, who would appear never to have published his results, was to continue a career which emphasized simulation using more accommodating computers. The relationship of his mechanical model to Fisher's and Phillips' hydraulic models is transparent. His method also seems, however, like a foreshadowing of Aumann's (1981) proposition of applying the concept of an automaton in modelling a player in a repeated game.

24 Smithies' note 6 stated that 'The need to return to Marshallian orthodoxy in this problem has been impressed on me equally by Lerner and Singer's geometry and by my own algebra'. Later writers using a Hotelling-style model have obviated this difficulty by appealing to Jevonsian or Edgeworthian utility functions rather than a Marshallian demand function to limit arithmetic awkwardness: Smithies' adherence to Marshallian methods seems to have been clearly misplaced.

25 In this section we discuss almost none of the succeeding literature. Triffin (1940) offers a standard discussion of both Chamberlin's and Robinson's books, and of much of the successive literature.

26 Kaldor (1938) felt and stated that the core theories of the two books were not significantly different. Robinson herself scarcely entered the fray.

4 STRATEGIC INTERDEPENDENCE: BILATERAL MONOPOLY

1 Debate about indeterminacy in the case of duopoly is discussed in Chapters 2 and 3, while this chapter contains an account of debate on the types of indeterminacy which can occur under bilateral monopoly. Curiously, while many economists have believed in a unique stable equilibrium in the case of duopoly, most have believed that bilateral monopoly, at least in Edgeworth's more general case, has indeterminate results. A more widespread concern with the Edgeworth model was the breadth of its applicability.

2 The core of a game or, more typically, an economy represented as a game is the set of post-play allocations (or imputations) which are equilibria. The concept of the core as general solution concept is due to Shapley (1952) and Gillies (1953) (published as Gillies (1959)).

3 Zeuthen's general position, that there is a unique equilibrium for every well-framed game, is discussed at greater length in Chapter 3.

4 Zeuthen's interest in differing degrees of competition between firms selling to another industry, particularly those based on proximity, correlates with his examination and extension of Hotelling's (1929) model, which was discussed in the previous chapter.

5 In fact, the core is a generalization of Edgeworth's contract curve, since a core can exist for games other than Edgeworth's trading game.

6 It has been known since Vickrey (1961) that with risk neutrality on the part of all participants, the results of Dutch and English auctions are identical. This concept had not been formulated when Edgeworth wrote, and it is far from clear that he would have wished to assume risk neutrality in any case.

7 It is well known that the box as we know it is due to Pareto (1896, §144[1]), while Pareto-optimality was developed by Edgeworth (1881). See Tarascio (1972).

8 We are indebted to Schmidt for this idea.

9 Walker (1995, 5) argues that Shubik (1959) on relationship between contract curve and core is 'limited' by Shubik's context of TU games, while Edgeworth's idea 'is more appropriately modelled as an NTU game'.

10 While Bowley's next chapter title, 'Multiple exchange', might seem to suggest that he discussed core convergence as Edgeworth had, this is not the case. Rather, he discussed general equilibrium and situations like those mentioned by Pareto, in which monopolists care about what they may buy with their proceeds.

11 It was in fact taken from Marshall to be printed as a pamphlet by Sidgwick, who feared that Marshall would lose credit to others inappropriately.

12 Marshall did analyse from a production point of view to some extent, even in 1923: he ruled out an offer curve which intersects any ray through the zero-trade origin more than once because ' . . . it would imply that [an amount] AB [of] bales from [Germany] are just capable of being sold for the expenses of producing [an amount] OB [of] bales from [England]: and also CD bales from [Germany] (which is the same as AB bales from [Germany]) are just capable of being sold for the

164

expenses of producing *OD* [greater than *OB*] bales from [England]. But this is impossible' (Marshall 1923, 334).

13 Marshall also mingled dynamics with a static trade model with multiple equilibria, in a fashion reminiscent of discussions of duopoly. He stated that 'It will always be for [the seller's] advantage to take an offer at once rather than to wait for a long time and then receive only a slightly increased amount' (1923, 133), then proceeded to a present value calculation, passing into a long pseudo-dynamic discussion in the context of the static diagram.

14 The same criticism as with Column (2) applies here.

15 Harsanyi (1956) showed that Zeuthen's solution to bargaining problem is equivalent to Nash's bargaining solution.

5 LEWIS CARROLL AND THE GAME OF POLITICS

1 Much of the material in this chapter has been previously published in slightly different forms, in M. A. Dimand (1994) and M. A. Dimand (1995).

2 In cooperative game theory, it is assumed that sets of players can make binding contracts with each other and thus form coalitions which are stable even when they would not be without binding contracts. The game is characterized by a set of players and a set of imputations (the payoffs made to coalitions in each possible coalition configuration).

  Nineteenth-century writers on proportional representation were thinking in coalitional terms. This is not unreasonable since it is groups who vote the same way who decide the outcome of elections, and the political parties which arose from this fact are genuine coalitions. Since there are no enforceable contracts between voters, or between voters and parties, a non-cooperative modelling of the issues surrounding voting itself may be more useful. Dodgson's model was non-cooperative between parties, with complete (and static) cooperation between a party and voters assumed at the second level.

3 This material has received little theoretical examination. While Hart's invaluable *Proportional Representation* (1992) discusses the history of the PR movement extensively, she approaches the material from the viewpoint of political history, concentrating on successive campaigns for PR rather than on the analysis used or on the merits of proposed systems. Until now, economists other than Duncan Black have paid little attention to the literature of PR. While Mueller (1989) analysed the scheme most frequently associated with Hare and included a section on PR, he did not discuss the nineteenth-century literature. Similarly, Tullock's (1972) discussion of PR does not address the early literature.

4 The Shapley value gives the expected marginal value of an agent's contribution (in this case, his vote) on the assumption that any coalition could occur.

5 For this reason I use 'he' as the generic pronoun throughout this chapter.

6 Also university graduates could vote for university burgesses – initially just for Oxford, Cambridge and Trinity College, Dublin, then for London University and then for the Combined English Universities and Combined Scottish Universities. University representation was abolished in 1948.

7 The concept of representation of the English voting theorists is that rejected by Burke in his *Letter to the Sheriffs of Bristol* (written when his stand as MP for Bristol on the American War of Independence was unpopular), where he argued that the MP owes his constituents the use of his judgement, not just his vote.

8 The PR theorists' habit of constructing distributions of party sympathy across districts to illustrate 'anomalies' in a given voting rule bears a strong similarity to

a custom of game theorists. Game theorists arguing the demerits of a particular equilibrium concept have long been in the habit of constructing examples of games in which the equilibria, according to that definition, look 'unreasonable'. In fact, each of these is a method of comparing equilibria.

9　However, if the minority consisted of the one-third plus $\varepsilon > 0$ of the electorate necessary to secure one seat, the number of voters disenfranchised would still be reduced.

10　The supposition that *all* electors' votes would be necessary to elect winning candidates depended on the false definition of the quota mentioned above. Under the correct definition of the quota where m seats were to be filled in a district, $1/(m+1)$ of the population would be unrepresented. Therefore, as Baily (1872, 6–7) noted, as the number of members per district increases, the number of wasted votes declines.

11　In fact, there is still evidence of substantially higher voter turnout under proportional representation than under majority rule (Mueller 1989, 223).

12　For example, if the issues are the amount of military spending and whether abortion should be legal, each platform consists of a number of dollars and a yes, no or 'sometimes' answer which can be coded as 1, 0 or 0.5. Consider an election in which there are three candidates for one seat. If A's platform is (5000,0) and B's is (4000,1), then the candidates can be represented by positions along a line only if C's platform is identical to A's or B's or is (α5000 + (1-α)4000, (1-α)1).

13　Courtney, who was Beatrice Webb's brother-in-law, joined Mill and H. Fawcett in supporting women's suffrage in the House of Commons.

14　Earlier empirical work in economics tends to be quite spotty and consists largely of tables of unanalysed data. Very little, even of that literature, focuses on the response of agents to varying incentives. Exceptions are van Thünen's remarkable work, and data gathered in pursuit of arguments surrounding the inception of the New Poor Law. Blaug (1963, 1964) criticizes the use of data in the New Poor Law literature.

15　Effectively, this is equivalent to setting an election problem in the second stage, where the first stage is one in which 'government effectiveness' is the payoff. Dodgson, who formulated a two-stage game, chose a very different first-stage objective, however.

16　See Riker (1992).

17　As a proper game-theoretic model, Dodgson's analysis was preceded only by Waldegrave's 1713 study of maximin play in the card game '*le Her*' and Cournot's 1838 treatment of duopoly behaviour. It was more or less contemporary with Bertrand's 1883 review of Cournot.

18　However, Black (1970, 26) contains a rather curious element: he stated that the problem Dodgson considered in *PPR* was 'isomorphic with this, the division in his own nature created by his love for Edith Denman'. Black (1958) similarly remarked that the earlier Dodgson voting pamphlets were his way of expressing turmoil over whether to marry Alice Liddell. We do not consider either speculation convincing.

19　Recall that the definition starts with the concept of the Droop quota (Droop 1868) – the minimum number of votes a candidate in a plurality rule election must have to be certain of winning. Where V votes have been cast to elect m candidates, the Droop quota is the least integer greater than $[V/(m+1)]$. In a race for three seats where 1,000 votes have been cast, a candidate may be sure he has been returned when 251 votes for him have been counted. Dodgson's idea, common to other nineteenth-century voting theorists, was that if a candidate received more votes than the Droop quota, the extra votes were 'wasted' and those who had cast them were not represented.

20 In the nineteenth-century PR literature in general, raising the cost of party organization to empower the individual voter was an explicit issue (Hart 1992), as noted above. Dodgson did not consider costly organization.

21 Indeed, recent controversy connected with PR and its aims suggests that public choice theorists might wish to turn to Dodgson's analysis of such systems.

22 Salisbury thought that the method was intended strictly to favour Conservatives, though he didn't mind that. (Dodgson protested that PR had no party bias. Salisbury, however, thought that the extant system in 1884 *always* favoured the Liberals (Hart 1992, 75)).)

6 EARLY MATHEMATICAL MODELS OF CONFLICT

1 Much of the material in this chapter has been previously published in slightly different form, in R.W. Dimand and M.A. Dimand (1994).

2 'Differential Games [were] developed by Rufus Isaacs in the early 1950s. They grew out of the problem of forming and solving military pursuit games. The first publications in this area were Rand Corporation research memoranda, by Isaacs, RM–1391 (30 November 1954), RM–1399 (30 November 1954), RM–1411 (21 December 1954) and RM–1486 (25 March 1955) all entitled, in part, Differential Games' (Walker 1995, 5).

   Christian Schmidt (1990) points out that Lanchester's and Richardson's work was, indeed, in the form of differential games, and it is startling to see how like some of their work games defined by Haywood (1954) are.

3 Coincidentally, Machiavelli also wrote a book entitled *The Art of War* of which Gilbert (1986, 23) says, 'For today's student of Machiavelli, *The Art of War* is not his most exciting book'. It was the only one of Machiavelli's political writings published during his lifetime, appeared in 21 editions in the sixteenth century, and influenced Clausewitz by its emphasis on analysing the general nature of war as the basis for studying specific situations. Machiavelli stressed the importance of a well-ordered state with good laws, as citizens would only fight and die for a government with which they were reasonably content, whereas for Sun Tzu, such concerns would be part of the Tao. Machiavelli held that the aim of war must be to defeat the enemy in the field, while Sun Tzu preferred to make actual battle unnecessary by making it evident which side would win.

4 Cleary explains the Way as signifying the Tao, which might, in this setting, be very roughly summarized as a sense of the balancing of things as they are.

5 Borel (1938) was to give the first explicit example of a Colonel Blotto game, which was not named until later: see Chapter 7. D. W. Blackett published in the first number of the *Naval Research Logistics Quarterly* on 'Some Blotto Games'.

6 A particularly amusing and sophisticated example is related by Jones (1978). At a time in World War II when English and German intelligence were continually assessing each other's scientific capabilities, English broadcast was being competently jammed by the German side. Jones, assigned to work out how to prevent this, advised that, first and foremost, English broadcast should continue as though no jamming was occurring. The German side, inferring that the English had found a method to nullify their jamming, desisted. Jones, an accomplished practical joker, had effectively bluffed the opponents that the English were 'of the type with the ability to nullify jamming' – at least by means of that instrument.

7 Kingsford (1960) and Rolt (1970) provide more biographical information on Lanchester.

8 The sense of urgency which actuated Richardson would seem to have had its parallel in later peace analysts. Notes for contributors in early issues of the *Journal of Conflict Resolution* stated that a specified payment from the author was necessary if she or he wished publication of her or his article rushed.

7
THE MINIMAX APPROACH TO NON-COOPERATIVE STRATEGIC GAMES FROM WALDEGRAVE TO BOREL

1 Ellsberg (1956) criticizes these approaches brilliantly. Mirowski (1991) links them with von Neumann's personality, which he finds curious.

2 A pure strategy is one which specifies an agent's behaviour with certainty at each node (or stage of the game), given all previous play up until that time (e.g. if Sally shows Mike that her choice is 'paper', he chooses 'scissors'). Recall that a mixed strategy is one in which a player plans *ex ante* to randomize over possible pure strategies (e.g. Mike should choose 'stone' with probability one-third, 'scissors' with probability one-third and 'paper' with probability one-third).

3 See Chapter 1.

4 Chapter 8 addresses the relationship between Bertrand's analysis of baccarat and other analyses of (recreational or gambling) games.

5 Leonard (1995, 733) notes the interesting fact that Zermelo, as well as von Neumann, worked on axiomatic set theory as a part of the so-called 'Hilbert programme'.

6 Backwards induction is a reasoning process followed by game theorists (and by implication, the agents they model) in solving a non-simultaneous game which is played in several stages. The concept is most easily explained for a finite multi-stage game. At each possible final stage of the game, one can work out the optimal move(s) of the player(s) whose move it is simply by looking at her (their) payoff(s). Therefore, for the player(s) whose move it is at a stage immediately before this, one can infer what her (their) payoffs will be if she (they) chooses (choose) to make a given final stage active. This permits prediction of what choice will be made at each possible penultimate stage. By iteration, one can move backwards up the game tree to solve the game at the first stage. Backwards induction can be used in an infinite game, but its use depends on defining the properties of the stage from which backwards induction is performed.

7 A subgame consists of a portion of a game tree whose first node is connected to the rest of the tree only through its predecessor. Kalmar's term 'script game' came from his relating a subgame to a starting position reached in a game of chess by correspondence – a starting position reached as a consequence of the previous 'script' produced by the correspondents.

8 Ville's proof is discussed at slightly greater length in the next chapter.

8

FROM GAMES OF PURE CHANCE TO STRATEGIC GAMES: FRENCH PROBABILISTS AND EARLY GAME THEORY

1 Much of the material of this chapter is to be published in slightly different form in Dimand and Dimand (forthcoming).

2 Some of the role of probability in the development of game theory is discussed in Chapter 1.

3 Ville's proof was still topological in part. The first completely elementary proof was that of Loomis (1946).

4 For other, less formal analyses of problems of this type, see Chapter 6.

5 Thus, Bertrand's analysis of baccarat lacks some of the sophistication of Waldegrave's solution to the card game '*le Her*', discussed in the next chapter. Waldegrave was so surprised at his answer, however, that he thought he must have been mistaken: Bertrand would seem not to have had this difficulty.

6 This problem, called 'the problem of points' by Todhunter (1865), was analysed by a number of earlier writers including Huygens and de Moivre. Arbuthnot's (1692) presentation was discussed in the first chapter.

7 See Chapter 3 for discussion of Hotelling's model.

9

VON NEUMANN AND MORGENSTERN IN HISTORICAL PERSPECTIVE

1 This chapter was published in somewhat different form in Dimand and Dimand (1995).

2 For our analysis of Böhm-Bawerk's discussion of an imperfect horse market, see Chapter 4.

3 Our analysis of Cournot (1838) occupies Chapters 2 and 4.

4 We discuss Edgeworth's contract curve and concern for indeterminacy in Chapter 4.

5 After Morgenstern's death, Simon read the memo which Morgenstern wrote to von Neumann when forwarding Simon's letter. Morgenstern wrote (in translation): 'I have . . . not thought a great deal about his points, but I am not very much impressed. It is pleasant, however, that he has occupied himself so intensively with the theory.' Simon later 'had a number of conversations with [Morgenstern] on organization theory, and with [von Neumann] on complex systems, artificial intelligence (he was skeptical) and automata theory, but with neither on game theory' (Simon 1995).

6 That Frisch felt this way is amusing in light of his work on strategic interdependence, which, however, included too much implicit *ceteris paribus* to be very serviceable (see Chapter 2).

BIBLIOGRAPHY

Note: Articles to be reprinted in *The Foundations of Game Theory* by M. A. Dimand and R. W. Dimand (eds), forthcoming from Edward Elgar Publishing, are marked with an asterisk *.

Anderson, O. (1949) 'Theorie der Glücksspiele und ökonomisches Verhalten', *Schweizerische Zeitschrift für Volkswirtschaft und Statistik* vol. 85, 46–53.

Anderton, C. H. (1989) 'Arms race modeling: problems and prospects', *Journal of Conflict Resolution* vol. 33 (2), 346–67.

Arbuthnot, J. (1692) *Of the Laws of Chance, or, a Method of Calculation of the Hazards of Game, Plainly Demonstrated, and Applied to Games at Present Most in Use, Which May Be Easily Extended to the Most Intricate Cases of Chance Imaginable*, London: Benjamin Motte.

Ardzrooni, L. (1934) 'Introduction' to Thorstein Veblen, *Essays in Our Changing Order*, New York: Viking.

Arrow, K. J. (1951) *Social Choice and Individual Values* New York: Wiley..

—— , Debreu, G., Malinraod, E. and Solow, R. M. (1991) *Cowles Fiftieth Anniversary*, New Haven, CT: Cowles Foundation for Research in Economics at Yale University.

Aumann, R. J. (1974) 'Subjectivity and correlation in randomized strategies', *Journal of Mathematical Economics* vol. 1, 67–96.

—— (1981) 'Survey of repeated games', in Aumann *et al.*, 11–42.

—— (1989) 'Game theory', in J. Eatwell, M. Milgate and P. Newman (eds) *The New Palgrave: Game Theory*, New York: W. W. Norton, 1–53.

—— (ed.) (1981) *Essays in Game Theory and Mathematical Economics in Honor of Oskar Morgenstern*, Zurich: Bibliographisches Institut.

Aumann, R. J. and Maschler, M. (1985) 'Game theoretic analysis of a bankruptcy problem from the Talmud', *Journal of Economic Theory* vol. 36, 195–213.

Bachelier, L. (1901) 'Théorie mathématique des jeux', *Annales de l'Ecole Normale Supérieure* 3rd series, vol. 18, 143–210.

Baily, W. (1872) *Proportional Representation in Large Constituencies*, London: Ridgway.

Baumol, W. J. and Goldfeld, S. (1968) *Precursors in Mathematical Economics: An Anthology*, Reprints of Scarce Works in Political Economy No. 19, London: London School of Economics.

Bayes, T. (1763) 'An essay towards solving a problem in the doctrine of chances', *Philosophical Transactions of the Royal Society* vol. 53, 370–418.

Bellany, I. (1975) 'The Richardson theory of "arms races": themes and variations', *British Journal of International Studies* vol. 1 (2), 119–30.

Bernheim, D. (1984) 'Rationalizable strategic behavior', *Econometrica* vol. 52, 1007–28.

170

Bernoulli, D. (1738) 'Specimen theoriae novae de mensura sortis', *Commentarii Academiae Scientiarum Imperialis Petropolitanae*, V: 175–92, trans. L. Sommer as 'Exposition of a new theory on the measurement of risk', *Econometrica* vol. 22 (1954), 23–36.

Berry, A. (1891) 'Alcune brevi povole sulla teoria del baratto di Marshall', *Giornale degli Economisti* (June).

*Bertrand, J. (1883) 'Review of Walras's *Théorie Mathématique de la Richesse Sociale* and Cournot's *Recherches sur les Principes Mathématiques de la Théorie des Richesses*', *Journal des Savants* (September), 499–508, trans. M. Chevaillier and reprinted in Magnan de Bornier (1992), 646–53.

—— (1924) *Calcul Des Probabilités, Éléments De La Théorie Des Probabilités*, 3rd edn, Paris: Gauthier-Villars.

Bewley, T. (1973) 'Edgeworth's conjecture', *Econometrica* vol. 41 (3), 425–52.

Black, D. (1958) *The Theory of Committees and Elections*, Cambridge: Cambridge University Press.

—— (1967) 'The central argument in Lewis Carroll's "The principles of parliamentary representation"', *Papers on Non-Market Decision Making* vol. 3 (Fall), 1–17.

—— (1969) 'Lewis Carroll and the theory of games', *American Economic Review* vol. 59 (May), 206–10.

—— (1970) 'Lewis Carroll and the Cambridge mathematical school of P.R.; Arthur Cohen and Edith Denman', *Public Choice*, vol. 8 (Spring), 1–28.

Blaug, M. (1963) 'The myth of the old Poor Law and the making of the new', *Journal of Economic History* vol. 23 (June), 151–84.

—— (1964) 'The Poor Law Report re-examined', *Journal of Economic History* vol. 24 (June), 229–45.

Böhm-Bawerk, Eugen van ([1914] 1959) *Capital and Interest, Volume II: Positive Theory of Capital, Book III: Value and Price*, trans. G. D. Huncke and H. F. Sennholz, South Holland, IL: Libertarian Press.

Borcherding, T. E. (1969) 'Discussion of Duncan Black (1969)', *American Economic Review* vol. 59 (May), 211–12.

Border, K. C. (1985) *Fixed Point Theorems with Applications to Economics and Game Theory*, Cambridge: Cambridge University Press.

*Borel, E. (1921) 'La théorie du jeu et les équations intégrales à noyau symétrique gauche', *Comptes Rendus de l'Académie des Sciences* vol. 173, 1304–8, trans. L. J. Savage as 'The theory of play and integral equations with skew symmetric kernels', *Econometrica* vol. 21 (1953), 97–100.

*—— (1924) 'Sur les jeux où interviennent l'hasard et l'habilité des joueurs', *Théorie des Probabilités*, Paris: Librairie Scientifique, J. Hermann, 204–24, trans. L. J. Savage as 'On games that involve chance and the skill of the players', *Econometrica* vol. 21 (1953), 101–15.

*—— (1927) 'Sur les systèmes de formes linéaires à déterminant symétrique gauche et la théorie générale du jeu', *Comptes Rendus de l'Académie des Sciences* vol. 184, 52–3, trans. L. J. Savage as 'On systems of linear forms of skew symmetric determinant and the general theory of play', *Econometrica* vol. 21 (1953), 116–17.

—— (1925–39) *Traité du calcul des probabilités et de ses applications*, 4 vols. in 18 fascicles, Paris: Gauthier-Villars.

—— (1938) *Applications des jeux de hasard*, tome 4, fascicle 2 of *Traité du calcul des probabilités et de ses applications*, rédigé par Jean Ville, Paris: Gauthier-Villars.

—— (1950) *Eléments de la théorie des probabilités*, trans. J. E. Freund as *Elements of the Theory of Probability*, Englewood Cliffs, NJ: Prentice-Hall, 1965.

Borel, E. and Chéron, A. (1940) *Théorie mathématique du bridge à la portée de tous*, Paris: Gauthier-Villars.

Boulding, K. E. (1962) *Conflict and Defense: a General Theory*, New York: Harper & Brothers for the Center for Research in Conflict Resolution, University of Michigan.

Bowley, A. L. (1924) *The Mathematical Groundwork of Economics*, Oxford: Oxford University Press.

*Braithwaite, R. B. (1955) *Theory of Games as a Tool for the Moral Philosopher*, Cambridge: Cambridge University Press.

Brams, S. J. (1980) *Biblical Games*, Cambridge, MA: MIT Press.

Brems, H. (1976) 'From the years of high theory: Frederik Zeuthen (1888–1959)', *History of Political Economy* vol. 8 (3), 400–11.

Brito, D. L. (1972) 'A dynamic model of an armaments race', *International Economic Review* vol. 13, 359–75.

Brouwer, L. E. J. (1912) 'Über Abbildung von Mannigfaltikeiten', *Mathematische Annalen* vol. 71, 97–115.

Chacko, K. G. (1950) 'Economic behaviour: a new theory', *Indian Journal of Economics* vol. 30, 349–65.

Chaigneau, N. and Le Gall, P. (1996) 'The French connection: the pioneering econometrics of Marcel Lenoir', in W. J. Samuels, C. Ménard *et al.* (eds), Aldershot: Edward Elgar Publishing.

Chamberlin, E. H. (1929), 'Duopoly: value where sellers are few', *Quarterly Journal of Economics* vol. 44, 63–100.

—— (1933) *The Theory of Monopolistic Competition*, Cambridge, MA: Harvard University Press.

Cherriman, J. B. (1857) 'Review of A. A. Cournot, *Recherches sur les Principes Mathématiques de la Théorie des Richesses*', *Canadian Journal of Industry, Science and Art* vol. 2, 185–94, reprinted in R. Dimand (1995), 567–78.

Chimenti, F. A. (1990) 'Pascal's wager: a decision-theoretic approach', *Mathematics Magazine* vol. 63 (5), 321–5.

Chipman, J. S. (1965a) 'A survey of the theory of international trade: Part 1, the classical theory', *Econometrica* vol. 33 (3), 477–519.

—— (1965b) 'A survey of the theory of international trade: Part 2, the neoclassical theory', *Econometrica* vol. 33 (4), 685–760.

Cho, I.-K. and Kreps, D. (1987) 'Signalling games and stable equilibria', *Quarterly Journal of Economics* vol. 102, 179–221.

Cleary, T. (trans.) (1988) *Sun Tzu, The Art of War*, Boston, MA and Shaftesbury, Dorset: Shambhala.

Coase, R. H. (1937) 'The nature of the firm', *Economica* vol. 4, 386–405.

—— (1960) 'The problem of social cost', *Journal of Law and Economics* vol. 3 (October), 1–44.

Cole, M. I. (1971) *The Life of G. D. H. Cole*, London.

Collard, E. A. (1975) *The McGill You Knew*, Don Mills, ON: Longman.

Collingwood, S. D. (1899) *The Life and Letters of Lewis Carroll*, New York: The Century Co., reprinted Detroit: Gale Research Company (1967).

Copeland, A. H. (1945) 'John von Neumann and Oskar Morgenstern's theory of games and economic behavior', *Bulletin of the American Mathematical Society* vol. 51, 498–504.

Cournot, A. A. (1838) *Recherches sur les principes mathématiques de la théorie des richesses*, trans. N. T. Bacon as *Researches into the Mathematical Principles of the Theory of Wealth*, New York: Macmillan (1927).

Courtney, L. H. (1876) 'Political machinery and political life', *Fortnightly Review* vol. 20 (July), 74–92.

—— (1879) 'The representation of minorities', *Nineteenth Century* vol. 6 (July), 141–56.

BIBLIOGRAPHY

Creedy, F. (1934) 'On the equations of motion of business activity', *Econometrica* vol. 2, 363–80.

Creedy, J. (1986) *Edgeworth and the Development of Neoclassical Economics*, Oxford: Basil Blackwell.

—— (1990) 'Marshall and international trade', in J. K. Whitaker (ed.) *Centenary Essays on Alfred Marshall*, Cambridge: Cambridge University Press.

David, F. N. (1962) *Games, Gods, and Gambling*, London: Charles Griffin.

Debreu, G. and Scarf, H. (1963) 'A limit theorem on the core of an economy', *International Economic Review* vol. 4 (3), 235–46.

de Montmort, P. R. (1713) *Essai d'analyse sur les jeux de hazard*, 2nd edn, Paris: Quilau.

*de Possel, R. (1936) *Sur la Théorie Mathématique des Jeux de Hasard et de Reflexion*, Paris: Hermann & Cie., Actualités scientifiques et industrielles, no. 436.

Dimand, M.A. (1994) 'C. L. Dodgson, public choice, and the mathematics of proportional representation', *History of Economics Review* vol. 22 (Summer), 16–23.

—— (1995) 'English voting theorists of the 19th century: an approach to cooperative game theory', *Economia delle Scelte Pubbliche (Journal of Public Finance and Public Choice)* vol. 1, 55–68.

Dimand, M. A. and Dimand, R. W. (forthcoming) *The Foundations of Game Theory*, 3 vols., Aldershot and Brookfield, VT: Edward Elgar Publishing.

Dimand, R.W. (1988) 'An early Canadian contribution to mathematical economics: J.B. Cherriman's 1857 review of Cournot', *Canadian Journal of Economics* vol. 21, 610–16.

—— (1995) 'Cournot, Bertrand and Cherriman', *History of Political Economy* vol. 27 (3), 563–78.

Dimand, R. W. and Dimand, M.A. (1992) 'The early history of the theory of strategic games from Waldegrave to Borel', in E. R. Weintraub (ed.) *Toward a History of Game Theory*, Durham, NC: Duke University Press, 15–27.

—— (1994) 'Early mathematical models of conflict: the contributions of Lanchester and Richardson', in K. I. Vaughn (ed.) *Perspectives on the History of Economic Thought*, Vol. IX, Aldershot and Brookfield, VT: Edward Elgar.

—— (1995) 'Von Neumann and Morgenstern in historical perspective', *Revue d'économie politique* vol. 105 (4), 540–57.

—— (forthcoming) 'From games of pure chance to strategic games: French probabilists and early game theory', in C. Schmidt (ed.) *Uncertainty in Economic Theory*, Aldershot and Brookfield, VT: Edward Elgar Publishing for l'Association Charles Gide pour l'Etude de la Pensée Economique.

*Dines, L. L. (1947) 'On a theorem of von Neumann', *Proceedings of the National Academy of Sciences, USA* vol. 33, 329–31.

Dodgson, C. L. (1884a) Letter to the *St James' Gazette* entitled 'Proportionate representation', 15 May, 5.

—— (1884b) Letter to the *St James' Gazette* entitled 'Proportionate representation', 19 May, 5–6.

—— (1884c) Letter to the *St James' Gazette* entitled 'Proportionate representation', 27 May, 5–6.

—— (1884d) Letter to the *St James' Gazette* entitled 'Proportionate representation', 5 June, 6.

—— (1884e) 'Parliamentary elections', *St James' Gazette*, 5 July, 5–6.

—— (1884f) 'Redistribution', *St James' Gazette*, 11 October, 3–5.

—— (1884g) *The Principles of Parliamentary Representation*, 1st edn, London: Harrison and Sons.

—— (1979) *The Letters of Lewis Carroll*, M. N. Cohen (ed.) (with the assistance of R. L. Green), London: Macmillan.

Dore, M. H. I., Chakravarty, S. and Goodwin, R. M. (eds) (1989) *John von Neumann and Modern Economics*, Oxford: Clarendon Press.

Downs, A. (1957) *An Economic Theory of Democracy*, New York: Harper & Row.

Droop, H. R. (1868) *On Methods of Electing Representatives*, London: Macmillan.

—— (1869) *On the Political and Social Effects of Different Methods of Electing Representatives*, n.p., read 10 March 1869.

—— (1871) *Proportional Representation as Applied to the Election of Local Governing Bodies*, London: Wildy & Sons, Law Booksellers and Publishers, and Manchester: Meredith & Ray.

—— (1881) 'On methods of electing representatives', *Journal of the Statistical Society* vol. 44 (June), 141–202.

*Edgeworth, F. Y. (1881) *Mathematical Psychics: An Essay on the Application of Mathematics to the Moral Sciences*, London: C. Kegan Paul (to be reprinted in part in *The Foundations of Game Theory*).

—— (1889) 'Opening [Presidential] Address for Section F of the British Association for the Advancement of Science', *Nature* vol. 40 (19 September), 496–509.

—— (1891) 'On the determinateness of economic equilibrium', as substantially recast in Edgeworth (1925), Volume II, 313–19.

—— (1894) 'The pure theory of international values', as restated in Edgeworth (1925), Vol. II, 3–60.

—— (1905) 'Review of *A Geometrical Political Economy* by H. Cunynghame', as reprinted in Edgeworth (1925), Vol. III, 136–44.

—— (1922) 'The mathematical economics of Professor Amoroso', *Economic Journal* vol. 32 (4), 431–57.

—— (1925) *Papers Relating to Political Economy*, 3 vols, London: Macmillan.

Ekelund, R. B. and Hébert, R. F. (1990) 'Cournot and his contemporaries: is an obituary the only bad review?', *Southern Economic Journal* vol. 57, 139–49.

*Ellsberg, D. (1956) 'The theory of the reluctant duellist', *American Economic Review* vol. 46, 909–23.

Fauveau, P.-G. (1864) *Considérations Mathématiques sur la Théorie de l'Impôt*, Paris: Gauthier-Villars.

—— (1867) 'Considérations mathématiques sur la théorie de la valeur', *Journal des Économistes*, 3rd series, vol. 5, 33–5.

Fawcett, M. G. (1871) *Two Essays on Proportional Representation by Mrs Fawcett*, London, which reprints 'Proportional Representation', *Macmillan's Magazine*, 22 September 1870, 1–8, and 'A short explanation of Mr Hare's scheme of representation', *Macmillan's Magazine*, 23 April 1871, 9–16.

Fisher, I. (1922) *The Making of Index Numbers*, Boston: Houghton Mifflin for the Pollak Foundation for Economic Research.

*Fisher, R. A. (1934) 'Randomisation, and an old enigma of card play', *Mathematical Gazette* vol. 18, 294–7.

Forchheimer, K. (1908) 'Theoretisches zum unvollständigen Monopole', *(Schmollers) Jahrbuch, für Gesetzgebung, Verwaltung und Volkswirthschaft im Deutschen Reich* vol. 32 (1), 1–12.

*Fréchet, M. (1953) 'Emile Borel, initiator of the theory of psychological games and its applications' and 'Commentary on three notes of Emile Borel', *Econometrica* vol. 21, 95–6 and 118–24.

—— (1965) 'La vie et l'oeuvre d'Emile Borel', *Monographies de l'Enseignement mathématique* 14, reprinted in *Oeuvres de Emile Borel*, Paris: Centre National de la Recherche Scientifique (1972), vol. I, 5–98.

Freedman, L. (1981) *The Evolution of Nuclear Strategy*, New York: St Martin's.

Friedman, J.W. (1992) 'The interaction between game theory and theoretical industrial economics', *Scottish Journal of Political Econocy* vol. 39(4), 353–73.

Frisch, R. (1933) 'Monopole – Polypole – la notion de force dans l'économie', *Nationalokonomisk Tidsskrift* vol. 71, 241–59.

Fudenberg, D. and Tirole, J. (1991) *Game Theory*, Cambridge, MA and London: MIT Press.

Gibbard, A. (1973) 'Manipulation of voting schemes: a general result', *Econometrica* vol. 41 (July), 587–602.

Gilbert, F. (1986) 'Machiavelli: the renaissance of the art of war', in Paret (1986), 11–31.

Gillies, D. B. (1953) *Some Theorems of N-Person Games*, Ph.D. thesis, Department of Mathematics, Princeton University.

*—— (1959) 'Solutions to general non-zero-sum games', in Luce and Tucker (eds) (1959), 47–85.

Goodwin, R. M. (1989) 'Swinging along the autostrada: cyclical fluctuations along the von Neumann Ray', in Dore, Chakravarty and Goodwin (eds) (1989), 125–40.

Granas, A. (1981) 'KKM-maps and their applications to nonlinear problems', in Mauldin (ed.) (1981), 45–61.

Granger, C. W. J. and Morgenstern, O. (1970) *The Predictability of Stock Market Prices*, Lexington, MA: D. C. Heath.

Greg, W. R. (1852a) 'The expected reform bill', *Edinburgh Review* vol. 95 (January), 213–80.

—— (1852b) 'Representative reform', *Edinburgh Review* vol. 96 (October), 452–508.

—— (1853) 'Parliamentary purification', *Edinburgh Review* vol. 98 (October), 566–624.

Grofman, B. (1987) 'Lewis Carroll', in J. Eatwell, M. Milgate and P. Newman (eds) *The New Palgrave: A Dictionary of Economics*, London: Macmillan.

*Guilbaud, G. Th. (1949) 'La théorie des jeux – contributions critiques à la théorie de la valeur', *Économie Appliquée* vol. 2, 275–319, trans. A. L. Minkes as 'The theory of games', *International Economic Papers* vol. 1, 37–65.

—— (1952) 'Les problèmes du partage matériaux pour une enquête sur les algèbres et les arithmétiques de la répartition', *Économie Appliquée* vol. 5, 93–137.

—— (1960) 'Faut-il jouer au plus fin? Notes sur l'histoire de la théorie des jeux', *La Décision*, Paris: Centre National de la Recherche Scientifique, 171–82.

—— (1968) *Eléments de la Théorie Mathématique des Jeux*, Paris: Dunod.

Guillebaud, C. W. (1961) Introduction and Notes to Marshall (1961).

Hall, R. and Hitch, C. (1939) 'Price theory and business behavior', *Oxford Economic Papers*. Reprinted in T. Wilson and P.W.S. Andrews (eds) *Oxford Studies in the Price Mechanism*, Oxford: Clarendon Press, 1951, 107–38.

Hare, T. (1857) *The Machinery of Representation*.

—— (1859) *A Treatise on the Election of Representatives, Parliamentary and Municipal*, further editions 1861, 1865, 1873.

—— (1866a) 'The keystone of parliamentary reform', *Fortnightly Review* o.s. vol. 3 (January), 559–65.

—— (1866b) 'Individual responsibility in representative government', *Fortnightly Review* o.s. vol. 4 (March), 350–8.

*Harsanyi, J. C. (1956) 'Approaches to the bargaining problem before and after the theory of games: a critical discussion of Zeuthen's, Hicks' and Nash's theories', *Econometrica* vol. 24, 144–57.

—— (1966) 'A general theory of rational behavior in game situations', *Econometrica* vol. 34, 613–634.

—— (1967–1968) 'Games with incomplete information played by "Bayesian" players, Parts I, II and III', *Management Science* vol. 14, 159–82, 320–34 and 486–502.

—— (1973) 'Games with randomly disturbed payoffs: a new rationale for mixed strategy equilibrium points', *International Journal of Game Theory* vol. 2, 1–23.

Hart, J. (1992) *Proportional Representation: Critics of the British Electoral System*, Oxford: Oxford University Press.

Haywood, Col. O.G. (1954) 'Military decision and game theory', *Operations Research Society of America* vol. 2, 365–85.

Heyward, E.R.J. (1941) 'H. von Stackelberg's work on duopoly', *Economic Record* vol. 17 (June), 99–106.

Hicks, J. R. (1935) 'Annual survey of economic theory: the theory of monopoly', *Econometrica* vol. 3, 1–20.

—— (1966) 'Linear theory', in *Surveys of Economic Theory* vol. 3, New York: St Martin's for American Economic Association and Royal Economic Society, 75–113.

Hildenbrand, W. (1993) 'Francis Ysidro Edgeworth: perfect competition and the core', *European Economic Review* vol. 37, 477–90.

Hill, A. V. (1960) *The Ethical Dilemma of Science and Other Writings*, New York: Rockefeller Institute Press; Oxford: Oxford University Press.

Hill, T. W. (1860) *Selections from the Papers of the Late Thomas Wright Hill, Esq. F.R.A.S.*, London: John W. Parker & Son.

Hollander, S. (1985) *The Economics of John Stuart Mill*, 2 vols, Toronto and Buffalo: University of Toronto Press.

Hotelling, H. (1929) 'Stability of competition', *Economic Journal* vol. 39, 41–57. Reprinted in Stigler and Boulding (1952), 467–84.

Hurwicz, L. (1945) 'The theory of economic behavior', *American Economic Review* vol. 36, 909–25. Reprinted in *A.E.A. Readings in Price Theory* (1952), by G. Stigler and K. Boulding (eds), Chicago: Richard D. Irwin, 505–26.

*—— (1953) 'What has happened to the theory of games?', *American Economic Review* vol. 65, 398–405.

*Isaacs, R. (1954) 'Differential games', Rand Corporation Research Memorandums RM-1391, RM-1399, RM-1411 and RM-1486.

Jones, R. V. (1978) *Most Secret War*, London: Hodder & Stoughton.

Jorland, G. (1987) 'The St. Petersburg paradox 1713–1937', in L. Kruger, L. Daston and M. Heidelberger (eds) *The Probabilistic Revolution*, Cambridge, MA: MIT Press, I: 157–90.

Justman, E. (1949) 'La théorie des jeux (Une nouvelle théorie de l'équilibre économique)', *Revue d'Economie Politique* vols 5–6, 909–25.

Kaldor, N. (1934), 'Mrs. Robinson's "Economics of imperfect competition" ', *Economica* n.s. vol. 1, 335–41.

—— (1935) 'Market imperfection and excess capacity', *Economica* n.s. vol. 2 (February), 33–50.

—— (1938) 'Professor Chamberlin on monopolistic and imperfect competition', *Quarterly Journal of Economics* vol. 52, 514–38.

—— (1989) 'John von Neumann: a personal recollection', foreword to Dore, Chakravarty and Goodwin (1989), vii–xi.

*Kalmar, L. (1928–9) 'Zur Theorie der abstrakten Spiele', *Acta Scientific. et Mathemat. Szegedensis* vol. 4, 65–85. Translated by J. Zantke.

Kaplan, F. (1983) *The Wizards of Armageddon*, New York: Simon & Schuster.

*Kaplanski, I. (1945) 'A contribution to von Neumann's theory of games', *Annals of Mathematics* vol. 46, 474–9.

Kaysen, C. (1946) 'A revolution in economic theory?', *Review of Economic Studies* vol. 14, 1–15.

—— (1952) 'The minimax rule of the theory of games, and the choices of strategies under conditions of uncertainty', *Metroeconomica* vol. 4, 5–14.

Kendall, M.G. (1963) 'Isaac Todhunter's *History of the Mathematical Theory of Probability*', *Biometrika* vol. 50, 204–5.

Kingsford, Peter W. (1960) *F. W. Lanchester, The Life of and Engineer*, London: Arnold.

Knobloch, E. (1987) 'Emile Borel as a probabilist', in L. Kruger, L. Daston and M. Heidelberger (eds) *The Probabilistic Revolution*, Cambridge, MA: MIT Press, I: 215–36.

Kolmogorov, A. N. (1933) *Grundbegriffe der Wahrscheinlichkeitsrechnung*, Berlin: Julius Springer Verlag. Translated by N. Morrison as *Foundations of the Theory of Probability*, New York: Chelsea Publishing, 1950.

Kramer, E. (1981) *The Nature and Growth of Modern Mathematics*, Princeton, NJ: Princeton University Press.

Kuhn, H. W. and Tucker, A. W. (eds) (1950) *Contributions to the Theory of Games*, I, Annals of Mathematics Studies, 28, Princeton, NJ: Princeton University Press.

*—— (1958) 'John von Neumann's work in the theory of games and mathematical economics', *Bulletin of the American Mathematical Society* vol. 64, 100–22.

Lanchester, F. W. (1916) *Aircraft in warfare*, London: Constable.

*—— (1956) 'Mathematics in warfare', excerpt from Lanchester (1916), reprinted in Newman (ed) (1956), 2138–57.

LeNoir, M. (1913) *Etudes sur la formation et le mouvement des prix*, Paris: Giard et Brière.

Leonard, R. J. (1992) 'Creating a context for game theory', in E. R. Weintraub (ed.) *Toward a History of Game Theory*, Durham, NC: Duke University Press, 29–76.

—— (1994) 'Reading Cournot, reading Nash: the creation and stabilisation of the Nash equilibrium', *Economic Journal* vol. 104 (May), 492–511.

—— (1995) 'From parlor games to social science: von Neumann, Morgenstern, and the creation of game theory 1928–1944', *Journal of Economic Literature* vol. 33 (June), 730–61.

Leontief, W. (1936) 'Stackelberg on monopolistic competition', *Journal of Political Economy* vol. 44 (August).

Leunbach, G. (1948) 'Theory of games and economic behavior', *Nordisk Tidsskrift för Teknisk økonomi* vols 1–4, 175–8.

*Loomis, L. H. (1946) 'On a theorem of von Neumann', *Proceedings of the National Academy of Sciences of the United States of America* vol. 32, 213–15.

Lubbock, Sir J., Courtney, L. H., Grey, A. and Westlake, J. (1885) 'Proportional representation: objections and answers', *Nineteenth Century* vol. 17 (February), 312–20.

Luce, R. D. and Raiffa, H. (1957) *Games and Decisions: Introduction and Critical Survey*, New York: Wiley.

Luce, R. D. and Tucker, A. W. (1959) *Contributions to the Theory of Games*, Volume IV (Annals of Mathematics Studies, 40), Princeton, NJ: Princeton University Press.

McDonald, J. (1950) *Strategy in Poker, Business, and War*, New York: W. W. Norton.

Machiavelli, N. (1965) *The Art of War*, trans. N. Wood, Indianapolis, Indiana: Bobbs Merrill.

McLean, I. and London, J. (1990) 'The Borda and Condorcet Principles: three medieval applications', *Social Choice and Welfare* vol. 7, 99–108.

Macrae, N. (1992) *John von Neumann*, New York: Pantheon Books.

Magnan de Bornier, J. (1992) 'The "Cournot–Bertrand Debate": a historical perspective', *History of Political Economy* vol. 24 (3), 623–56.

Majeski, S. J. and Jones, D. L. (1981) 'Arms race modeling: causality analysis and model specification', *Journal of Conflict Resolution* vol. 25 (2), 259–88.

Marschak, J. (1946) 'Neumann's and Morgenstern's new approach to static economics', *Journal of Political Economy* vol. 54, 97–115.

Marshall, A. (n.d. [c. 1872–1874]) 'Essay on international trade', in Marshall (1975).

—— (1879) *The Pure Theory of Foreign Trade (and Other Portions of Economic Science Bearing on the Principle of Laissez Faire)*, as reprinted in Marshall (1975).

—— (1923) *Money Credit and Commerce*, London: Macmillan.

—— (1961) *Principles of Economics*, 9th (Variorum) edn, C. W. Guillebaud (ed.), London: Macmillan for The Royal Economic Society.

—— (1975) *The Early Economic Writings of Alfred Marshall, 1867–1890*, 2 vols, introduced by J. K. Whitaker (ed.), London: Macmillan for The Royal Economic Society.

Marshall, J. G. (1853) *Minorities and Majorities: Their Relative Rights*, London: Ridgway.

Martin, J. B. (1874) 'The elections of 1868 and 1874', *Journal of the Statistical Society* vol. 37 (June), 193–225.

Mauldin, R. D. (ed.) (1981) *The Scottish Book: Mathematics from the Scottish Café*, Boston, Basel and Stuttgart: Birkhäuser.

*Mayberry, J. P., Nash, J. F. and Shubik, M. (1953) 'A comparison of treatments of a duopoly situation', *Econometrica* vol. 21 (1), 141–54.

Ménard, C. (1978) *La Formation d'une Rationalité Économique: A. A. Cournot*, Paris: Flammarion.

Mill, J. S. ([1871] 1923) *Principles of Political Economy*, London: Longmans, Green.

Mirowski, P. (1991) 'When games grow deadly serious: the military influence on the evolution of game theory', in C. D. Goodwin (ed.) *Economics and National Security, History of Political Economy*, Supplement to vol. 23, Durham and London: Duke University Press, 227–56.

—— (1992) 'What were von Neumann and Morgenstern trying to accomplish?', in E.R. Weintraub (ed.) (1992), 113–47.

—— (1994) *Edgeworth's Writings on Chance, Probability and Statistics*, Lanham, MD: Rowman.

Morgenstern, O. (1928) *Wirtschaftsprognose*, Vienna: Julius Springer Verlag.

—— (1931) 'Mathematical Economics', in *Encyclopedia of the Social Sciences*, New York: Macmillan, vol. 5, 364–8.

—— (1935a) 'The time moment in value theory', trans. in A. Schotter (ed.) (1976), 151–67.

*—— (1935b) 'Vollkommene Voraussicht und wirtschaftliches Gleichgewicht', *Zeitschrift für Nationalökonomie* vol. 6 (3), August, 337–57, trans. F. H. Knight, 'Perfect foresight and economic equilibrium', reprinted in A. Schotter (ed.) (1976), 169–83.

—— (1941) 'Professor Hicks on value and capital', *Journal of Political Economy* vol. 49 (3), 361–93. Reprinted in A. Schotter (ed.) (1976), 185–217.

—— (1948) 'Oligopoly, monopolistic competition, and the theory of games', *American Economic Review: Papers and Proceedings* vol. 38, 10–18.

—— (1951) 'Abraham Wald, 1902–1950', *Econometrica* vol. 19 (4), 361–7. Reprinted in A. Schotter (ed.) (1976), 493–7.

*—— (1976a) 'The collaboration of Oskar Morgenstern and John von Neumann on the theory of games', *Journal of Economic Literature* vol. 14, 805–16.

—— (1976b) *Selected Economic Writings of Oskar Morgenstern*, A. Schotter (ed.), New York: New York University Press.

Morgenstern, O. and Thompson, G. L. (1976) *Mathematical Theory of Expanding and Contracting Economies*, Lexington, MA: D. C. Heath.

Morse, Philip M. and Kimball, George E. (1951) *Methods of Operations Research*, Cambridge, MA: Technology Press of MIT and New York: Wiley.

Mueller, D. C. (1989) *Public Choice II*, Cambridge: Cambridge University Press.

*Nash, J. F. (1950a) 'Equilibrium points in *n*-person games', *Proceedings of the National Academy of Sciences* vol. 36, 48–9.

*—— (1950b) 'The bargaining problem', *Econometrica* vol. 18, 155–62.

*—— (1951) 'Non-cooperative games', *Annals of Mathematics* vol. 54, 286–95.

*—— (1953) 'Two person cooperative games', *Econometrica* vol. 21, 128–40.

Newman, J. R. (ed.) (1956) *The World of Mathematics*, 4 vols, New York: Simon & Schuster.

Newman, P. (1990) 'The great barter controversy', in J. K. Whitaker (ed.) *Centenary Essays on Alfred Marshall*, Cambridge: Cambridge University Press.

Nichol, A.J. (1934) 'A re-appraisal of Cournots' theory of duopoly price', *Journal of Political Economy* vol. 42(1): 80–105.

Niehans, J. (1992) 'Heinrich von Stackelberg: relinking German economics to the mainstream', *Journal of the History of Economic Thought* vol. 14 (2), 189–208.

Niou, E. M. S. and Ordeshook, P. C. (1990) 'A game-theoretic interpretation of Sun Tzu's *The Art of War*', California Institute of Technology Social Science Working Paper 738.

Nymeyer, F. (1973) 'Experiments with matching buy and sell orders in different ways', Supplement I to *Value and Price: An Extract from Böhm-Bawerk*, South Holland, IL: Libertarian Press, 187–204.

Ordeshook, P. (1986) *Game Theory and Political Theory: An Introduction*, Cambridge: Cambridge University Press.

Ortmann, A. and Meardon, S. J. (1995) 'A game-theoretic evaluation of Adam Smith's TMS and WN', in I. Rima (ed.) *The Classical Tradition in Economic Thought: Proceedings of the 20th History of Economics Society Meetings*, Aldershot and Brookfield, VT: Edward Elgar, 43–62.

Owens, L. (1989) 'Mathematicians at war: Warren Weaver and the Applied Mathematics Panel, 1942–1945', in D. Rowe and J. McCleary (eds) *The History of Modern Mathematics, vol. 2: Institutions and Applications*, New York: Academic Press.

Paret, P. (ed.) with the collaboration of Craig, G. A. and Gilbert, F. (1986) *Makers of Modern Strategy from Machiavelli to the Nuclear Age*, Princeton, NJ: Princeton University Press.

Pareto, V. (1896) *Cours d'Economie Politique*, Lausanne: F. Rouge.

Pascal, B. (1950) *Pensées*, with an English translation, brief notes and introduction by H. F. Stewart, New York: Pantheon Books.

Pearce, D. (1984) 'Rationalizable strategic behavior and the problem of perfection', *Econometrica* vol. 52, 1029–50.

Pigou, A. C. (1905) 'Appendix A: On the extent to which wage bargains between industrial combinations are indeterminate', to *The Principles and Methods of Industrial Peace*, London: Macmillan.

—— (1908) 'Equilibrium under bilateral monopoly', *Economic Journal* vol. 18, 205–20.

—— (1912) *Wealth and Welfare*, London: Macmillan.

—— (1948) *Economics of Welfare*, 4th edn, London: Macmillan.

Popper, K. (1976) *Unended Quest: An Intellectual Autobiography*, La Salle, IL: Open Court.

Prékopa, András (1980) 'On the development of optimization theory', *American Mathematical Monthly* vol. 87 (7), 527–42.

Rapoport, A. (1957) 'Lewis F. Richardson's mathematical theory of war', *Journal of Conflict Resolution* vol. 1 (3), 249–99.

179

—— (1960) *Fights, Games, and Debates*, Ann Arbor: University of Michigan Press.

—— (1974) *Conflict in Man-Made Environment*, Harmondsworth: Penguin.

Rashevsky, N. (1948) *Mathematical Theory of Human Relations*, Bloomington, IN: The Principia Press.

Rees, M. (1980) 'The mathematical sciences and World War II', *American Mathematical Monthly* vol. 87 (8), 607–21.

Reid, G. (1979) 'Forchheimer on partial monopoly', *History of Political Economy* vol. 11 (2), 303–8.

Rellstab, U. (1992) 'New insights into the collaboration between John von Neumann and Oskar Morgenstern on the *Theory of Games and Economic Behavior*', in E. R. Weintraub (ed.) *Toward a History of Game Theory*, Durham, NC: Duke University Press, annual supplement to *History of Political Economy* vol. 24, 77–93.

*Richardson, L. F. (1919) *The Mathematical Psychology of War*, Oxford: W. Hunt.

—— (1935a) 'Mathematical psychology of war', *Nature* vol. 135, 830–1.

—— (1935b) 'Mathematical psychology of war', *Nature* vol. 136, 1025.

—— (1938) 'The arms race of 1909–13', *Nature* vol. 142, 792–3.

—— (1939) *Generalized Foreign Politics*, Cambridge: Cambridge University Press.

—— (1946) 'Chaos, international and intermolecular', *Nature* vol. 158, 135.

—— (1950a) 'Mathematics of war and foreign politics', in T.H. Pear (ed.) *Psychological Factors of Peace and War*, London: Hutchinson. Reprinted in J. R. Newman (ed.) (1956), 1240–53.

—— (1950b) 'Statistics of deadly quarrels', in T. H. Pear (ed.) *Psychological Factors of Peace and War*, London: Hutchinson. Reprinted in J. R. Newman (ed.)(1956), 1254–63.

—— (1951) 'Could an arms race end without fighting?', *Nature* vol. 168, 567–8, 920.

—— (1957) 'A bibliography of Lewis Fry Richardson's studies of the causation of wars with a view to their avoidance', *Journal of Conflict Resolution* vol. 1 (3), 305–7.

—— (1960a) *Arms and Insecurity*, Rashevsky, N. and Trucco, E. (eds), Pittsburgh, PA: The Boxwood Press, and Chicago: Quadrangle Books.

—— (1960b) *Statistics of Deadly Quarrels*, Wright, Q. and Lienau, C. C. (eds), Pittsburgh, PA: The Boxwood Press, and Chicago: Quadrangle Books.

Richardson, S. A. (1957) 'Lewis Fry. Richardson (1881–1953): a personal biography', *Journal of Conflict Resolution* vol. 1 (3), 300–4.

Riker, W. (1992) 'The entry of game theory into political science', in E. R. Weintraub (ed.) (1992).

Rives, N. W., Jr. (1975) 'On the history of the mathematical theory of games', *History of Political Economy* vol. 7, 549–65.

Robinson, J. (1933) *The Economics of Imperfect Competition*, London: Macmillan.

Robinson, J. B. (1951) 'An iterative method of solving a game', *Annals of Mathematics* vol. 54, 296–301.

Rothschild, K. W. (1947) 'Price theory and oligopoly', *Economic Journal* vol. 57, 299–320. Reprinted in G. Stigler and K. Boulding (1952), 440–64.

Ruist, E. (1949) 'Spelteori och ekonomiska problem', *Economisk Tidsskrift* vol. 2, 112–17.

Russell, B. A. W. (1914) *War, the Offspring of Fear*, London: Union for Democratic Control.

Samuelson, P. A. (1989) 'A revisionist view of von Neumann's growth model', in M. Dore, S. Chakravarty and R. Goodwin (eds) *John von Neumann and Modern Economics*, Oxford: Clarendon Press, 100–22.

Satterthwaite, M. A. (1975) 'Strategy-proofness and Arrow's conditions: existence and correspondence theorems for voting procedures and social welfare functions', *Journal of Economic Theory* vol. 10 (April), 187–217.

Schenzler, C., Siegfried, J. J. and Thweatt, W. O. (1992) 'The history of the static equilibrium dominant firm price leadership model', *Eastern Economic Journal* vol. 18, 171–86.

Scherer, F. M. (1980) *Industrial Market Structure and Economic Performance*, 2nd edn, Boston: Houghton Mifflin.

Schmidt, C. (1990) 'Game theory and economics: an historical survey', *Revue d'Economie Politique* vol. 100 (5), September–October, 589–618.

—— (1992) 'Concurrence, concours des producteurs et modes d'organisation de la production chez Antoine Augustin Cournot', *Economies et Sociétés* vol. 16 (3), 71–99.

Schmidt, C. and Blackaby, F. (1987) *Peace, Defence and Economic Analysis: Proceeding of a Conference held in Stockholm jointly by the International Economic Association and the Stockholm International Research Institute*, Houndmills, Basingstoke, Hampshire and London: Macmillan.

Schotter, A. (ed.) (1976) *Selected Economic Writings of Oskar Morgenstern*, New York: New York University Press.

Schumpeter, J. A. (1930) 'Preface' to Zeuthen (1930), vii–xiii.

—— (1954) *History of Economic Analysis*, edited from manuscript by E. B. Schumpeter, New York: Oxford University Press.

*Shapley, L. S. (1952) 'Notes on the *n*-person game III: some variants of the von Neumann–Morgenstern definition of solution', Rand Corporation Research Memorandum RM-817.

—— (1953) 'A value for *n*-person games' in H. Kuhn and A. W. Tucker (eds) *Contributions to the Theory of Games*, vol. 2, Princeton, NJ: Princeton University Press, 307–17.

*Shubik, M. (1955) 'A comparison of treatments of a duopoly problem (Part II)', *Econometrica* vol. 23, 415–31.

—— (1959a) 'Edgeworth market games', in A. W. Tucker and R. D. Luce (eds) *Contributions to the Theory of Games*, vol. IV, Princeton, NJ: Princeton University Press, 267–78.

—— (1959b) *Strategy and Market Structure: Competition, Oligopoly, and the Theory of Games*, New York: Wiley.

—— (1982) *Game Theory in the Social Sciences*, Cambridge, MA: MIT Press.

—— (1987) 'The uses, value and limitations of game theoretic methods in defence analysis', in C. Schmidt and F. Blackaby (1987), 53–84.

—— (1989) 'Antoine Augustin Cournot', in J. Eatwell, M. Milgate and P. Newman (eds) *The New Palgrave: Game Theory*, New York and London: W. W. Norton.

—— (1992) 'Game theory at Princeton, 1949–1955: a personal reminiscence', in E. R. Weintraub (ed.) (1992), 151–64.

Sidgwick, W. C. (1884) Letter to the *St James Gazette*, 6 June, 5.

Simaan, M. and Cruz, J. B., Jr. (1975a) 'Formulation of Richardson's model of the arms race from a differential game viewpoint', *Review of Economic Studies* vol. 42, 67–77.

—— (1975b) 'Nash equilibrium strategies for the problem of armament race and control', *Management Science* vol. 22, 96–105.

*Simon, H. (1945) 'Review of *The Theory of Games and Economic Behavior*, by J. von Neumann and O. Morgenstern', *American Journal of Sociology* vol. 27, 558–60.

—— (1982) *Models of Bounded Rationality* vol. 2, Cambridge, MA: MIT Press.

—— (1991) *Models of My Life*, New York: Basic Books.

—— (1995) Private letter, dated 4 April. Quoted by permission.

Smith, A. (1759) *The Theory of Moral Sentiments*. Reprinted Oxford: Clarendon Press, 1976; Indianapolis: Liberty Fund, 1981.

—— (1776) *The Wealth of Nations*. Reprinted Oxford: Clarendon Press, 1976; Indianapolis: Liberty Fund, 1981.

Smithies, A. (1941) 'Optimum location in spatial competition', *Journal of Political Economy* vol. 49, 423–39. Reprinted in G. Stigler and K. Boulding (1952), 485–501.

*Smithies, A. and Savage, L. J. (1940) 'A dynamic problem in duopoly', *Econometrica* vol. 8, 130–43.

Stackelberg, H. von (1934) *Marktform und bleichgewicht*, Vienna and Berlin: Julius Springer.

—— ([1948] 1952) *Grundlagen der theoretischen Volkswirtschaftslehre*. With an introduction by A. T. Peacock (trans.) *The Theory of the Market Economy*, New York: Oxford University Press.

*Steinhaus, H. (1925) 'Definitions for a theory of games and pursuit' (in Polish), *Mysl Akademicka*, Lwów, 1: 13–14, E. Rzymovski (trans.) with introduction by H. Kuhn, *Naval Research Logistics Quarterly* (1960), 105–8.

Stigler, G. (1947) 'The kinky oligopoly demand curve and rigid prices', *Journal of Political Economy* vol. 55, 432–49. Reprinted in G. Stigler and K. Boulding (1952), 410–39.

Stigler, G. and Boulding, K. (eds)(1952) *A.E.A. Readings in Price Theory*, Chicago and Homewood, IL: Richard D. Irwin.

Stigler, S. M. (1986) *The History of Statistics: The Measurement of Uncertainty Before 1900*, Cambridge, MA: Belknap Press of Harvard University Press.

Stone, J. R. N. (1948) 'The theory of games', *Economic Journal* vol. 58, 185–201.

Sun Tzu (1988) *The Art of War*, T. Cleary (trans.), Boston and Shaftesbury, Dorset: Shambhala.

Sutton, J. (1993) 'Echoes of Edgeworth: the problem of indeterminacy', *European Economic Review* vol. 37, 491–9.

Sweezy, P. (1939) 'Demand under conditions of oligopoly', *Journal of Political Economy* vol. 47, 568–73. Reprinted in G. Stigler and K. Boulding (1952), 404–9.

Tarascio, V. J. (1972) 'A correction: on the genealogy of the so-called Edgeworth–Bowley Diagram', *Western Economic Journal* vol. 10, 193–7.

Taylor, J. G. (1979) 'Recent developments in the Lanchester Theory on combat', in *IFORS Proceedings*, K. B. Haley (ed.), Amsterdam: North-Holland, 773–806.

Theocharis, R. D. (1990) 'A note on the lag in the recognition of Cournot's contribution to economic analysis', *Canadian Journal of Economics* vol. 23 (4), 923–33.

—— (1993) *The Development of Mathematical Economics: The Years of Transition: From Cournot to Jevons*, London: Macmillan.

Todhunter, I. (1865) *A History of the Mathematical Theory of Probability from the Time of Pascal to that of Laplace*, Cambridge: Cambridge University Press. Reprinted Bronx, NY: Chelsea Publishing (1965).

Triffin, R. (1940) *Monopolistic Competition and General Equilibrium Theory*, Cambridge, MA: Harvard University Press.

Tullock, G. (1972) *Toward a Mathematics of Politics*, Ann Arbor: University of Michigan Press.

Ulam, S. (1981) 'An anecdotal history of the Scottish book', in R. D. Mauldin (ed.) (1981), 3–16.

*Ville, J. (1938) 'Sur le théorie générale des jeux où intervient l'habilité des joueurs', in E. Borel *et al.* (1925–1939), vol. 4, *Applications des jeux de hasard*, Fasc. 2, 105–13.

Viner, J. (1937) *Studies in the Theory of International Trade*, New York: Harper & Row.

—— (1946) 'The implications of the atomic bomb for international relations', *Proceedings of the American Philosophical Society* vol. 90(1).

Vives, X. (1993) 'Edgeworth and modern oligopoly theory', *European Economic Review* vol. 37, 463–76.

*von Neumann, J. (1928a) 'Sur la théorie des jeux', *Comptes Rendus de l'Académie des Sciences* 186.25 (18 June), 1689–91.

*—— (1928b) 'Zur théorie der gesellschaftsspiele', *Math. Annalen* vol. 100, 295–320, in S. Bargmann (trans.) as 'On the theory of games of strategy', *Contributions to the Theory of Games* vol. 4, A. W. Tucker and R. D. Luce (eds) *Annals of Mathematics Studies* 40, Princeton, NJ: Princeton University Press (1959), 13–42.

—— (1937) 'Über ein Oikonomisches Gleichungssystem und eine Verallgemeinerung des Brouwerschen Fixpunktsatzes', *Ergebnisse eines Mathematischen Seminars* in K. Menger (ed.), Vienna, G. Morton (trans.) as 'A model of general economic equilibrium', *Review of Economic Studies* vol. 13 (1945), 1–9.

*—— (1953) 'Communication on the Borel Notes', *Econometrica* vol. 21, 124–5.

von Neumann, J. and Morgenstern, O. (1944, 1947, 1953) *The Theory of Games and Economic Behavior*, Princeton, NJ: Princeton University Press.

—— (1967) *The Theory of Games and Economic Behavior*, New York: John Wiley & Sons.

*Wald, A. (1945a) 'Statistical decision functions which minimize the maximum risk', *Annals of Mathematics* vol. 46, 265–80.

*—— (1945b) 'Generalization of a theorem by von Neumann concerning zero-sum two-person games', *Annals of Mathematics* vol. 46, 281–6.

—— (1947) '*Theory of Games and Economic Behavior* by J. von Neumann and O. Morgenstern', *Review of Economic Statistics* vol. 39, 47–52.

—— (1950) *Statistical Decision Functions*, New York: John Wiley & Sons.

*Waldegrave, J. (1713) Minimax solution to 2-person, zero-sum game, reported in letter from P. de Montmort to N. Bernoulli, with introduction by H. Kuhn (trans.) in *Precursors of Mathematical Economics*, W. J. Baumol and S. Goldfeld (eds), London: London School of Economics (1968), 3–9.

Walker, P. (1995) 'An outline of the history of game theory', Discussion Paper No. 9504, Department of Economics, University of Canterbury, Christchurch, New Zealand.

Walker, P. and Martin, O. (1996) Comment on Dimand and Dimand (1992), *History of Political Economy* 29.

Wallace, I., Wallechinsky, D. and Wallace, A. (1983) *Significa*, New York: E. P. Dutton.

Weintraub, E. R. (ed.) (1992) *Toward a History of Game Theory, History of Political Economy*, supplement to vol. 24, Durham and London: Duke University Press.

Weyl, H. (1935) 'Elementare Theorie der konvexen Polyeder', *Commentarii Mathematici Helvetici* vol. 7, 290–306, in H. W. Kuhn (trans.) as 'The elementary theory of convex polyhedra', *Contributions to the Theory of Games* vol. 1, H. W. Kuhn and A. W. Tucker (eds) *Annals of Mathematics Studies* 24, Princeton, NJ: Princeton University Press (1950), 3–18.

*—— (1950) 'Elementary proof of a minimax theorem due to von Neumann', *Contributions to the Theory of Games* vol. 1, H. W. Kuhn and A. W. Tucker (eds) *Annals of Mathematics Studies* vol. 24, Princeton, NJ: Princeton University Press (1950), 19–26.

Whitmore, W. F. (1953) 'Edison and operations research', *Journal of the Operations Research Society of America* vol. 1, 83–5.

Wright, Q. (1942) *A Study of War*, Chicago: University of Chicago Press.

Zermelo, E. (1913) 'Über eine Anwendung der Mengenlehre auf die theorie des Schachspiels', *Proceedings, Fifth International Congress of Mathematicians* vol. 2, 501–4.

Zeuthen, F. (1930) *Problems of Monopoly and Economic Warfare*, Else Zeuthen (trans.), London: George Routledge & Sons.

*—— (1933) 'Theoretical remarks on price policy: Hotelling's case with variations', *Quarterly Journal of Economics* vol. 47, 231–53.

INDEX